100 THINGS
YOU WILL
NEVER FIND

100 THINGS YOU WILL NEVER FIND

LOST CITIES, HIDDEN TREASURES,
AND LEGENDARY QUESTS

DANIEL SMITH

Quercus

Contents

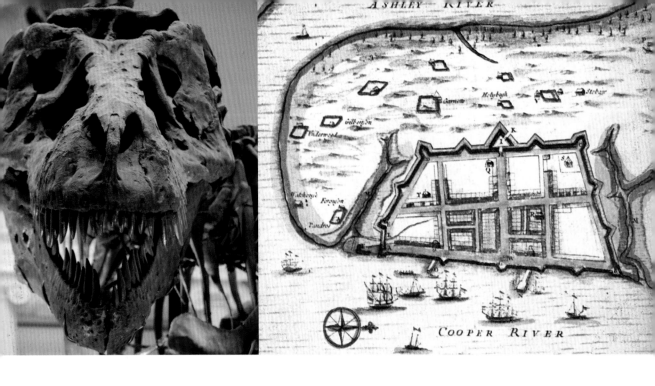

Introduction

"There will always be a lost dog somewhere that will prevent me from being happy."

La Sauvage—Jean Anouilh

All of us at one time or another suffer the frustration of losing something essential to us. The keys carelessly discarded as we step through the front door. The show tickets dutifully filed in the really safe place that has now escaped our memory. The check that needs to be paid into the bank today. On occasion, these small-scale losses are almost enough to make you lose your mind.

When I was growing up, my mother taught me that if I had misplaced something I should address St. Anthony, the patron saint of lost things, for help. There was even a short rhyme she taught me to facilitate communication:

"St. Anthony, St. Anthony, please help me find what belongs to me."

To this day, if I have failed to find a lost wallet despite hunting high and low, I force myself to stop, take a deep breath, and make the same old appeal. And more often than not, it seems to do the trick. Whether this is because I have taken a moment to gather my thoughts and resume the search more methodically, or whether there is some real saintly intervention involved, I shall leave the reader to decide.

Yet there are times when we just have to accept that something really is gone. No matter how long and hard you seek, you simply cannot find it—even with St. Anthony's help. That missing pen lid, the receipt for those pants a couple of sizes too small or—perhaps most devastatingly of all—the cell phone you were sure that you put down just over there. Rarely, though, are any of these losses as grave as they might seem in the moment.

But every now and again, there is a loss that really is significant. It may

seriously impact the fortunes of an individual, or extract a cost from society as a whole. A few, it is safe to assume, leave our entire civilization severely diminished.

The hundred losses detailed in the pages of this book range in size and severity from a single gem stone to a whole colony of people, via video cassettes, works of art, racehorses, and fleets of aircraft. Each loss has its own unique and fascinating story, at the center of which is always the same enduring mystery: what was the object's ultimate fate?

Some of the disappearances that follow have inspired elaborate conspiracy theories that strain the bounds of credibility, while others are rooted in stories that are no less moving for their apparent mundanity. Among the various tales, you will find grand narratives of greed and criminality, high politics and low treachery, ambition and tragedy, calumny, and calamity. It is fair to say that all life is here, just waiting for you to reveal it.

Of course, every loss also presents an opportunity: the chance to undertake a quest to recover it. Life itself, let us not forget, is something of a quest for all of us at one level or another, whether we are searching for love, self-knowledge, wisdom, material wealth, respect, or something else entirely. From

the Holy Grail of Arthurian legend to Captain Flint's trove in *Treasure Island* and the Horcruxes of *Harry Potter*, questing after lost things is also a recurring motif throughout the history of our culture.

What all of these stories tell us is that the seeking is just as important —sometimes even more so—than the act of finding. While the desire to recover and retrieve may be the motivation that drives a quest, it is the twists and turns and forks in the road along the way that most fascinate. If King Arthur's knights had set out from Camelot early one morning, only to be back by lunchtime with the Grail safely in their possession, it would have been a dull story indeed. It was, of course, the adventures they undertook, the difficult decisions they were forced to make, and the heartfelt introspection that all this induced that keeps Arthur and his court fresh and relevant to us still.

The American singer-songwriter, author, and actor Jimmy Buffett, put it neatly:

"Searching is half the fun: life is much more manageable when thought of as a scavenger hunt as opposed to a surprise party."

Amelia Earhart's airplane

WHAT IT IS The plane flown by pioneering female pilot Earhart
WHY YOU WON'T FIND IT The aircraft lost contact with ground control

An aviation pioneer and feminist icon, Amelia Earhart set off on a 29,000-mile (47,000-kilometer) around-the-world flight around the world in 1937, accompanied by navigator Fred Noonan. Somewhere over the Pacific Ocean, their plane crashed and neither Earhart, Noonan, nor the aircraft was ever found.

Born in 1897 in Kansas, Amelia Earhart's life as a bona fide American heroine began in 1920 when a short flight at an airfield prompted her to learn to fly herself. Two years later she became the 16th woman to receive a pilot's license from the Fédération Aéronautique Internationale. When, in 1932, she became the first female to fly solo across the Atlantic Ocean, her legendary status was secured. Five years later she set out to circumnavigate the world along the equator. It should have been her crowning achievement but instead its tragic end ensured she remains at the center of one of the most enduring mysteries of the 20th century.

Plans for the journey began in 1936, when Earhart gained the backing of her employers at Purdue University. Aviation manufacturers Lockheed built a twin-engined monoplane—a Model 10 Electra —to her exacting specifications, while two experienced flyers, Fred Noonan and Harry Manning, were chosen to share navigational duties, each responsible for a different leg of the trip. A first attempt in March 1937 ended almost before it began due to mechanical problems, but a second attempt commenced from Miami on June 1.

By the end of the month, the Electra had reached the Pacific island of New Guinea, about three-quarters of the way through its epic journey. Earhart set off on the next leg with Noonan on July 2, heading for uninhabited Howland Island in the middle of the Pacific Ocean, but they would never make it. Radio contact was lost shortly after Earhart established her position close to the Nukumanu Islands, about 800 miles (1,300 kilometers) from where they had taken off.

A US Coast Guard vessel, *Itasca*, was responsible for maintaining communications. An hour after her last broadcast, a rescue operation swung into action but after several days searching over an area covering hundreds of thousands of square miles, no sign of the plane or her crew was found. On July 19 the mission—at that time, the most expensive

PIONEERING SPIRIT Previous page: *Amelia Earhart's feats of daring captivated America and made her a national sweetheart.*
Above: *An aerial view of Gardiner Island, where it is thought that Earhart and her copilot Fred Noonan may have met their ends.*

search-and-rescue operation in US history—was called off. Earhart's husband, George Putnam, privately funded further searches, but to no avail. Despite the absence of a body, Earhart was pronounced dead on January 5, 1939.

Ever since, there has been no shortage of opinion as to what might have happened to the intrepid adventuress, her navigator, and their plane. It has been proposed, for instance, that Earhart was using her flight to spy on Japanese Pacific territories on behalf of Washington. Forced to crash-land, the story goes, she was captured by the Japanese and either imprisoned or executed. However, few but the most hardy conspiracy theorists put much faith in such a hypothesis. Even more unlikely is the theory, put forward in a 1970 book, that Earhart did not die on the trip but took up a new life in New Jersey under an assumed name.

So what other possibilities are there? It is perfectly feasible that the Electra ran into technical problems and crashed into the sea in an unknown location. It seems likely that the aircraft's radio system was not working very well and we know the plane was short on fuel. Some investigators also suspect that there may have been some problems with the flight plan that Noonan was following.

Yet perhaps the strongest evidence suggests that Earhart and Noonan made an emergency landing on a reef close to the uninhabited Gardiner Island (now known as Nikumaroro and part of the Pacific island nation of Kiribati), about 350 miles (560 kilometers) from Howland Island. This is a line of inquiry that the International Group for Historic Aircraft Recovery (TIGHAR) has been following since the 1980s after discovering a report from the 1940s that a British official had found a buried skeleton on the island which may have belonged to a tall, white woman.

In 2013, TIGHAR announced that sonar imaging had revealed an anomaly 590 feet (180 m) below Gardiner Island's coastal waters—an unusual structure with a size and shape comparable to that of an Electra. This ties in with a photo taken by a British naval officer in the area in 1937 showing what many have long believed was the wreckage from Earhart's plane. On the island itself, TIGHAR has also recovered handmade tools, plexiglass fragments consistent with the type used by Lockheed, and a jar that may have contained freckle cream of the sort favored by Earhart. All of this points to the fact that she and Noonan made it to the island alive and spent some time there before presumably dying from unknown causes. But with neither their bodies nor the recovered wreck of the aircraft to prove it, the mystery will live on for some time.

The Romanov Imperial Easter Eggs

WHAT THEY ARE Ornate jeweled eggs given as gifts by the Russian imperial family
WHY YOU WON'T FIND THEM They were mislaid or misappropriated during the rule of Josef Stalin

Nothing better represents the decadence of Russia's ruling Romanov dynasty than the remarkable Imperial Easter Eggs. Created for them by the legendary jeweler Carl Fabergé from 1886 until the family's demise in the Russian Revolution of 1917, each egg was a work of art and they are today valued at millions of dollars each. But of the 50 that Fabergé is known to have created, only 42 are accounted for.

The giving of decorated eggs to loved ones at Easter was a long-standing Russian tradition, but never on the scale to which the Romanovs became accustomed. The very first of the Imperial Eggs was commissioned by Tsar Alexander III, who presented it to his wife, Empress Maria Feodorovna, in 1885. Crafted by Fabergé in his St. Petersburg studio (reputedly with input from the Tsar himself), the finished egg (roughly 2.5 inches or 6 cm tall) was a thing of wonder. Known as the Hen's Egg, it is made of gold and encased in a white enamel shell. When opened, a golden yolk is revealed containing a bejeweled hen. This in turn can be opened up, and once revealed a miniature "imperial crown" in gold and diamonds, with a ruby pendant at its center (sadly crown and pendant are both now lost).

After the success of this initial gift, Fabergé was given complete artistic freedom, with the single condition that each egg should contain a surprise (and a rather more extravagant one than the package of candies we might hope for today!). When Alexander III died in 1894, the tradition was continued by his son, Tsar Nicholas II. In fact, he doubled the order so that he could present one each to his wife, Tsarina Alexandra Fedorovna, and his mother, the Dowager Tsarina.

With the exceptions of 1904 and 1905, when the Russo-Japanese War was in full swing, Fabergé faithfully fulfilled his commission until 1917. However, his final two eggs were never presented to their intended recipients after the revolution forced Nicholas's abdication in March 1917. The Romanov dynasty was ended once and for all a year later when its principal members were executed by the Bolsheviks. Fabergé, meanwhile, fled Russia for Switzerland.

The new government under Lenin ransacked the former imperial palaces and sent their treasures to Moscow. It would seem that the eggs spent the next several years crated up within the walls of the Kremlin. However, after Lenin died in 1924, Stalin formulated a plan to sell the eggs to foreign buyers to

raise revenue. Fabergé's son, Agathon, was even briefly released from prison to value them, only to be returned when he was deemed to have overvalued them.

From 1927 onward, many of the eggs left the country, often raising a mere fraction of their true value at auction. The largest privately owned collection, totaling nine eggs, was assembled by Malcolm Forbes of the legendary American business dynasty. In 2004, it was sold en masse to Russian gas and oil tycoon Viktor Vekselberg, for US$100 million. The biggest collection of all comprises the ten still held by Moscow's Kremlin Armory Museum.

Today, there are eight eggs whose whereabouts are unknown. Together they would surely command US$100 million at a conservative estimate. Chronologically, these are:

• The 1886 Hen with Sapphire Pendant— "a hen of gold and rose diamonds taking a sapphire egg out of a nest" according to the imperial archive.
• The 1888 Cherub with Chariot—in which an angel pulls a chariot containing an egg, within which is a clock.
• The 1889 Necessaire—containing a diamond-encrusted manicure set.
• The 1896 Alexander III—containing a dozen miniature paintings of scenes relevant to Nicholas and Alexandra's courtship.
• The 1897 Mauve Enamel—a gift for the Dowager Tsarina containing three miniature pictures.
• The 1902 Empire Nephrite—another gift for the dowager, this one containing a portrait of her husband.
• The 1903 Danish Jubilee—another for the dowager, with portraits ofher parents.
• The 1909 Alexander III Commemorative —yet another of the dowager's, enclosing a gold bust of her husband.

So where might these delicate treasures be hidden today? It is possible, but unlikely, that some are simply lost within the labyrinthine vaults of the Kremlin. More probably, they went into private collections in the 1920s and 1930s, perhaps bought for hundreds of dollars rather than the millions they are worth now. Indeed, unwitting descendants may perhaps still have one sitting on a mantel or up in the attic, little realizing the overlooked fortune in their hands.

Lost fossils of the Bone Wars

WHAT THEY ARE Rare dinosaur bones from the American West
WHY YOU WON'T FIND THEM Many were destroyed as part of a 19th-century academic feud

The opening up of the Western United States in the mid-1800s paved the way for a stampede that became known as the Great Dinosaur Rush. Evidence of prehistoric life was discovered at an extraordinary rate, with dozens of new species of dinosaur identified. At its center were two men, Othniel Marsh and Edward Cope, whose personal rivalry inspired great leaps forward but several acts of gross vandalism, too.

Marsh and Cope were vastly contrasting figures. Cope, born into a wealthy background, was the epitome of the amateur gentleman naturalist. Marsh had humbler roots, but was propelled into academia by his vastly rich uncle, the philanthropist George Peabody. Marsh became Yale's first professor of paleontology, while Cope, who could turn from charming to irascible in the blink of an eye, established himself at Philadelphia's Academy of Natural Sciences. Marsh, furthermore, was a Darwinist, while Cope was not.

Initially, relations between the two men were amicable, and in the 1860s they both worked the rich fossil seams of the Great Plains region. Any sense of camaraderie, however, was crushed forever in 1869 when Marsh pointed out that Cope had incorrectly assembled one of his finds so that the skull had been placed where the tail should be. A humiliated Cope attempted to buy up all copies of the paper detailing his horrible mistake, while Marsh did all he could to keep it available.

With the gloves off, tactics became ever less palatable. The rivals attacked each other's work and good name in print, bribed third parties to obstruct the other's operations, and employed teams of fossil-hunters who spied on each other and regularly descended to physical violence. Even more gravely, they were not above the theft of bones, and had a reckless penchant for dynamite. In short, priceless paleontological specimens were destroyed simply to prevent the other side from getting their hands on them or to throw them off a particular scent. Such activities were an appalling abuse of the academic code, carried out in the pursuit of self-glorification.

Cope died in 1897 and Marsh two years later. By the end of their respective careers, Cope had named 56 new species of dinosaur, and Marsh 80. Yet the public feuding had cost them their fortunes and their reputations, too. Most unforgivable of all, though, was the willful destruction of prehistoric artefacts. They discovered much, but we can never know how much more was lost.

The Davidoff-Morini Stradivarius

WHAT IT IS A priceless musical instrument
WHY YOU WON'T FIND IT It was stolen in New York in 1995

There is no greater name in the world of musical instruments than that of Italian violin-maker Antonio Stradivari (1644–1737). The much-loved violinist Erika Morini was fortunate enough to own a particularly fine example of his work until it was stolen from her New York apartment in 1995. The incident remains listed among the FBI's Top Ten Art Crimes.

Born in Austria in 1904, Erika Morini made her professional debut at the age of 12, and performed in New York for the first time in 1921. Recognized as one of the leading violinists of her age, in 1924 she was presented with her Stradivarius by her father, who had bought it in Paris. The instrument, made in 1727, is one of about 650 examples of his craft that remain in existence, and had previously belonged to the great 19th-century cellist, Karl Davidoff.

Morini performed regularly with her Stradivarius until she retired in 1976, after which time it is thought that she never picked up a violin again. By 1995, she was 91 years old and her health was failing. In October that year she was hospitalized suffering with heart problems. But while she lay dying, somebody broke into her apartment on Fifth Avenue (presumably using keys, since there was no evidence of forced entry) and stole not only the violin but also personal papers, artworks, and scores from a locked closet. A value of US$3 million was put on the violin alone.

Morini died the following month, still unaware of the crime since her loved ones decided against burdening her with the news. While the crime against Morini was a particularly heartless one, it was by no means unique. In 2010, for instance, the Korean violinist Min-Jin Kym had her US$1.8 million 1696 Stradivarius stolen while she ate a sandwich at a London railway station. The thieves utterly failed to grasp the value of what they had swiped and later tried to sell it for $167 before being caught and sent to prison.

Sadly Kym's violin also remains missing—the latest addition to a long list of instruments reported stolen and never seen again. These include the 1712 Karpilowsky (stolen in 1953), the 1734 Arnes (stolen in 1981), the 1735 Lamoureux-Zimbalist (stolen in 1981), the 1714 Colossus (stolen in 1998), the 1709 King Maximilian (stolen in 1999), and the 1714 Le Maurien (stolen in 2002). In the case of the Davidoff-Morini, it was perhaps a blessing that Erica Morini did not live to endure her loss.

Recipe for Chartreuse

WHAT IT IS The formula for the liqueur distilled by French monks
WHY YOU WON'T FIND IT You need to be one of only two monks permitted access to it

A liqueur produced in the Voiron region of France by the Carthusian order of monks, Chartreuse was first bottled in 1764, but is based on a recipe given to the monks more than a century and a half before. Packing a taste-punch that combines sweetness and spice, the drink is manufactured from 130 different herbs and other botanical products. It is said that only two monks know the recipe at any one time.

Today, Chartreuse is sold commercially in three forms, none of which are for the fainthearted: yellow (80 proof); green (110 proof); and green or yellow V.E.P. ("Vieillissement Exceptionnellement Prolongé" or "Exceptionally Prolonged Aging"; 138 proof). In 1605, François-Annibal d'Estrées, Marshal of King Henri IV's artillery, presented a recipe for the "elixir" to the Chartreuse monks at Vauvert in the outskirts of Paris. It is thought to have been devised by an alchemist in the previous century as a medicinal "cure-all."

Alas, the formulation proved so complex that the monks were initially unable to produce the tonic. In the early 1700s the recipe found its way to the order's mother house near Grenoble and was subjected to new and intense study. At last, in 1737, an apothecary called Frère Jerome Maubec untangled its mysteries and came up with a practical production method, selling the medicine to a small clientele around Grenoble. Realizing that people were getting a taste for the elixir, the monks brought a slightly watered-down "green" version to the market in 1764. It was an immediate hit.

Manufacture stopped for a period when the monks were expelled from the country during the French Revolution, and in 1810 the secret recipe narrowly escaped an order by Napoleon that it be shared with the state. A slightly sweeter, yellow Chartreuse was introduced in 1838, and a new distillery was built near the Fourvoirie monastery in 1860.

However, the monks were once again expelled from France in 1903, and their drink's trademark was transferred to a private company, while the monks continued production from Spain, selling this version as "Une Tarragone." However, the private distillers were unable to replicate the monks' beverage and went bankrupt in 1923. The monks were gifted back the trademark by some well-wishers, and resumed their work at Fourvoirie until a landslide caused catastrophic damage in 1935 and operations were transferred to Voiron, where they continue today.

JFK's brain

WHAT IT IS The brain of revered former US President John F. Kennedy
WHY YOU WON'T FIND IT Once key evidence in the investigation into his assassination, it later disappeared

Even half a century after the event, there is nothing quite like the assassination of the US President John F. Kennedy to get the blood pumping in a conspiracy theorist. Was it the CIA that killed him, or the Mafia, the Cubans, or the Kremlin? The fact is, this was a crime littered with multiple mini mysteries, among the most curious of which is the fate of the president's brain.

When JFK was gunned down in Dallas, Texas, on November 23, 1963, it sent shock waves around the planet. The leader of the Free World—who just a year earlier had pulled us back from the brink of mutual self-destruction in the Cuban Missile Crisis—was gone, and with him died the hopes of a generation.

Within hours of the shooting, disgruntled former marine and petty criminal Lee Harvey Oswald was arrested for the murder. The following year, the official inquiry into the assassination, the Warren Commission, concluded that Oswald was guilty and had acted alone. However, Oswald never saw the due process of a criminal trial because by then he, too, was dead, shot by a shady underworld figure, Jack Ruby, a mere two days after the slaying of the President. Any hopes that the Warren Commission's judgment would bring closure to the case were short-lived. It was merely the first staging post on a trail that twisted and turned with countless conspiracy theories, some credible and others far less so.

But while "conspiracy nuts" may be easy to mock, the official files on the Kennedy killing are littered with gaps and inconsistencies that provide grist to the mill of the doubters and cynics. One of the key questions is just how many shots were fired—and from where? Oswald is supposed to have been located on the sixth floor of the Texas School Book Depository at Dealey Plaza, from where he fired at least three shots into the back of the presidential car. So if it could be proved, for instance, that Kennedy had suffered a bullet wound to the front of his head, the idea of Oswald as the lone gunman would fall apart.

As such, the findings of the autopsy— carried out at the Bethesda Naval Hospital in Maryland—are of crucial importance. But ever since its report was released, there have been doubts about its findings. Some have been argued that an injury to Kennedy's throat was not, as the autopsy concluded, a bullet exit wound, but rather an entry wound. Others have also pointed out the unlikely trajectory of the so-called "magic bullet,"

supposedly responsible for injuries to both the president and his copassenger, the Texas governor John Connally.

Doubts about the lone gunman theory grew, and in 1978 the House Select Committee on Assassinations (HSCA) found the shooting was probably the result of a conspiracy. Oswald fired the fatal shots, it reported, but others were also involved. In 1992, the US government established the Assassination Records Review Board, charged with making all official records available to the public. It was not the Board's job to pass any judgment on the veracity or credibility of the evidence, but in 1998 one of its chief analysts, Douglas P. Horne, put his personal conclusions on record.

In Horne's opinion, autopsy photographs of Kennedy's brain in the National Archives came from someone other than Kennedy. The implication was clear— the official photos gave a misleading record of the president's brain injury and, thus, the circumstances of the shooting. However, there is no chance of examining Kennedy's actual brain—

despite being preserved at the time, all trace of it was lost in 1965.

On April 22 that year, JFK's brother Robert (himself assassinated in 1968)—requested that autopsy material including the brain be transferred from the custody of presidential physician Dr. George Burkley, to his brother's former personal secretary, Evelyn Lincoln, for safekeeping. In 1966, the material was transferred back to the government— but now, it did not include the brain.

From then until now, the fate of JFK's brain has never been publicly explained. A reasonable assumption is that Robert Kennedy had it buried with his brother's body when it was reinterred at Arlington, Virginia, in March 1967, but we cannot be sure. Robert was certainly known to be fearful that it might be put on public exhibition in the future as a macabre souvenir of one of the darkest episodes in American history. But in securing the dignity of his fallen brother, he may also have inadvertently prolonged the confusion surrounding the circumstances of his death.

The Story of the Kelly Gang

WHAT IT IS The original feature movie
WHY YOU WON'T FIND IT Only about a quarter of the movie is known to exist

If you thought that the full-length movie was born in Hollywood, then you'd be wrong. The very first feature movie was actually made in Australia—suburban Melbourne to be precise. Filmed in 1906, it took as its subject the Australian folk hero and bush-ranging killer, Ned Kelly. But sadly for us, no complete copies of this landmark cultural work have survived to the modern day.

Cinema was still a distant dream when Ned Kelly was killed in a shoot-out at the Glenrowan Hotel in 1880 while sporting his iconic suit of homemade armor, but his story has provided wonderful scope for movie-makers ever since. Leading a ruthless gang on a crime spree through the Australian Bush that challenged the authority of the colonial powers, he was nothing more than a thug to some, while others saw him as a latter-day Robin Hood.

An early Australian movie exhibitor, Charles Tait, was perhaps the first to realize how Kelly's story might suit the burgeoning cinematic art form. He invited his brothers, John and Nevin, and two colleagues, Millard Johnson and William Gibson, to join him as coproducers of the movie (and, more importantly, its principal financiers). Charles himself came up with a script and took on directing duties, while Frank Mills was brought in to star as Ned, Elizabeth Tait played his sister Kate, and Nicholas Brierley took the role of Joe Byrne, a notorious member of the gang.

Working with a budget equivalent to around US$1,000, Tait produced a movie that lasted for more than an hour—an extraordinary feat at a time when the average movie lasted no more than ten minutes. *The Story of the Kelly Gang* premiered at Melbourne's Athenaeum Hall on Boxing Day 1906 and provoked an immediate response. Some adored it, while others questioned its glorification of a murderer whose killing spree had ended less than 30 years previously. But regardless of taste, the movie was a major commercial success, playing to packed houses throughout the country and bringing in perhaps US$25,000 for its backers. There were at least six prints in circulation, with showings often accompanied by a live narrator and live sound effects. There were even reports that it was inspiring copycat criminals—in 1907, five children in the state of Victoria apparently robbed a photographic studio and held up a group of fellow schoolchildren.

Also in 1907, the movie went international, opening in New Zealand

and Britain, where it was publicized as "the longest film ever made." Yet cinema moved so quickly that it was not long before its impact began to fade. By the end of the Second World War, not a single complete copy of the movie was known to survive.

Then in 1976, several short fragments—consisting of no more than a few frames each—were found in a private collection in Adelaide. A couple of years later another private collection—this time in Melbourne—yielded some more material and, in 1980, a further discovery was made on a Melbourne garbage dump. By the turn of the millennium, the Australian National Film and Sound Archive (NFSA) had painstakingly restored ten minutes of the movie—less than one-sixth of its original length. A few more minutes, the longest single surviving sequence, turned up in 2006 at the UK's National

Film and Television Archive (now called the BFI National Archive). So a century after its historic release, NFSA was able to extend its edit to just over 17 minutes of film—about a quarter of the complete movie. The following year *The Story of the Kelly Gang* was inscribed on UNESCO's Memory of the World Register.

It is a sad fact that today not only is the movie barely known outside the world of academic movie historians, it is not even the most famous movie about Ned Kelly. Yet it is heartening that efforts continue to eventually restore it to its original glory. Further sequences may well lie in a movie archive somewhere, perhaps wrongly cataloged. Who knows, there may even be a complete copy tucked away and long forgotten in someone's attic or basement—a foundation stone of the modern movie business just waiting to delight (or appal) once more.

Loch Ness Monster

WHAT IT IS A reputed monster inhabiting the famous Scottish lake
WHY YOU WON'T FIND IT If Nessie is not simply myth, it is certainly highly elusive

Loch Ness is a vast freshwater lake in Scotland, and an area of exquisite natural beauty. Yet there has long been rumor that beneath its placid surface resides a monster of the deep. For the past eighty years, the Loch Ness Monster has been the keystone of a veritable microindustry. So what are your chances of seeing the infamous "Nessie"?

The loch (a traditional Scots Gaelic word for a lake or sea inlet) measures some 22.5 miles (36 kilometers) long, 1.5 miles (2.5 kilometers) wide, and 750 feet (230 meters) deep. It is the second largest lake in Scotland by area after Loch Lomond, but thanks to its depth it contains the largest volume of water by far—so there's certainly plenty of room to hide a monster or two. The truth is, however, that there is very little in the way of solid fact concerning Nessie. The most we can say with confidence is that it is a cryptid—an animal whose existence is disputed. It thus joins the ranks of speculative creatures alongside the likes of the Yeti, the Bunyip, and the Beast of Bodmin Moor.

Those who do believe in the creature claim that it is supported by historical evidence going back for a millennium—in the seventh century, for instance, Adomnán, Abbot of Iona, wrote in his *Vita Columbae* ("*Life of Columba*") of a burial in the vicinity of the River Ness of a man who had been savaged by a "water beast" while out swimming.

However, our modern fascination with the Loch Ness Monster has a rather more recent heritage. In April 1933, a certain Mr. and Mrs. Mackay were driving past the Loch when the good lady spied a large, black creature circling in the water. "Stop!" she screamed at her husband, before exclaiming, "The beast!" The sighting was reported in the *Inverness Courier* in early May 1933 and some three months later the same paper carried the story of George Spicer and his wife. They too had been driving around the Loch when they saw "the nearest approach to a dragon or prehistoric animal that I have ever seen in my life."

By the end of the year, the widely read *Daily Express* newspaper produced the first purported photograph of the creature. The following year saw the appearance of the so-called "Surgeon's photo," showing something emerging from the Loch that does look decidedly strange even if not irrefutably monstrous. It was supposedly taken by one Colonel Robert Wilson (he did not wish his name

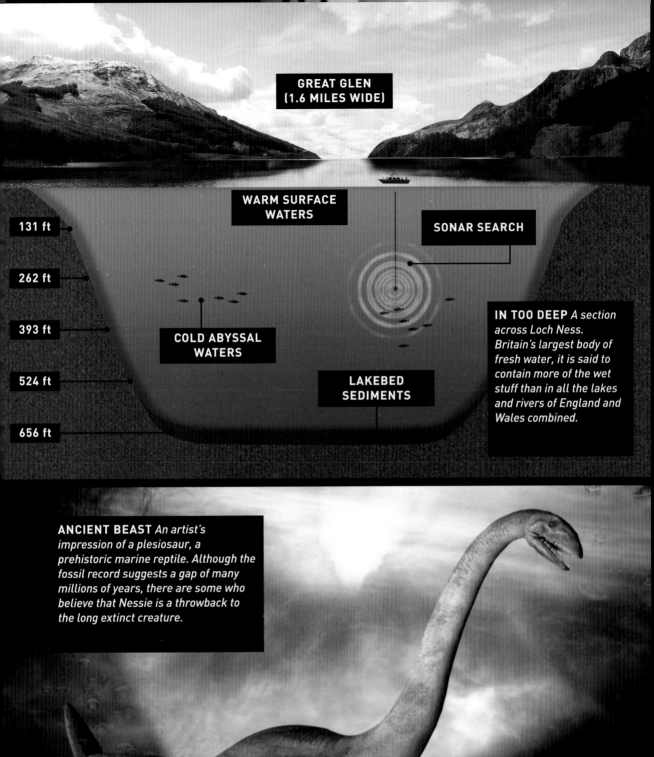

GREAT GLEN
(1.6 MILES WIDE)

WARM SURFACE
WATERS

SONAR SEARCH

131 ft

262 ft

393 ft

COLD ABYSSAL
WATERS

524 ft

LAKEBED
SEDIMENTS

656 ft

IN TOO DEEP *A section across Loch Ness. Britain's largest body of fresh water, it is said to contain more of the wet stuff than in all the lakes and rivers of England and Wales combined.*

ANCIENT BEAST *An artist's impression of a plesiosaur, a prehistoric marine reptile. Although the fossil record suggests a gap of many millions of years, there are some who believe that Nessie is a throwback to the long extinct creature.*

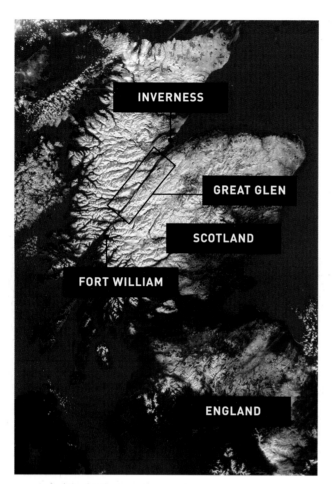

MONSTER'S LAIR? *Loch Ness lies at the northeastern end of the Great Glen, a fault line bisecting the Highlands. The monster legend has proved a great boon to the local tourism industry for decades, and shows no signs of waning.*

Believers have often claimed that the Loch Ness Monster is most likely a type of plesiosaur, a marine reptile that first appeared over 200 million years ago. However, plesiosaurs died out some 65 million years ago, and Loch Ness only formed about 10,000 years ago—did a Triassic throwback somehow survive for all these years tucked away in the Scottish Highlands? Scientific rationality would strongly suggest no.

Others think the loch is home to some long-forgotten species of giant fish. There are certainly eels in these waters, so perhaps Nessie is an outsized example of one of those. Then there are those who suggest that we are actually dealing with a seal or perhaps even a long-necked newt.

The cynics, though, have other ideas. For the best part of a century, Nessie has been a phenomenal money-spinner, attracting vast numbers of visitors to the loch. It has also been pointed out that a great many of the reported sightings have come from local café and hotel owners (Mrs. Mackay herself was a hotel manageress). So for the nonbelievers, Nessie is merely a creature of the imagination—if not a hoax then simply a trick of the light or some quite normal occurrence such as a rotting Scots pine rising to the water's surface.

Submersible vessels and cutting-edge sonar technology have in recent years failed to settle the argument once and for all. And until science does, there will still be plenty of souls scouring the waters of Loch Ness for the monster they are convinced resides there.

to be in the public domain hence the "Surgeon's photo" moniker) early on the morning of April 19, 1934. For years it was regarded as the best evidence of Nessie's existence, but several decades later it was unveiled as a hoax—this monster, at least, had in fact been a toy submarine with a hand-crafted neck and head attached.

Yet today there are still plenty who believe that something strange lives in the loch. The faithful are bolstered by numerous other photographs as well as video apparently capturing Nessie's image. There are well over a thousand reported sightings on record too. So if the story isn't one grand hoax, what sort of creature might we be dealing with?

Roanoke Colony

WHAT IT IS One of England's earliest attempts at settlement in North America

WHY YOU WON'T FIND IT Virtually all trace of the settlement and its inhabitants disappeared

In 1584, Walter Raleigh—that great explorer, aristocrat, and adventurer —was granted a charter by Queen Elizabeth I to establish a colony in Virginia. The intention was that both Raleigh and his monarch would reap a share of the wealth available in the New World. So began the remarkable story of Roanoke, which would go down in history as the "Lost Colony."

Raleigh inherited the scheme for an English settlement in the New World from his half-brother Sir Humphrey Gilbert, who had died in 1583 after putting the wheels in motion. The great buccaneer planned to use the colony as both a trading center and a jumping-off point for privateers to attack treasure-laden Spanish galleons. Roanoke Island (now part of North Carolina) was explored in 1584 by an expedition sent by Raleigh, and identified as a potentially suitable location, but Raleigh had no desire to oversee its establishment himself, instead dispatching a fleet of five ships under the command of Sir Richard Grenville. They left Plymouth on April 9, 1585 and, after a difficult first few months in which they razed a nearby Native American village in retaliation for an alleged theft, established themselves.

Grenville headed back to England in August 1585, leaving behind 108 men under the leadership of one Ralph Lane, with orders to build up a colony in the northern part of the island. Grenville promised to return by April 1586 with new supplies and more settlers. In the meantime, Lane set about building a fort and acquainting himself with the local area and its people. By the middle of 1586, however, there was still no sign of Grenville and relations with some of the local tribes had deteriorated so badly that the colonists had to fight off an attack on the fort. Fortunately, Sir Francis Drake passed by on his way back from a Caribbean jaunt around this time and agreed to transport the colonists back to England. When Grenville finally arrived and discovered the colony abandoned, he too promptly turned tail, leaving 15 men to maintain a claim on the colony. But after further attacks from local tribesmen, they soon fled.

In August 1587, the burned remains of the settlement were discovered by 115 or so new settlers sent from England. Undeterred, they set about building a new village, with John White (one of the original colonists two years earlier) as governor. On August 18, a baby, Virginia Dare, was born—the first child of English parents born in the Americas. Yet

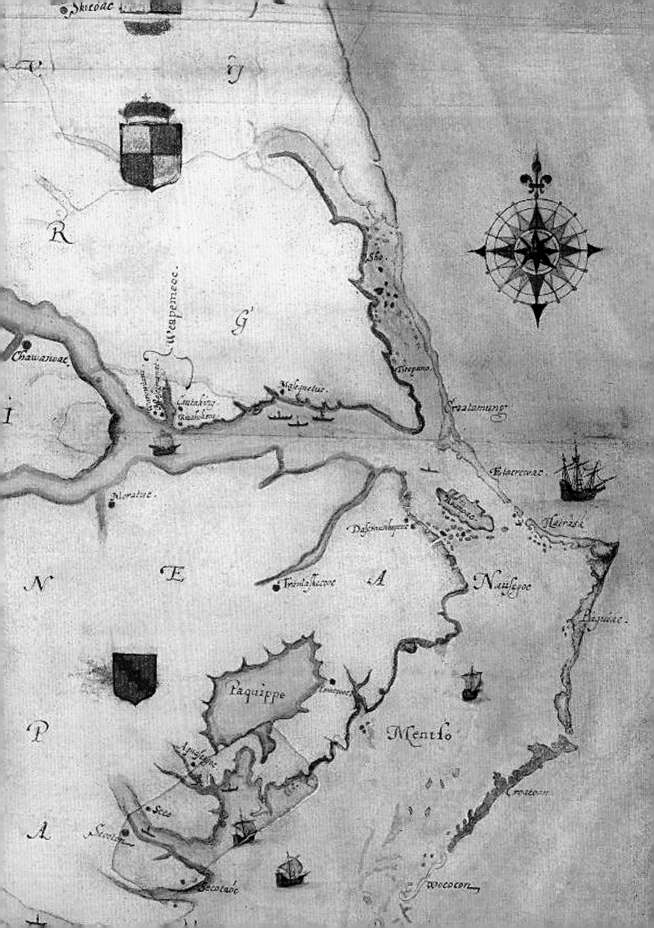

BRAVE NEW WORLD? Above: *A portrait of Sir Walter Raleigh from 1588. In a lifetime of epic adventure, he rose to become one of Elizabeth I's favorites, but was executed by her successor, James I. Opposite: A 1585 chart of the North American coast around Roanoke (the island shown in pink near the center), drawn by English mapmaker John White.*

reference to a friendly local tribe that led White to ponder whether his people had gone to stay with them. However, he was unable to establish whether or not this was indeed the case.

Over the following years, what was left of the colony was either swallowed up by the earth or lost to coastal erosion. Twenty years after the second settlement of Roanoke, England finally established a permanent settlement at Jamestown, Virginia, and Roanoke might have been entirely forgotten were its mystery not so gripping. So what might have happened to the lost colonists?

Some have speculated that Native Americans, tired of years of bad blood, did away with the interlopers, though this does not tally with the lack of signs of violence. Conversely, others have suggested that relations improved so much that the colonists moved inland and married into the local tribe—a hypothesis that may soon be tested by DNA analysis. Climatologists, meanwhile, believe the colony endured a terrible three-year drought from 1587 to 1589, so perhaps the colonists simply grew tired of waiting for White to return and perished at sea as they sought to escape. Or perhaps they were successful in relocating, possibly to nearby Haterras Island or another part of Roanoke (a theory given credence by the 2012 discovery of a contemporary map suggesting the presence of a second fort on the island).

Others have blamed Spanish troops from Florida for murdering the settlers, possibly because they were under the impression that the colony was far more successful (and a greater threat to their interests) than it ever really was. Yet we know that the Spanish authorities were almost as baffled as the English by what had happened at Roanoke.

relations with the neighbors remained as bad as ever, and White was persuaded to return to Britain to seek help.

His return was delayed by war between Spain and England, and when he finally made it back to Roanoke in August 1590, he found the colony abandoned. This time, there was no evidence of violence, nor was there any Maltese Cross—the agreed symbol should they have been forced to leave. Indeed, the buildings seemed to have been abandoned in an organized way, suggesting some sort of preplanning. On one of the fort's posts was carved a single word: "Croatoan"—a

10 Paititi

WHAT IT IS A legendary "lost city" of the Incas
WHY YOU WON'T FIND IT Supposedly buried deep in the Amazon jungle, it has eluded explorers for centuries

The Inca empire was the largest in pre-Columbian South America, awash with gold and silver vital to their religious rites, and Paititi was its legendary "City of Gold," supposedly a depository for fabulous treasures. Though it is by no means certain whether the stories about it are apocryphal, if Paititi did exist, it is likely to have lain deep in the Peruvian Amazon.

Spanish Conquistators first encountered the Inca peoples in the 1520s. Relations were cordial at first, but within a few years the situation became far more tense as the Incas realized that these pale-skinned interlopers brought death and destruction in their wake. Manco Inca, installed as a puppet king by the Spanish, soon turned against his overlords, and in 1539 established a jungle stronghold at Vilcabamba, whose fall in 1572 effectively marked the end of the Inca empire. But it has long been suggested that Vilcabamba was just one of several discreet jungle settlements, packed with stocks of gold and silver.

Another of these, according to legend, was Paititi—a sort of Incan El Dorado. According to the Incan myth of Inkarri, the Spanish executed the last true Incan king, chopped up his body, and buried the various pieces around Peru. One day the pieces will be reunited and he will become one again, supposedly heralding a return of Incan power. The Inkarri is also said to have founded and spent his later life in Paititi, having previously established the cities of Q'ero and Cusco. Those who believe in the existence of Paititi were given a boost in 2002 with the discovery of a remarkable document in the archives of the Jesuit Order in Rome. This was an early 17th-century letter from Father Andre Lopez, Rector of the Jesuit College in Cuzco, describing his dealings with the residents of a city called "Payititi," founded by those fleeing Spanish rule. The document described sophisticated buildings and temples lined with gold.

But when it comes to locating the city today, there is little in the way of solid consensus. In recent decades, academics and explorers have extended their search area from Peru into neighboring northern Bolivia and southwest Brazil. In 2007, there were well publicized claims that ruins found in southern Peru were the remains of the lost city. The discovery was met with cautious excitement by the academic community and welcomed with open arms by the regional tourist industry. Few, though, are convinced that the search has reached its conclusion.

LOST WORLD *A view across jungle-covered Peruvian hills to the Stairs of Intipata, a recently discoverd series of agricultural terraces carved out of the hillside some 9,200 feet (2,800 m) above sea level. Who knows what other settlements lie hidden in such inaccessible terrain?*

11 Holy Grail

WHAT IT IS The "Holy Grail" for all treasure-seekers
WHY YOU WON'T FIND IT Many have tried, few claim success, and even fewer are believed

Perhaps the most sought-after of all the "lost things" in this book, the Holy Grail has become a synonym for any elusive target. Casting aside the Dan Brown generation's alternative takes on the nature of the Grail, it is traditionally understood to be a vessel (usually a cup, plate, or bowl) used by Christ at the Last Supper. And there is no shortage of places that claim to be its home.

In the Bible, the Grail barely warrants a mention within the much broader story of Christ's life and teachings, but by the Middle Ages, it had become less a historical object and more a mythical icon with apparently miraculous properties. Its legend owes much to the mixing of Christian and Celtic traditions: 12th-century French writer Chrétien de Troyes sowed the seeds in his epic poetry, adding the romantic figure of King Arthur (see page 172) to the mix. Chrétien described it thus: "The grail was made of the finest pure gold, and in it were set precious stones of many kinds, the richest and most precious in the earth or the sea."

Theories propagated that it resided in Glastonbury in England, taken there by Joseph of Arimathea, the man who gave up his own tomb for the crucified Jesus. Another popular notion, still held by some, is that the Grail formed part of the mysterious treasure of the Knights Templar (see page 53). So any aspiring Grail-hunter must attempt to answer three fundamental questions on their quest: Is there really such a thing as the Holy Grail? If so, what exactly is it? Finally, where is it? Let's look at some of the claimants:

• Related to the belief that the Grail came to Britain courtesy of Joseph of Arimathea, the so-called Nanteos Cup in Wales has its advocates. A bowl of olive wood, it came into the possession of monks from Glastonbury, who took it to Wales during Henry VIII's dissolution of the monasteries. It eventually found its way to the Powell family, who kept it for many years in their Nanteos Mansion, not far from Aberystwyth. Today, the mansion is a hotel, but the bowl is rarely seen in public.

• Arculf, an Anglo-Saxon pilgrim, claimed in the seventh century to have seen a chalice from the Last Supper in a chapel not far from Jerusalem. Double-handled and made of silver, it has never been found. Jerusalem, and the Temple Mount in particular—is regularly cited as the Grail's home. Another theory points out that Jerusalem historically had an extensive network of underground tunnels ideal for secreting treasures.

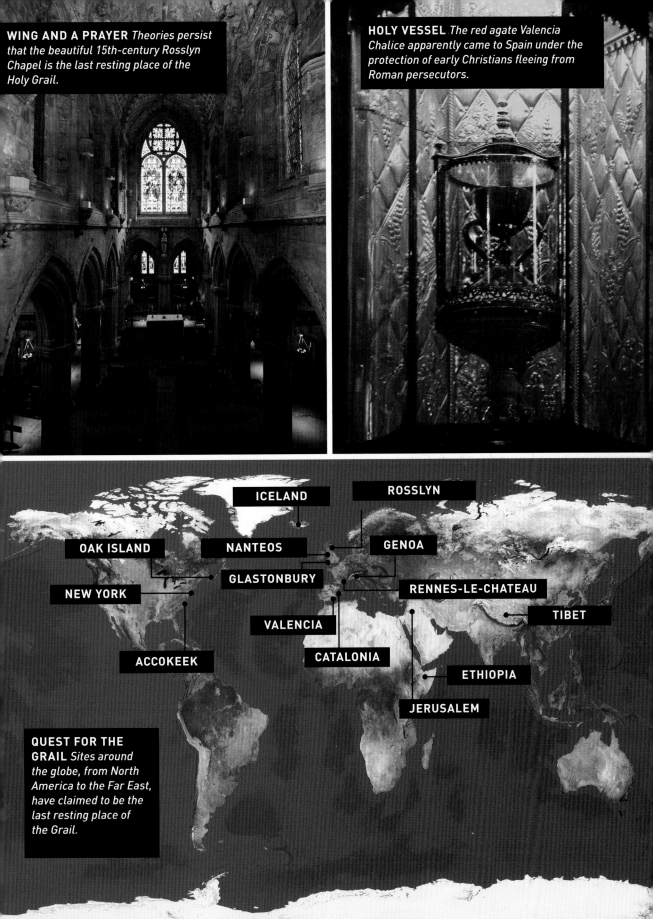

WING AND A PRAYER *Theories persist that the beautiful 15th-century Rosslyn Chapel is the last resting place of the Holy Grail.*

HOLY VESSEL *The red agate Valencia Chalice apparently came to Spain under the protection of early Christians fleeing from Roman persecutors.*

ICELAND

ROSSLYN

OAK ISLAND

NANTEOS

GENOA

GLASTONBURY

NEW YORK

RENNES-LE-CHATEAU

TIBET

VALENCIA

CATALONIA

ACCOKEEK

ETHIOPIA

JERUSALEM

QUEST FOR THE GRAIL *Sites around the globe, from North America to the Far East, have claimed to be the last resting place of the Grail.*

GOSPEL TRUTH *Leonardo da Vinci painted* The Last Supper *on the wall of Santa Maria della Grazie in Milan during the 1490s. Although a chalice is conspicuously absent from the painting, some have interpreted the grail as a platter or dish, similar to the one Leonardo shows in front of Christ.*

• The Antioch Chalice, discovered at Antioch in modern-day Turkey in 1911, is now in the collection of the New York Metropolitan Museum of Art. Though much of the fabric of the object postdates Christ's life, there is evidence that its inner lining was made around the right period. However, even the Met itself regards claims that it is the Holy Grail as "ambitious."

• Italy's San Lorenzo Cathedral, meanwhile, is home to the Genoa Chalice, which entered the historical record in the 12th century. Its claims to greatness, though, were hit when the emerald vessel was damaged after Napoleon demanded it be sent to Paris, and it was revealed to be made less of emerald and more of green glass.

• Then there is the Valencia Chalice in Spain, on display in the Catedral de Santa Maria. A red agate vessel, it has been dated to both the right era and part of the world and continues to be used on occasion in papal masses.

• Alternatively, the castle of the Fisher King—who in the Arthurian legends is charged with protecting the Grail—has been identified by some as being located on Montserrat, a mountain in Catalonia. This has given rise to speculation that the Grail might lie in the grounds of the nearby Benedictine abbey of Santa Maria de Montserrat.

• Other theories link the Grail to stories we have already explored in this book—was it among Templar treasures supposedly spirited away to Rosslyn Chapel in Scotland, or Oak Island in Nova Scotia? Or did it fall into the hands of the Cathar sect of Languedoc and end up secreted at Rennes-le-Château?

• Perhaps more unlikely still is the claim of Accokeek in Maryland. According to local folklore, the Grail came to the town in the first decade of the 17th century, deposited by a Jesuit priest who had stowed away on a ship captained by the English explorer, John Smith.

Of course, many are convinced that the Grail lies somewhere else altogether. Should you be the one lucky enough to turn it up, you will face one last challenge—convincing the world that your grail is *the* Grail.

Franklin's lost fleet

WHAT IT IS A mid-19th century expedition to find the Northwest Passage **WHY YOU WON'T FIND IT** Rescue parties have consistently failed to track it down

In 1845, Captain John Franklin set off from England for the Canadian Arctic in a bid to plot the last unmapped section of the Northwest Passage. He took with him two ships and 133 men, but by 1850 all of them had disappeared, apparently without trace. It was a story that caused a furore in Victorian Britain, and almost 170 years later the vessels and most of the men remain lost.

The search for the Northwest Passage—an alternative route taking sailors from the Atlantic to the Pacific Ocean via the northern coast of North America—had obsessed the maritime nations of Europe for centuries. Franklin's first journey to survey the Arctic shoreline was in 1819, and he undertook a second from 1825–27. Following that trip he was knighted and appointed Lieutenant-Governor of Van Diemen's Land (modern Tasmania).

Though almost 60, Franklin was invited to lead a new expedition in search of the Northwest Passage in 1845. Setting off on May 19, it was to be among the best equipped in history, with two technologically advanced vessels—HMS *Erebus* and HMS *Terror*—134 experienced and capable crew, and food supplies sufficient for at least five years. In early July, the party was reduced in number from 134 to 129 when Franklin sent home five men while docked in Greenland. The last verified sighting of the expedition came at the end of the same month when the crews of two whalers, *Prince of Wales* and

Enterprise, spotted *Erebus* and *Terror* in Baffin Bay, Canada.

Franklin was a significant public figure in Britain, so there was naturally great interest in the expedition's progress. When three years passed without word, the Admiralty came under pressure, not least from Franklin's wife Jane, to send a rescue mission. Eventually, one land expedition and two seafaring missions were launched in 1848, and a reward of $33,288 was also offered for anyone who could find the lost vessels. Such was the pull of the prize that by 1850 there were some 13 British and American ships engaged in tracing the party.

At the end of that year, search parties finally found signs of the expedition, discovering a few personal effects and the graves of three crewmen on Beechey Island in the Wellington Channel. Over the next few years more of the crew's possessions were recovered, along with oral testimony from the native Inuit population. When Dr. Rae of the Hudson Bay Company

DOCUMENTARY EVIDENCE *The 1859 search party uncovered this chilling document in a cairn on King William Island. Franklin's own progress report (in the middle) has been superseded by a scribbled record of the increasingly desperate situation around the outer margins.*

of 24 men had died, including Franklin himself on June 11, 1847.

Further expeditions over the remainder of the 19th century and into the 20th gradually built up a picture of what had occurred by recording physical evidence (including bodies and graves) and interviewing the Inuit. In the early 1980s a team from Alberta University concluded that the men had been killed by a combination of hypothermia, pneumonia, tuberculosis, scurvy, starvation and, in some cases, lead poisoning. The latter may have stemmed either from faulty food cans or water pipes. From cut marks evident on bone samples, the academics also concluded that the stories of cannibalism were likely true.

It was a dismal end to an ambitious and seemingly well-prepared adventure, and Franklin maintained the status of a hero among his Victorian contemporaries. Nevertheless, his body—and those of most of his men—remain undiscovered, lost to the elements or lying in unmarked graves. As for the ships, it is likely they were smashed by the ice and lost beneath the waves long ago.

published a selection of their evidence in 1854, he came to a grim conclusion. After the ill-fated expedition became stranded "... it is evident that our wretched Countrymen had been driven to the last dread alternative—cannibalism—as a means of prolonging existence."

The entire party were officially declared dead in 1854 but Lady Franklin wanted to know more. In 1859, she sponsored an expedition that discovered two messages on King William Island. The first, dated May 28 1847, stated that both *Erebus* and *Terror* had spent the previous winter off the coast there. "Sir John Franklin commanding the Expedition," it read. "All well." However, the second message, written in the margins of the first and dated April 25 1848, disclosed that the vessels had become trapped in ice and been abandoned. By that stage, a total

13 Shakespeare's *Love's Labour's Won*

WHAT IT IS A proposed lost play by the "Swan of Avon"
WHY YOU WON'T FIND IT No manuscript of the play has ever been produced as evidence of its existence

There is a surprising amount of debate around just how many plays William Shakespeare wrote. While few disagree with his authorship of the 37 included in most modern *Complete Works*, he is regularly cited as the sole or coauthor of several other extant plays, and is sometimes credited with a further two "lost plays," one of which—*Love's Labour's Won*—seems to have vanished without trace.

While Shakespeare is today the most revered writer in the English language, he made little effort in his lifetime to preserve his works in printed form. He wrote for the stage, freely adapting and overhauling his works as each specific production demanded, and was apparently unconcerned with posterity. Indeed, were it not for the efforts of a few friends who produced the *First Folio* of 36 plays in 1623, seven years after his death, many more of his works might have been utterly lost to us. Since then, academics have largely agreed that Shakespeare penned at least half of *Pericles, Prince of Tyre*, bringing the total of the accepted "canon" to 37.

Several more plays sometimes attributed to him (at least in part) remain the focus of heated dispute, including *Edward III*, *Sir Thomas More*, *Edmund Ironside*, and *The Two Noble Kinsmen*. But there are also two "lost plays"—both of them credited to Shakespeare in near-contemporary records, but neither of which have survived in their original form. *The History of Cardenio* was listed in a 1653 entry in the Stationers' Register (an official log of copyright) as the work of Shakespeare and John Fletcher. In 1727 a certain Lewis Theobald published a play called *Double Falsehood*, which he claimed was based on three original manuscript versions of Shakespeare's *Cardenio*, which itself borrowed heavily on Cervantes's *Don Quixote* for plot. Many modern experts now agree that Theobald's work contains several fragments of Shakespeare within it, so this "lost play" may be considered at least partially rediscovered. The same cannot be said of *Love's Labour's Won*.

The first reference to it comes from an essay of 1598 by one Francis Mere, a cleric and teacher, who mentions it in a short list of Shakespeare's comedies. *Love labour won*, as he called it, followed directly after *Love labour lost*, suggesting that he hadn't simply miswritten the title of that other similar-sounding canonical work.

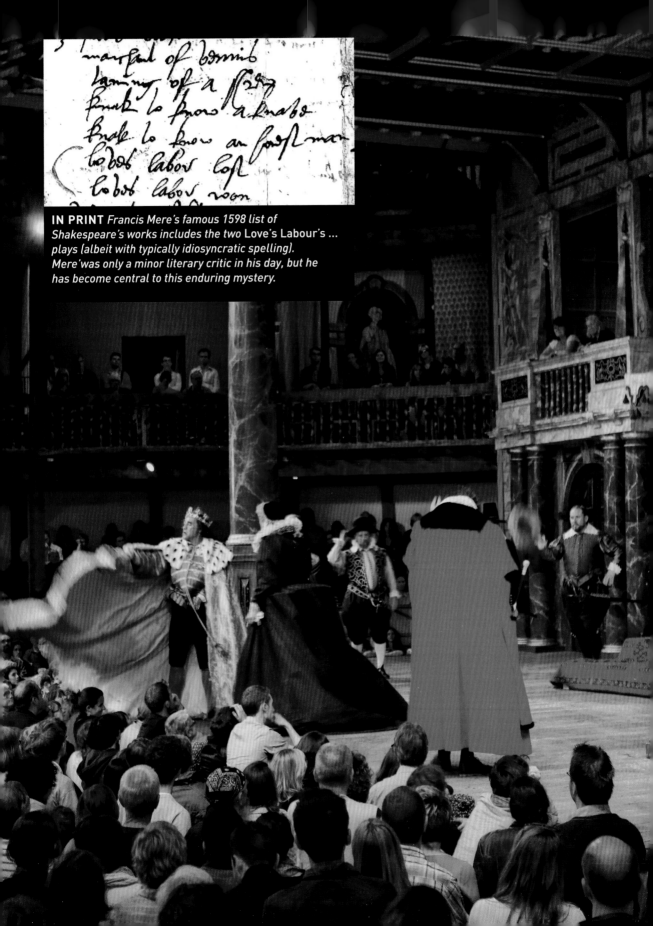

IN PRINT *Francis Mere's famous 1598 list of Shakespeare's works includes the two* Love's Labour's ... *plays (albeit with typically idiosyncratic spelling). Mere'was only a minor literary critic in his day, but he has become central to this enduring mystery.*

GLOBAL VIEW *A view of the original Globe Theatre, built in Southwark on the south side of the River Thames in 1599 by the Lord Chamberlain's Men, of whom Shakespeare was an employee. If he did write a play called* Love's Labours Won, *then there is a good chance that it would have been performed here. Today a modern replica stands close to the site.*

To take the latter conjecture first, while Mere's list may have included *Love's Labour's Lost*, his list omits another great comedy that had certainly been written by that stage, namely *The Taming of the Shrew*. Others have suggested that *Love's Labour's Won* was an alternative title for *Much Ado About Nothing*, which some critics have suggested has distinct correlations with *Love's Labour's Lost* and was produced very close to the time that Mere was writing. Some have even been posited that the lost play was not a comedy at all, but a version of the tragedy *Troilus and Cressida*.

On the other hand, those who support the argument that *Love's Labour's Won* was a unique work and not merely an alternative title point not only to the play's sequel-like name, but also to the manner in which *Love's Labour's Lost*, its presumed counterpart, concludes. At the climax, our heroes—the king of Navarre and his high-born companions Berowne, Dumaine, and Longaville—are told by their respective loves to wait for a year before seeing them again, as a test of their fidelity. There is none of the neatness that characterizes the endings of many Shakespearean works, and indeed, it would be fair to say that the story is crying out for a sequel.

A further reference to the play only came to light in the mid-20th century, found in the 1603 records of a bookseller called Christopher Hunt.

If we are to accept that this was indeed a play by Shakespeare, we may reasonably make one of two assumptions. Either it was a totally original work (though surely somehow linked to the aforementioned *Love's Labour's Lost*), or it was a work that came down to us with a different title. There are advocates aplenty for both arguments.

All of which tends to give credence to the idea that there is an authentic lost Shakespeare play written at some time before Mere's 1598 essay. Conceivably, Shakespeare was typically slack about preserving a copy of the text himself, and when no one else did, the play disappeared forever. But perhaps some alert actor or stagehand did grab a copy and kept hold of it. If they did, then whoever finds it can expect to become a very wealthy individual indeed.

Raoul Wallenberg

WHO HE IS A Swedish war hero who saved thousands of Jews from the Nazis **WHY YOU WON'T FIND HIM** Last known to have been held in Moscow's Lubyanka Prison, his fate is the subject of conjecture

Raoul Wallenberg is regarded as one of the greatest heroes of the Second World War, his work to save thousands of Jews from the Nazi gas chambers winning him countless international honors. Yet just what happened to him is uncertain. Last seen in January 1945, when, where and how he died (and, if not naturally, at whose hands) has never been satisfactorily established.

Born into a prominent Swedish family in 1912, Wallenberg studied in Paris before graduating in architecture from the University of Michigan in 1935. On returning to Sweden, he entered business and in 1936 began working for a trading company run by a Hungarian Jew, Kálmán Lauer. As the 1930s neared their end, Hungary came increasingly within the German sphere of influence and introduced a raft of anti-Semitic laws. Since his boss could not be sure of safety in his homeland, Wallenberg frequently found himself acting as Lauer's representative in Budapest.

In 1944, Hitler ordered the occupation of Hungary, establishing a puppet government and ordering the deportation of Jews to the concentration camps as part of the "Final Solution." Around June of that year Wallenberg was approached by the US-Founded War Refugee Board who asked him to move to Hungary and work on a program to assist the Jewish population there. By the time he was assigned to the Swedish diplomatic corps in Budapest a month later, there were just 230,000 Jews left in the country—almost 400,000 less than at the beginning of the year. Along with fellow diplomats, Wallenberg set about issuing fake Swedish papers to the remaining Jews, stating that they were to be repatriated and thus exempt from transportation. He also rented a swathe of real estate and declared the buildings protected by diplomatic immunity. These buildings housed around 10,000 Jews in safety, while Wallenberg gained a reputation for courage in the face of extreme intimidation from Nazis and Hungary's own Fascists, the Arrow Cross Party. While estimates differ, the efforts of Wallenberg (and a network of several hundred associates) saved the lives of anything from 15,000 to 100,000 people.

With Soviet troops threatening the German occupiers by the end of 1944, Wallenberg had to use all his diplomatic skills to prevent a last-ditch attempt by the Nazis to exterminate or transport Hungary's remaining Jews. The Soviets,

however, were wary of him, suspecting links to Western intelligence agencies.

On January 17,1945, Wallenberg was summoned to the city of Debrecen by the Soviet authorities. What happened next remains highly contentious. The Swedish authorities were informed that Wallenberg was under Soviet protection. He was then transported to Moscow, where he was held in Cell 123 of the infamous Lubyanka Prison. In March, Hungarian radio (now controlled by the Kremlin) falsely reported that Wallenberg and his driver had been

killed in a car accident en route to Debrecen two months earlier. By 1947, Moscow was telling the government in Stockholm they had no trace of him, suggesting he must have been killed in the chaos of the Germans' final days in Budapest, or at the hands of Nazi or Arrow Cross agents.

Ten years later, however, a new story emerged when the Kremlin released documentation apparently dating to July 17, 1947 stating that Wallenberg had died in his Moscow cell from a heart attack or similar complaint. Yet many doubted

PLACE OF NO RETURN? *Moscow's Lubyanka Building (left) was the notorious headquarters of the Soviet KGB security agency. After showing remarkable bravery fighting the Nazis in the Second World War, Wallenberg (above) was taken here—but thereafter his fate is unclear.*

this official version of events. There was much suspicion that his death was in no way natural but that he had been, in fact, executed or assassinated.

Several former prisoners of the Soviet regime claimed that Wallenberg had not been killed at all but had remained within the Gulag system, possibly into the 1980s. Theories abounded that he was held in the hope that he could be used as leverage in negotiations with the West, and that there were plans in the 1950s to use him in a show trial. It is possible that he was originally kept

alive with such aims in mind but, as the Cold War took grip, Moscow felt that a "disappearance" was the easiest option.

The search continues, spearheaded by members of Wallenberg's family who remain convinced that the answers to the mystery lie in Russian, Swedish, or Hungarian archives. In 2012, the Russian security services reiterated that his case remains open and that the post-Soviet government has no part in an official cover-up. It is to be hoped that the truth about one of the 20th century's true heroes will one day come to light.

A translation of the Cascajal block

WHAT IT IS A key to the earliest written language in the Americas
WHY YOU WON'T FIND IT Thus far, only one inscription using the language has been discovered

The chance discovery of an inscribed stone tablet by workmen in Mexico in the late 1990s seemed to open a window onto an ancient writing system lost for close to three millennia. Though not all academics are convinced by its authenticity, it potentially provides evidence of the oldest known written language in the Americas. The only problem is, nobody knows what it says.

Discovered by road builders excavating an ancient mound at Cascajal near San Lorenzo in the Mexican state of Veracru, the block weighs some 26 pounds (12 kg) and measures 14 x 8 x 5 inches (36 x 21 x 13 cm) It is inscribed with 62 symbols, made up of some 28 individual markings.

It was not until 2006 that academics studying the block revealed their findings to the world. They concluded that the tablet was evidence of a writing system in use in the New World around 900 BC. Previously, the oldest known writing (from the Zapotec civilization) dated to about 500 BC. The Cascajal text originates from the Olmec, a Mesoamerican people who inhabited a swathe of land along the Gulf of Mexico from around 1200 BC. Their artistic works, most notably enormous sculpted heads, had long been known, but never before had there been any indication that they used a written language.

When details of the find were published in the journal *Science*, they sparked a fierce debate. Its mixture of symbols—including ears of corn, seashells, insects, and abstract shapes—left many in no doubt that it qualified as writing. Others, though, were less convinced. They were uncomfortable that it had been removed from the ground in an unsupervised manner and that it had been attributed to the Olmec through fragments of ceramics found alongside it, rather than by dating the stone itself.

Furthermore, other Mesoamerican writing systems tend to be written vertically, whereas the Cascajal text forms broadly horizontal lines. In fact, it has precious few similarities with any other known ancient writing from the region, such as that of the Mayans. And if this was evidence of a written language, why has no one found any other examples?

In the absence of an Olmec "Rosetta Stone," we may have a long wait for answers. Is it too much to hope that a construction worker will one day stumble upon the key by another roadside?

Hangar 18

WHAT IT IS An alleged depository for evidence of alien life
WHY YOU WON'T FIND IT According to the faithful, "they" don't want us to find it

For those arguing that extraterrestrials have visited Earth, there is a frustrating lack of conclusive evidence. Believers more often than not cite the legendary Roswell incident of 1947—but where is the evidence for this alleged alien crash-landing? Many UFOlogists suspect that it is contained within the mysterious and elusive "Hangar 18."

One of the most curious things about this storehouse of alleged alien treasure is that not only do people argue over whether it exists, but even those who support its existence still cannot agree on where exactly it is. Two sites, however, are regularly put forward— some are sure the hangar is (or at least, was) located at the Wright-Patterson Air Force Base in Ohio. This base opened in 1917 not far from Dayton, and between 1947 and 1969 was the headquarters for Project Blue Book, a study conducted by the US Air Force to examine data from reported UFO sightings and determine whether they represented a threat to national security. The project ultimately concluded there was no proof that any UFO ever posed such a threat, or originated extraterrestrially. However, the fact that the study happened at all has bolstered those who claim Hangar 18 existed and was filled with other-worldly material.

An alternative view identifies the hangar as a building within Area 51—part of a United States Air Force facility in Southern Nevada, thought to be attached to the Edwards Air Force Base in California. Covering 21,000 acres in the Nevada Desert, Area 51 was a weapons testing area in the Second World War and has been used for developing cutting-edge military technology since at least the 1950s. Amid such heightened secrecy, suspicion is sure to follow, and rumors have abounded over the years that the US government has used Area 51 to conduct research into such outré areas as time travel and weather control. But the most enduring of all the rumors concern the events said to have taken place in Roswell, New Mexico in 1947.

In July of that year, a press release from the Army Air Field at Roswell stated, astonishingly, that an unidentified object had been recovered there. It followed several weeks of reports from civilians of a disklike object in the skies. The media soon got their teeth into the story, and public interest was well and truly piqued by the time the military decided to retract its statement. In years to come, declassified papers would suggest that

TOP SECRET
Main picture: *An aerial view of the Wright-Patterson Air Force Base, near Dayton, Ohio. A one-time center of government-run UFO investigations, could it also be the home of the purported Hangar 18?*

KEEP OUT! *The boundary of Nevada's Area 51 is littered with signs warning off anyone tempted to set foot on to the restricted ground. Such ferocious security has inevitably given rise to all sorts of speculation as to what secrets are kept there.*

the UFO was nothing more than a secret surveillance balloon, but by then there were plenty of people convinced that a large-scale cover-up was in action.

By the 1970s, the Roswell Incident was at the heart of a mini-industry catering to ardent conspiracy theorists. It was variously claimed that not only had a UFO crash-landed in New Mexico, but it was successfully recovered by the government, studied, and reverse engineered. "Where on earth do we think technological developments such as the Stealth bomber originate?" argued some. In the late 1980s, a man named Bob Lazar announced he had been a physicist at Area 51 and had witnessed no less than nine alien spacecraft stored on site. Even more startling were suggestions that the Roswell craft contained one or more alien visitors, though opinion varies as to whether

they were alive or dead. Talk of a movie showing an autopsy conducted on one of the extraterrestrial crew has also refused to go away. Certain conspiracy theorists are convinced that the Roswell debris is stored at Area 51, perhaps in a vast underground complex of tunnels and warehouses centered around the notorious Hangar 18.

Whatever the truth of Hangar 18 and its purported contents, it has become a rallying point for both those who distrust their earthly masters and those convinced there is sentient life beyond our planet. It was even the subject of a song by heavy metal band Megadeath. In truth, we know very little about Hangar 18. It could be in Ohio or perhaps in Nevada. But perhaps its most likely home is somewhere deep in our collective imagination.

Treasure of the Knights Templar

WHAT IT IS The alleged trove of the famous Crusader Order
WHY YOU WON'T FIND IT We are not sure what we are looking for, let alone where it is

For fans of conspiracy theories, few organizations capture the imagination like the Order of the Knights Templar. In just under two centuries, the Templars established themselves as one of the world's richest and most powerful organizations, only to fall from grace in spectacular circumstances. Rumors abound of stores of valuable and important treasure, but where might it have ended up?

The Poor Fellow-Soldiers of Christ and the Temple of Solomon, better known as the Knights Templar, were founded by Hugues de Payens around 1119 to assist the passage of Christians on their way to the Holy Land. Jerusalem's Crusader King, Baldwin II, gave permission for the knights to base themselves on the city's Temple Mount, ancient site of the Temple of Solomon.

A decade later, the organization received the official sanction of the Roman Catholic Church, and as a result, began to attract large financial donations from the wealthy across Europe. Its ranks swelled with the sons of many prominent families, and in the years that followed, the Vatican granted it unprecedented powers that put it above all authority expect that of the papacy itself.

Some suspected that Templar influence over the church was the result of something the knights had discovered in Jerusalem—there was talk that they had found the Holy Grail, the Ark of the Covenant, or secret documentation that

shed new light on the life of Christ. One thing that all the rumors agreed on was that they were in possession of something of quite extraordinary value.

Templar operations expanded from merely protecting pilgrims into areas such as banking (although the knights retained all their skills as an awesome fighting force). Visitors to the Holy Lands could deposit their worldly goods with the knights ahead of a pilgrimage, and the order became a major lender to European monarchies. The order also bought up swathes of land in both Europe and the Middle East, earning yet more revenue from the agriculture and industry that took place on its property.

The entire island of Cyprus belonged to the Templars, and it was here that the order relocated in the late 13th century after a sustained downturn in its fortunes. Reversals against Muslim forces had seen the order lose much of its land and some of its reputation, but it remained enormously wealthy. This

TREASURE HOUSE? *A view of the mysterious Tour Magadala at Rennes-le-Château in the Languedoc region of France. Just what did the village's 19th-century priest, Bérenger Saunière, uncover here?*

HOLY SMOKE *This image of the execution of two Templars (one of them probably Grand Master Jacques de Molay) comes from the medieval* Grandes Chroniques de France, *composed by the monks of Saint-Denis. The fall of the Templars was sudden and brutal, but according to all accounts, the knights took the secrets of their treasure to their graves.*

was in dangerous contrast to King Philip IV of France, who found himself mired in debt to them. Embittered, he planned his revenge, and on Friday, October 13, 1307 hundreds of knights, including the Templar Grand Master Jacques de Molay, were arrested and charged with heresy by Pope Clement V. Much of the evidence was undoubtedly trumped up at Philip's behest: accused of, among other things, homosexual relations and spitting on the cross, dozens of the Templars were burned at the stake. De Molay himself was executed in 1314—two years after

Philip had persuaded Clement to disband the order.

But when Philip's soldiers went in search of the Templar treasury, they discovered it gone. One of the knights, John de Châlon, testified that following a tip-off about the mass arrests in 1307, three wagons laden with gold, silver, and precious stones had been smuggled out of Paris and loaded onto Templar ships. If this did indeed happen, then the fleet's ultimate destination is unclear. Some have suggested that the fleeing Templars headed for Scotland, while others favor Spain or Croatia as more likely locations. A few have even suggested that the Templars made a pre-Columbian voyage to the Americas, depositing their treasure on Oak Island off the coast of Nova Scotia.

There is also Rennes-le-Château, in France's Languedoc region. Here, it is said that a local priest named Bérenger Saunière discovered buried treasure while renovating his church in the late 1800s. Exactly what he found—if anything at all—is not clear, but since the 1950s his story has gained popular currency, not least through the 1982 book *The Holy Blood and the Holy Grail* that influenced Dan Brown's global hit, *The Da Vinci Code*. Inevitably, some are convinced that Saunière found nothing less than the lost Templar treasure.

What we know for sure is that the Knights Templar built up a vast hoard of both wealth and power, and that the order's end was sudden and messy— fertile ground for those who believe in a secret and lost treasure. But the barriers to uncovering the truth are immense. Not only is its location uncertain, but its true nature is equally murky. For those with the desire, this is a treasure that lets you choose your own conspiracy theory.

The Mahogany Ship

WHAT IT IS A mooted shipwreck off the coast of Australia

WHY YOU WON'T FIND IT Sightings ended in the 1880s and no firm evidence for its existence has ever been produced

Between the 1830s and 1880s, there were regular reports of the wreck of an unusual, dark-wood ship in the waters off Victoria, Australia. If proven to exist, the "Mahogany Ship" could rewrite the history of European exploration on the continent. However, so far no one has been able to locate it, leading to suspicions that it may be no more than the product of local legend.

The first of the relevant sightings seems to date to 1836, according to details recorded by author George Dunderdale in 1898: "*In January, 1836, Captain Smith, who was in charge of the whaling station at Port Fairy, went with two men, named Wilson and Gibbs, in a whale boat to the islands near Warrnambool, to look for seal ... On this journey they found the wreck of a vessel, supposed to be a Spanish one, which has since been covered by the drifting sand.*"

Over the ensuing decades, rumors grew of a large, old-fashioned wreck in the waters west of Warrnambool, toward Port Fairy in southwest Victoria. It was usually described as constructed from a dark, mahogany-like wood, and possibly of Spanish origin. Some 30 sightings were recorded, often differing in details. Then, in the 1880s, they came to an end, and it was assumed that the Mahogany Ship was now entirely hidden beneath layers of sand.

The first concerted attempt to rediscover the Mahogany Ship, made in 1890 by a local historian called Joseph Archibald, met with a notable lack of success, starting a trend that continues to the present day despite the use of cutting-edge technology and offers of rewards from the Victorian government. There have been occasional exciting finds, such as a 6.6-foot (2-m) length of white oak discovered in 2000, but no firm connections to the Mahogany Ship have ever been established.

Those convinced that tales of the vessel are more than simply folklore have come up with various theories over the years. It has been suggested that the ship was not Spanish at all but, variously, Dutch, Arabic, or Chinese in origin—or possibly even a whaling boat. Another idea is that convicts built it to attempt an escape from Tasmania. Perhaps most intriguing of all, though, is the suggestion—laid out in detail in Kenneth McIntyre's 1977 book *The Secret Discovery of Australia*—that it was part of a Portuguese fleet wrecked in 1522—250 years before Captain Cook claimed credit for the first European exploration of Australia's east coast.

WRECKED *No contemporary images of the Mahogany Ship exist but this retrospective depiction was painted by the Australian artist, Thomas Clark (1814–83).*

VICTORIA

WARRNAMBOOL

MELBOURNE

PORT FAIRY

PIONEERS? *Speculation suggests that the Mahogany Ship was a European, Asian, or Arabian wreck. Victoria received numerous international visitors hoping to establish links with Australia but were the Mahogany Ship's crew among the first to arrive?*

TASMANIA

19 Pythagoras's complete works

WHAT THEY ARE The lifelong labors of one of the ancient world's great thinkers
WHY YOU WON'T FIND THEM No authentic written records of his teachings and philosophy survive

His name has struck fear into the hearts of schoolchildren for millennia yet the man responsible for countless "must try harder" comments has failed to leave us any of his own homework. As the first man to call himself a "philosopher" (literally, a lover of wisdom), there can be few such influential figures whose entire original work has disappeared.

Pythagoras was born on the Greek island of Samos around 570 BC, and died some 75 years later at Metapontum, a city in Magna Graeca (southern Italy). He is best known to us today as the man behind the famous theorem about right-angled triangles, but there was much more to him than that one rule of geometry. An intrepid traveler in his youth, he worked extensively in the fields of mathematics, politics, music, astronomy, medicine, and philosophy. In addition, he was a noted mystic and, having established himself in the Magna Graeca city of Croton around 530 BC, effectively became leader of a secretive and ascetic philosophical school (Pythagoreanism) that saw reality in terms of mathematical relationships. Such ideas were hugely influential in his own lifetime, but the Pythagoreans were attacked by their enemies and effectively supressed in his later years.

It is difficult, too, to overestimate his enduring impact. Many academics believe that Plato was greatly indebted to his teachings, while Bertrand Russell once said: "It is to this gentleman that we owe pure mathematics." Yet not a single word he wrote has survived. Instead, his ideas are known solely through the work of others, mostly writing centuries after he died. Even some of the extant texts attributed to him in antiquity are now suspected of having been forgeries.

Pythagoras worked in an age where the oral tradition ruled, and his thinking spread primarily by word of mouth. So we must look to the writings of the likes of Plato (fifth to fourth centuries BC), Aristotle, Aristoxenus, Diogenes Laërtius, and Heraclides Ponticus (all fourth century BC) as well as later writers such as Iamblichus (second to third century AD) for a sense of his teachings. Today, however, some question how many of the ideas attributed to him are actually the work of others—if some of his original manuscripts came to light now by some miracle, it might allow us once and for all to discern just how great a contribution he made to the development of human knowledge. The tale also serves as an object lesson for pupils everywhere: always show your working!

Jules Rimet Trophy

WHAT IT IS The original soccer World Cup
WHY YOU WON'T FIND IT It was stolen in 1983

Soccer is the true global game, reaching every corner of the planet, and the pinnacle for any player is to lift the World Cup. Since the competition's inauguration in 1930, only a few hundred have had the good fortune to do so. When Brazil won the competition for a then-record third time in 1970 they were given the original trophy for keeps. Alas, it was stolen while on public display 13 years later.

In 1930, Uruguay became the first winners of the World Cup in a tournament played on their home turf. The trophy itself, made of gold-plated sterling silver, depicted the Greek goddess of Victory, Nike, supporting an octagonal cup. Standing some 14 inches (35 cm) tall and weighing in at 8.4 pounds (3.8 kg), it was created by the renowned French sculptor, Abel Lafleur. In 1946, the cup was officially renamed as the Jules Rimet Trophy, in honor of the French president of FIFA (world soccer's governing body) who oversaw the tournament's creation.

The cup had already had a couple of close shaves with oblivion before it finally disappeared for good. In 1938, Italy became World Champions at the last tournament to be played before the onset of the Second World War. At the time, FIFA's vice president was an Italian called Ottorino Barassi, and he squirreled the trophy away from a bank vault in Rome and hid it in a shoe box under his bed for the duration of the war to keep it out of the reach of the Nazis.

The trophy's next drama occurred in England in 1966, when it was put on display at Westminster City Hall in London during the build up to that year's tournament. A mix of uniformed and plain-clothes police kept guard over it, but while the exhibition was not open to the public, the cup was briefly left unattended. At around ten past midday on Sunday, March 20, guards noticed that the back of its display case had been broken into and the trophy taken.

A couple of days later, the chairman of the English Football Association received part of the cup's removable lining through the mail—along with a ransom demand for $25,000. By now, the story was dominating the headlines but there was scant progress in recovering the precious treasure until the heart-warming intervention of a black-and-white Collie dog by the name of Pickles.

While out walking with his owner, David Corbett, on March 27 in Upper Norwood, a suburb of southeast London, Pickles sniffed out a package wrapped in

FETCH, BOY!
Pickles the dog enjoys some press attention after discovering the stolen soccer World Cup in a hedge while out for a walk with his owner. Unfortunately, Pickles was unavailable to help the Brazilian police 17 years later.

newspaper and tied with string, hidden in a hedge. To Mr. Corbett's surprise, it turned out to contain the Jules Rimet Trophy. Pickles instantly became a national celebrity, and while no one was ever convicted of the theft, one man, Edward Betchley, was found guilty of demanding money with menaces.

In 1970, the much-traveled trophy finally retired after Brazil won the tournament for a third time: in accordance with Rimet's original wishes, any nation achieving this was to receive the cup in perpetuity. Brazil had dominated that year's tournament in Mexico with a style and panache never before seen, marshaled by perhaps the greatest player that ever lived, Pelé. So it seemed fitting that the Jules Rimet Trophy should go on permanent display at the offices of the Brazilian Football Confederation (CBF) in Rio de Janeiro. It was replaced by an entirely new tournament trophy, sculpted by Italian Silvio Gazzaniga, but sadly the original was not to be granted a long and peaceful retirement.

Although displayed behind bulletproof glass, the cabinet in which it sat was somewhat lightweight. On the evening of December 19, 1983 the CBF's offices were raided by a gang of thieves. They tied up a guardsman, removed the trophy cabinet from the wall, and made off into the night. The theft became a source of great shame to many in the soccer-mad nation. Several suspects were arrested, but no one was charged until three Brazilians and an Argentine were eventually convicted of the heist *in absentia*. The cup itself was never found, and is widely believed to have been melted down shortly after it was stolen. If true, it was a sad end for an object worth far more as a symbol of sporting greatness than as scrap metal.

Thanks to the craftsmanship of German company Wilhelm Geist and Son of Hanau, a replica was presented to Brazil in 1984. As for the trophy that World Cup winners receive today, it remains the property of FIFA and is no longer passed from winning nation to winning nation.

King John's crown jewels

WHAT IT IS "Bad" King John's regalia
WHY YOU WON'T FIND IT They were lost on an ill-fated journey across England

One of the most reviled figures in English history, "Bad" King John also suffered the indignity of mislaying a large slice of his worldly wealth shortly before his death. Though credible contemporary accounts of exactly what happened to the crown jewels are scant, his decision to send his baggage train on a route subject to fast-changing tides appears to have been a fateful one.

King John of England has never had a very good reputation. He was always seen as a poor second-best to his older brother King Richard the Lionheart, especially after trying to usurp power while Richard was fighting in the Crusades. After succeeding Richard legitimately in 1199, he oversaw the loss of vast swathes of land to France, and in a bid to restore his name and dominions, he ruthlessly set about raising revenues, earning a reputation as a cruel and vindictive monarch among all strata of society. Indeed, the nation's barons were so angered by his feudal antics that they eventually forced him to sign the Magna Carta limiting his powers. Even after his death, John's image took a battering, especially in the legends of Robin Hood.

During the fall of 1216, John found himself under attack on all sides. There were French troops in England, his own barons were hostile, the King of Scotland was intent on invasion, and the masses held him in contempt. Around this time, he was shuttling between Lincolnshire and East Anglia in a bid to rid those areas of rebels. On October 9 he arrived at Bishop's Lynn (now King's Lynn) in Norfolk, where he received extravagant hospitality. Unfortunately, it was perhaps a little too extravagant as he soon fell ill with dysentery. Despite this, he was intent on getting back on the road and within a few days he and a train of more than 2,000 troops and servants were headed for Newark in Nottinghamshire. They set off across the Fens, a large expanse of marshland, but John—feeling ever more poorly—decided to go via the Cambridgeshire market town of Wisbech. His army took a slightly quicker route via The Wash, a large estuary where Norfolk and Lincolnshire meet.

Unfortunately, John's train included a large number of horse-drawn wagons laden with luggage including the crown jewels. These were slow-moving at the best of times and may have additionally had to contend with quicksand. So when the tide started coming in fast, they stood little chance of escape. Quite where disaster struck is not certain, though most historians believe it was in

NORTH SEA

NEWARK

LINCOLNSHIRE

ROUTE OF JEWELS

THE WASH

SUTTON BRIDGE

WISBECH

BISHOP'S LYNN

ROUTE OF KING JOHN

NORWICH

EAST ANGLIA

CAMBRIDGE

LOST LEGACY *A 15th-century depiction of Queen Matilda (1102–67), Holy Roman Empress, Queen of Germany, and disputed Queen of England. The jewelry she accumulated during her dramatic life is said to have been among the riches lost in The Wash by her grandson.*

LONDON

the vicinity of what is now Sutton Bridge, a few miles north of Wisbech and west of Bishop's Lynn. In his *History of England*, composed in the 1250s, the chronicler Matthew Paris described the event thus: "... *he [John] lost there irretrievably the carts and packhorses bearing his booty and loot, and all his treasure and household effects.*" Nor were things about to get any better for John: during the journey, his health deteriorated and he died at Newark on October 19 1216. He was buried shortly afterward at Worcester, without any of his regalia.

Exactly what was lost in the calamity has never been entirely clear. Certainly, John had accumulated significant amounts of jewelry and plate from the monastic houses he visited during 1215 and 1216. The luggage train was also believed to have included the regalia that his grandmother, Queen Matilda, had as queen of Germany. Yet some academics cast doubt on whether John would have allowed such riches to travel separately from himself. Was the story actually a fiction designed to hide the fact that he had already disposed of much of his wealth to pay mercenaries? Or had he perhaps used the crown jewels as security for essential loans? Another theory suggests that John kept the crown jewels with him, but was poisoned by a Cistercian monk (perhaps with links to the Knights Templar—see page 53), who stole the jewels to sell on the European mainland.

Even if we take the story at face value, there is little chance of recovering the lost riches, since they would now lie beneath a layer of silt several feet deep. Nonetheless, both treasure-hunters and historians carry on their investigations undeterred. Researchers from the University of Nottingham, for instance, have taken soil samples in a bid to establish the exact route of the train. If they are successful, it might at least give us a better idea of the precise location where King John lost his wealth.

Score of *Thespis*

WHAT IT IS The first operatic collaboration of Gilbert and Sullivan
WHY YOU WON'T FIND IT Apart from a few short sections, there is no trace of the score after 1897

With works such as *The Mikado*, *The Pirates of Penzance*, and *HMS Pinafore*, W.S. Gilbert and Arthur Sullivan became the undisputed kings of the comic opera. They collaborated on a total of 14 productions over a 25-year period at the end of the 19th century, but the score for their debut work, *Thespis*, is frustratingly lost except for a few short extracts.

With Gilbert responsible for the words and Sullivan for the music, *Thespis, or The Gods Grown Old*, was a "Grotesque Opera in Two Acts" telling the story of an ancient Greek acting troupe—led by Thespis, who was according to legend, the first actor. The show follows the troupe as they swap roles with the gods of Mount Olympus. As might be expected, pandemonium ensues. The play opened at London's Gaiety Theatre on December 26, 1871, with Sullivan himself conducting.

It had been the idea of the theater's impresario, John Hollingshead, to bring Gilbert and Sullivan together for a festive entertainment—both were individually well known to him, but both men were also very busy, with numerous other works premiering in the capital and around the country. By their own admission, *Thespis* was written rather hurriedly. Gilbert would later note, "it was a crude and ineffective work, as might be expected, taking into consideration the circumstances of its rapid composition." Nevertheless, it

received a relatively warm reception from both audiences and critics, and ran for a perfectly creditable 63 performances. Despite this, it was never performed again during the lifetimes of its creators.

Only a single song, "Little Maid of Arcadee," was published at the time, and Gilbert and Sullivan did not collaborate again until *Trial by Jury* in 1875. It was not until the 1950s that there was a concerted attempt to put on a new production of *Thespis*, but by that time the score had been lost for 50 years or more. All that we have left today is "Little Maid of Arcadee," another song called "Climbing Over Rocky Mountain" (whose music was reused in *The Pirates of Penzance*), and some music that accompanied a ballet in Act II. It may be that a complete score still exists, but some suspect that Sullivan quietly disposed of it, regarding it as a lesser work. Alternatively, some musicologists believe he recycled much of the music for use in later shows. In which case, we may be a lot more familiar with the music of *Thespis* than we ever imagined.

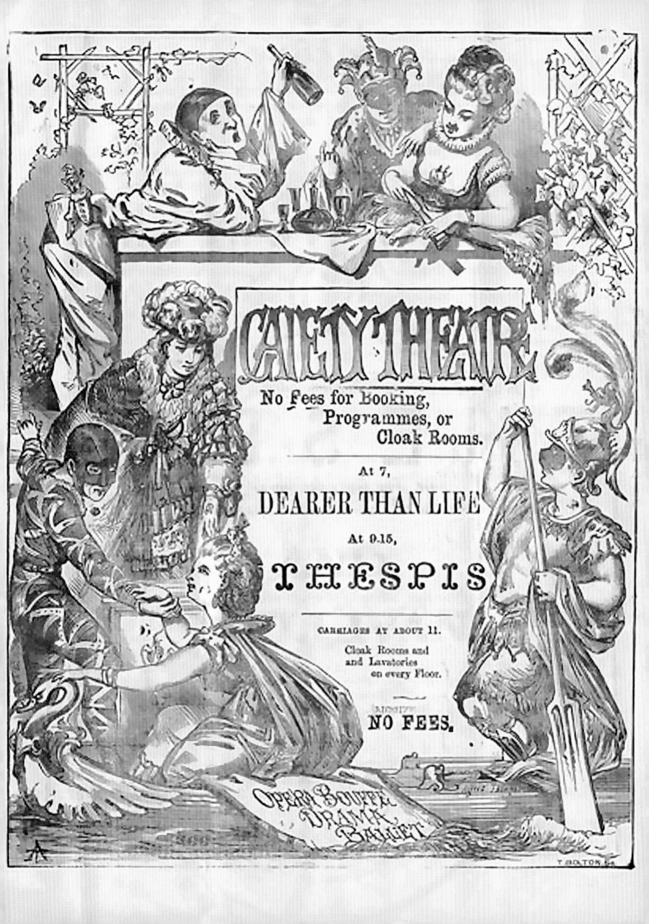

Kusanagi-no-Tsurugi

WHAT IT IS One-third of the Imperial Regalia of Japan
WHY YOU WON'T FIND IT Though it is claimed to be at the Shinto Atsuta Shrine, no one has seen it for centuries

Kusanagi-no-Tsurugi (or Grass-Cutting Sword) is a legendary weapon originating from within a dreaded eight-headed serpent, which forms part of the Japanese Imperial Regalia, alongside a jewel (*Yasakani no Magatama*) and a mirror (*Yata no Kagami*). It is said to reside out of the public gaze at the sacred Atsuta Shrine in Aichi prefecture, but whether it still exists is up for debate.

According to ancient myth, the serpent *Yamata-no-Orochi* blighted the life of a well-to-do family, eating seven of eight daughters in successive years. The father offered his last daughter's hand in marriage to a warrior, Susanoo, if he could kill the beast. After subduing Orochi with rice wine, Susanoo cut off each of his eight heads and then started on his tails. Within one of these, he discovered the sword. It subsequently passed to his sister, and then became part of the regalia used to legitimize the Japanese emperors. Prince Yamato Takeru later used it to cut down grass that had been set on fire by one of his enemies during a hunting trip, giving the sword its famous name. After suspicions that it had brought a curse upon a later emperor, it was deposited at the Atsuta Shrine at the end of the seventh century.

According to some sources, the sword was thrown into the sea in the 12th century by an individual on the losing side of the dynastic war that then raged in Japan between the powerful Minamoto and Taira clans. Another version suggests that it sank in a ship along with the monk who had stolen it, one narrative saying it remains beneath the waves and another claiming it was washed ashore and recovered by priests who returned it to Atsuta.

The last person to have publicly claimed to have seen the sword was a priest during the Edo period (which ran from 1603 to 1868), who described a weapon of white metal and a little less than 3 feet (90 cm) in length. It is also claimed that this priest later died as a result of a curse associated with the sword. At the last imperial coronation, of Akihito in 1989, the new emperor apparently received the sword, though it remained hidden from view throughout the entire ceremony.

So did *Kusanagi-no-Tsurugi* ever exist? If it did, was it lost almost 1,000 years ago? And what is it that dwells at Atsuta and is used to bless emperors? Today, it is widely accepted that the Shrine houses nothing more than a copy of the original sword of legend.

Pi-Ramesse

WHAT IT IS A lost capital of ancient Egypt
WHY YOU WON'T FIND IT It was effectively uprooted and moved in the second millennium BC

Can a city be in two places at once? In the case of Pi-Ramesse, one of the great cities of ancient Egypt, the answer is "sort of." The capital city of the 19th Dynasty pharaoh Ramesses the Great (reigned 1279–1213 BC) was relocated wholesale after his death, leaving archaeologists with the difficult task of piecing together a picture of the town from two different sites.

Ramesses II is arguably the most celebrated of all the leaders of ancient Egypt. The harbor town of Pi-Ramesse was founded by his father, Seti I, but it was Ramesses who transformed it into a new capital, taking the place of Thebes and Memphis.

The city's heyday lasted until 1078 BC, but the branch of the Nile on which it sat gradually dried up, and the capital relocated to the newly built city of Tanis. The new site remained an important city until it was finally abandoned in the sixth century AD. Archaeologists began excavating the ruins in the 19th century, and by the 1930s had identified numerous buildings and monuments whose inscriptions convinced many that this was in fact Pi-Ramesse. This inevitably caused huge confusion—here was the fabric of one of the great cities of history, in a location where it simply should not have been.

The mystery endured for several decades, until in the 1960s Austrian Egyptologist Manfred Bietak realized

it could be explained by tracing the historical changes in the course of the Nile. His excavations at two sites yielded remarkable results—not only did he identify the modern town of Tell el-Dab'a as Avaris, capital of Egypt from 1650–1580 BC, but he also established that the true site of Pi-Ramesse lay beneath the present-day city of Qantir. When the move to Tanis occurred, the authorities simply moved statues, obelisks, temples, and other buildings from the old capital to the new. Today, little evidence of the old city is visible above ground at Qantir, but geophysical survey techniques have revealed the ghostly outline of a metropolis centered around a great temple, with roads built on a grid system, domestic dwellings ranging from the ramshackle to the splendid, and a complex of lakes and canals.

So an extraordinary situation exists of a city in two places at once: the outline of Pi-Ramesse survives in its original location, while the buildings and monuments that gave it life are to be found in another place entirely.

ABANDONED *The ruins of the former capital of Ancient Egypt, Tanis, were rediscovered in the 19th century. But it took another century for archaeologists to realize that its architects had recycled much of the fabric of Pi-Ramesse, confounding later historians.*

MEDITERRANEAN
SEA

TANIS

AVARIS

NILE DELTA

ALEXANDRIA

QANTIR

CAIRO

GIZA

FAIYUM

MONUMENT BUILDER *Pharaoh Ramesses II had an enormous number of statues and buildings constructed in his honor, emphasizing his majesty. Perhaps the most stunning are the giant depictions seen at Abu Simbel.*

LOWER EGYPT

Beagle 2

25

WHAT IT IS A spacecraft designed to seek out life on Mars

WHY YOU WON'T FIND IT Contact was lost six days before it was scheduled to land

The Beagle 2 mission held out hope for all small-scale space enthusiasts. Overseen by an alliance of British universities, it was a low-budget project (by space exploration standards anyway) and its public face, Professor Colin Pillinger of the Open University, was an archetypally eccentric space scientist. Alas, though, the mission ended in disaster when Beagle 2 disappeared off the radar.

Beagle 2 was a module developed by the United Kingdom as part of the European Space Agency's (ESA) Mars Express mission in 2003. The aim was to land the craft on the surface of the Red Planet, where it would operate for six months, recording local geology, atmosphere, and climate. Most importantly of all, though, it would search for evidence of either current or prehistoric Martian life.

The module was named in honor of HMS *Beagle*, the ship that had carried Charles Darwin on his landmark voyages of the 1830s. Just as Darwin's discoveries exponentially increased our understanding of life on Earth, it was hoped Beagle 2 might do the same for Mars. After several years of work, Mars Express launched from a site in the Central Asian republic of Kazakhstan on June 2, 2003. On December 19, the orbiter spacecraft released Beagle 2 for its onward journey to the surface. It should have landed on Christmas Day, sending a signal back to Earth. But as the world watched intently, there was only deafening silence.

After a search lasting several weeks, the management team declared Beagle 2 officially missing on February 6. There were several different theories as to what had gone wrong: it's possible Beagle never landed at all but burned up in the Martian atmosphere, or even bounced off it completely; alternatively, the parachute and airbags designed to protect it on impact may have malfunctioned.

In December 2005, almost exactly two years after the world last heard from Beagle 2, there were reports from ESA of something spotted on the Martian surface very close to the module's intended landing site. Unfortunately, there has been no subsequent confirmation of whether this is indeed the spacecraft—another disappointment for the mission crew who could have taken some solace from knowing that they at least managed to land on target. Meanwhile, the Mars Express Orbiter continues to function, alongside several other spacecraft carrying orbital surveys. If Beagle 2 made it to Mars, there is a good chance it may yet be found.

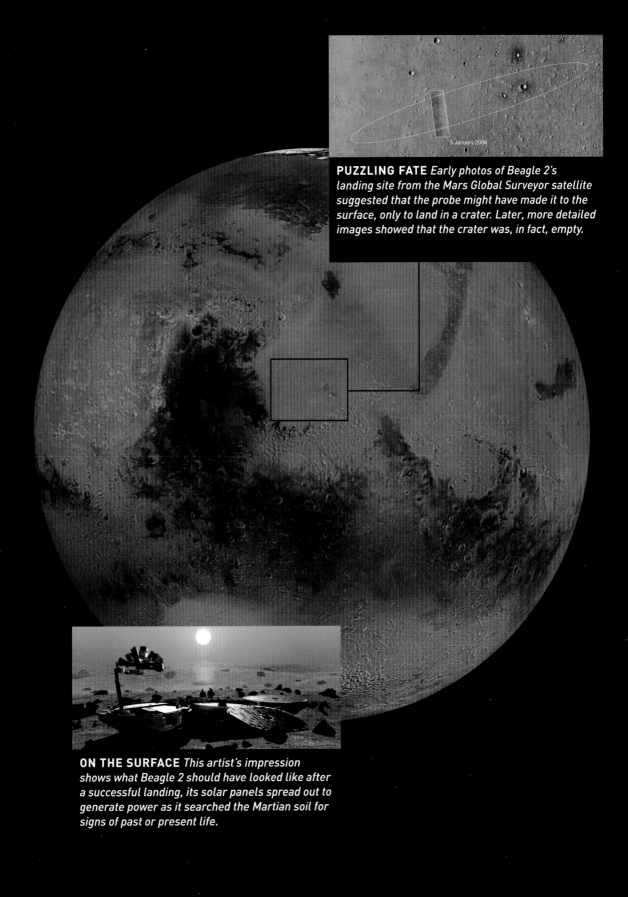

PUZZLING FATE *Early photos of Beagle 2's landing site from the Mars Global Surveyor satellite suggested that the probe might have made it to the surface, only to land in a crater. Later, more detailed images showed that the crater was, in fact, empty.*

5 January 2004

ON THE SURFACE *This artist's impression shows what Beagle 2 should have looked like after a successful landing, its solar panels spread out to generate power as it searched the Martian soil for signs of past or present life.*

26

Blackbeard's treasure

WHAT IT IS Legendary pirate booty
WHY YOU WON'T FIND IT Only Blackbeard and the Devil know where it is …

Arguably the most fearsome pirate of them all, Edward Teach terrorized the Caribbean and the American East Coast in the early 18th century under the infamous name of Blackbeard. Following his death, conflicting stories began to circulate about the fate of his treasure. If he did conceal it (and not, as some believe, simply spend it all) then someone may yet find themselves very rich.

Born in England around 1680, Edward Teach is thought to have acted as a privateer during Queen Anne's war against the French (1702–13) before joining the Bahama pirate crew of Benjamin Hornigold. He developed an almost demonic image, his nickname coming from prodigious facial hair that he tied in braids. His greatest success came in 1717 when he seized a large warship, *La Concorde*, from French slave-traders as it sailed off the coast of Martinique. He promptly renamed it *Queen Anne's Revenge* and began attacking other ships in the area to fill his coffers with gold. Before long he had assembled a small pirate navy patrolling the coasts of Virginia and the Carolinas.

In May of 1718, Blackbeard blockaded Charleston, South Carolina, but the following month his flagship ran aground at Beaufort on the North Carolina coast. He was given safe harbor by the governor of North Carolina, but in November 1718 was intercepted by ships under Lt. Robert Maynard, acting for Virginia governor, Alexander Spotswood.

Blackbeard met a grisly end, put to the sword and then shot for good measure. Finally, he was decapitated and his head mounted at the front of Maynard's ship.

But Maynard found very little in the way of treasure on Blackbeard's ships, and it has long been thought that the pirate had already hidden stashes of loot at various locations around North Carolina. Some believe that he buried a chest beneath a tree somewhere on Ocracoke Island, and others suggest that there is treasure to be found near his home in Bath. There are tales that two fishermen found three iron kettles filled with gold coins here in the 1930s, reburying the money to claim later. Alas, if the story is to be believed, one of the fishermen died and floods ensured the surviving partner was unable to find the hiding place again. Meanwhile, in 1996 a wreck that many archaeologists believed to be *Queen Anne's Revenge* was identified. Again, though, there were no pieces-of-eight or chests filled with glittering gems —if Blackbeard did deposit his loot for a rainy day, he hid it well.

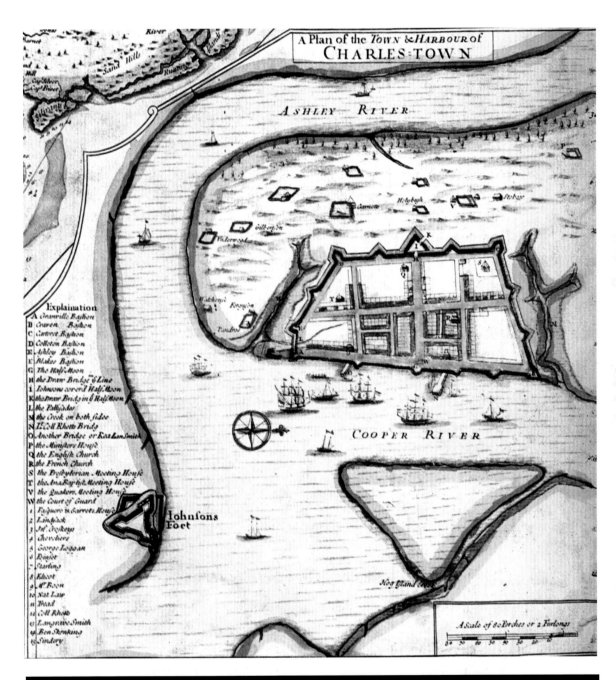

TREASURE MAP *A contemporary map of 18th-century Charleston, believed by many to be the last resting place of Blackbeard's treasure. The blockade of the city was Blackbeard's last major triumph before his enemies caught up with him. When asked where his booty could be found, he was reported to have said that only he and the Devil knew where it was, and whichever of them lived longer would claim it.*

Tybee Island bomb

WHAT IT IS A Cold War-era
nuclear bomb
WHY YOU WON'T FIND IT
It was ditched in the sea
after a midair collision

In 1958, a US Air Force plane dropped a nuclear bomb into the waters off the coast of the US state of Georgia. If it was fully operational and had it exploded, it would have unleashed a destructive power a 100 times greater than the bomb dropped on Hiroshima. It has been lost ever since, prompting much discussion as to just what level of threat it poses.

The story began on February 4, 1958, when a USAF B-47, piloted by Major Howard Richardson, was loaded with the bomb and sent on a long-distance training flight from the Homestead Air Force Base in Florida. A little after midnight on the morning of February 5, the bomber was cruising over North Carolina and Georgia when an F-86 Sabre fighter collided with it, ripping a hole in the wing and nearly knocking an engine off its mounting. The F-86 pilot ejected to safety, but Richardson aimed to land his aircraft. Fearful that his payload might detonate in the process, he sought and was granted permission to ditch the bomb. Flying over the sea not far from the bustling city of Savannah, he dropped it into the shallow waters around Tybee Island—the easternmost point of the state—before executing a perfect emergency landing at the Hunter Air Force Base.

The bomb, needless to say, did not detonate, and a rescue mission involving the Air Force and the US Navy swung rapidly into action. But by April 16, the search had drawn a blank. The Mark 15 bomb was by no means small, measuring 13 feet (4 m) long and weighing 7,500 pounds (3,400 kg), but it was thought to lie hidden in thick layers of silt somewhere in Wassaw Sound.

The Air Force insisted that although the bomb carried 396 pounds (180 kg) of conventional high explosives as well as enriched uranium, the capsule necessary to start a reaction had been removed for safety reasons: in other words, it was nonoperational. This line, however, has been repeatedly challenged. Whether or not the bomb is capable of exploding, its loss raises other concerns. Firstly, there is the ongoing fear that it could fall into the wrong hands. Then there is the risk of radioactive contamination. As an Air Force report concluded in 2001, while the bomb lies beneath feet of sand and mud, there is little reason to worry. But should it become exposed to seawater as a result of shifting sands, it might easily corrode and allow the uranium to spill into the environment with potentially devastating consequences.

SWEPT FOR ACTION *The B-47 Stratojet was the world's first swept-wing bomber. Operational for 12 years following its introduction in 1953, it was generally regarded as a reliable aircraft, and normally carried a three-man crew.*

2335

U.S. AIR FORC

U.S. AIR FORCE

FRIENDLY FIRE *The B-47's mission was relatively straightforward until the catastrophic collision with a Sabre. Had the pilot not had the foresight to ditch his payload, the city of Savannah might have been devastated.*

NORTH CAROLINA

ATLANTIC OCEAN

SOUTH CAROLINA

SAVANNAH

CHARLESTON

TYBEE ISLAND

GEORGIA

JACKSONVILLE

FLORIDA

MIAMI

HOMESTEAD AIR
FORCE BASE

CUBA

28

Kitezh

WHAT IT IS The "Russian Atlantis"
WHY YOU WON'T FIND IT The city is rumored to lie beneath a lake in Nizhny Novgorod, Russia

According to legend, Yuri II, Grand Prince of Vladimir, commanded the construction of a beautiful new city on the Volga River in central Russia, which became not just a center for trade but also a spiritual hub. Alas, Kitezh soon attracted the attentions of marauding Tartars, but before they were able to take the holy city, it submerged itself in the waters of Lake Svetloyar, where it remains to this day.

Prince Yuri is said to have ordered the construction of the twin town of Little and Great Kitezh in the early years of the 13th century, after falling in love with the Volga region. Kitezh was renowned for its white stone churches and golden domes. But in 1238 Yuri's lands were invaded by the Mongol forces of Khan Baty, who captured many cities and razed them to the ground. Eventually Yuri and his diminished forces retreated to Kitezh, but Little Kitezh quickly fell to the invaders and Khan Baty's men were amazed to see that Great Kitezh had no fortifications at all. With its inhabitants praying fervently, the Mongols were about to attack when water suddenly burst from the ground and completely swallowed up the city.

The tale of this miraculous escape was passed down through the centuries and tradition has it that on a quiet day you can still hear the sound of the town's many church bells ringing beneath Lake Svetloyar, and even voices singing hymns. Some claim to have seen the lights of religious processions in the water, as well as the image of Kitezh's magnificent buildings. Certainly, the lake has retained a grip on the imagination of numerous pilgrims who claim that its waters have medicinal properties and the area is blessed with particular spiritual power. During the Second World War, its shores became a shrine for mothers praying for the safe return of children fighting on the Eastern front.

The story of the submerged town first appeared in print toward the end of the 18th century in the *Kitezh Chronicle*, a book that is believed to be based on the oral traditions of the Old Believers (a breakaway group from the Russian Orthodox Church). Folklore has it that the city and its inhabitants will rise from the lake just before the end of the world. If you wish to see the lake for yourself, it is to be found close to the village of Vladimirskoye in the Voskresensky District of Nizhny Novgorod in the northeast of Russia. But there is no guarantee that you will find evidence of Kitezh while you are there—it is said to only reveal itself to the pure of heart.

DEEP WATERS Main image: *Lake Svetloyar, fabled home of the lost city, today backs on to a protected conservation area.* Inset: *A group of "Old Believers"—a Russian Orthodox sect who believe that Kitezh will rise from the lake to herald the Day of Judgment.*

NIZHNY NOVGOROD

MOSCOW

LAKE SVETLOYA

THE VOLGA RIVER

VOLGOGRAD

RUSSIA

LAND OF MYSTERY *Kitezh is said to have been located in Voskresensky, today one of 43 districts that make up the Russian province of Nizhny Novgorod. Almost half of the province is made up of forests.*

British Guiana 1c Magenta

29

WHAT IT IS The world's rarest stamp
WHY YOU WON'T FIND IT Unseen by the public since the 1970s, its last known owner died in 2010

Philatelists—those who practice the collection and study of stamps—like nothing more than a rarity. To discover a stamp that has been printed upside down, back-to-front, in the wrong color, or with a misprint is a cause for great celebration. So imagine the allure of a stamp of which there is only one known example in existence. Step forward, the British Guiana 1c Magenta.

British Guiana (known today as Guyana) was a British territory in the Caribbean until it achieved independence in 1966. In the mid-19th century, its mail system relied on stamps shipped from printers in the UK, but in 1856 the island ran out of stamps before a new shipment had arrived. Postmaster general, E.T.E. Dalton, asked the producers of the colony's principal newspaper to run off an emergency batch that could be used until the official supply arrived.

Two denominations were needed: 4 cent stamps for use on letters, and 1 cent stamps for newspapers. Both were printed in black on magenta paper, and, since they lacked perforations, were cut by hand from large sheets. To the casual observer, they were not much to look at—the 1c stamp featured a ship inside a frame and the territory's Latin motto, *Damus Petimus Que Vicissim* ("We give and expect in return"), alongside the value of the stamp and the country of issue.

But as anyone who has ever found their hands smudged after a flick through the morning headlines knows, a newspaper press is not the cleanest of machines. Dalton was unhappy with the quality of the stamps produced and feared that they could be easily forged. So he decreed that each stamp sold should be initialed by a post office clerk.

Fortunately, the shipment from Britain soon arrived, and the island's authorities dispensed with the unsatisfactory backup stamps. We might never have heard anything more of the British Guiana 1c were it not for the eagle-eye

of a 12-year-old aspiring philatelist called Vernon Vaughan, who in 1873 was looking through a pile of his uncle's old correspondence. The 1c stamp jumped out at him for its unfamiliarity, not least its octagonal shape. It had been postmarked and initialed on April 4, 1856 in Demarara on the island's northern coast by a clerk named E.D. Wright. Time had not been kind to the stamp, but Vernon soaked it off the envelope and, realizing it was nowhere to be found in the official catalogs, sold it to a local collector, N.R. McKinnon, for 6 shillings.

In 1878, McKinnon sold his collection for $200, and the new owner passed the 1c Magenta to experts in London for inspection. They determined that it was quite unique, and it duly sold later that year for the mighty sum of $250. It passed on through several more hands, including a museum in Berlin, before finding its way to France as part of war reparations after the First World War. In 1922, American collector Arthur Hind paid US$36,000 for it at auction, outbidding Briain's King George V.

In 1970, it was purchased by a group of American investors for US$280,000, and displayed around the world over the following decade. Then, in 1980, it was sold again, this time to John DuPont, a member of the wealthy Pennsylvania dynasty. He paid the eyewatering sum of US$935,000 and withdrew it from public exhibition, but in 1997 the stamp's story took a new and strange twist. DuPont was a philanthropist with a range of interests, including amateur sport. He was particularly passionate about wrestling, and had done much to fund the sport. In the process, he had become good friends with Dave Schultz, who had won gold in free wrestling at the 1984 Los Angeles Olympics. But in 1996, for reasons unknown, DuPont shot Schulz dead. A defense of insanity was rejected,

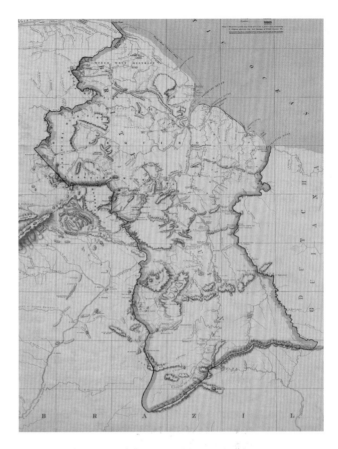

OUTPOST OF EMPIRE *British Guiana was a British Colony from 1814 until 1966, when it became independent Guyana. A government-run system for the issuing of postage stamps and delivery of mail was in operation from the early 1850s.*

and DuPont remained behind bars until his death in 2010.

The stamp, meanwhile, suffered its own incarceration at a Philadelphia bank. DuPont's will, unsuccessfully disputed by his niece and nephew, left Bulgarian wrestler Valentin Yordanov as principal beneficiary. The fate of the stamp, however, is unknown. In the meantime, a German by the name of Peter Winter announced in 1999 that he had unearthed a *second* 1c Magenta, apparently in the possession of a Romanian dancer. His claim split experts, however, with London's Royal Philatelic Society among those claiming the new find a forgery.

Mozart and Salieri's *Per la ricuperata salute di Ophelia*

WHAT IT IS A musical collaboration between two notorious rivals
WHY YOU WON'T FIND IT The score disappeared long ago

The intense competition between composers Wolfgang Amadeus Mozart and Antonio Salieri is one of the most infamous rivalries in high culture. There has even been a persistent rumor that Salieri murdered Mozart. Yet the relationship between the two was considerably more nuanced than many assume, and the primary evidence for this comes in the form of a collaborative lost cantat.

Austrian-born Mozart's genius was recognized early with his travels across Europe as a child prodigy. By the time he died in 1791 aged 35, he had produced a body of work that arguably marks him out as the greatest composer of all time. Salieri, an Italian who was born a few years before Mozart and lived to 75, had a star that shone brightly for much of his life but faded in the 19th century. Today, he is best known as Mozart's embittered nemesis in the Oscar-winning 1984 movie, *Amadeus*. The movie was a reworking of Peter Schaffer's earlier play, which itself drew upon a 19th-century poem by Alexander Pushkin. But does the fiction reflect the facts?

Salieri moved to Vienna as a young man and became a firm favorite of Emperor Joseph II. The composer of more than 40 operas, he held a number of important posts. Indeed, it is possible that—as an Italian—his success upset local composers, possibly contributing to the later denigration of his reputation. He certainly beat Mozart to at least one teaching post, and Mozart would later blame the initial lukewarm reception for his opera *Figaro* on "Salieri and his tribe."

Yet there is also strong evidence for long periods when the two men got along. Shortly before his death, Mozart wrote to his wife of how he had taken Salieri to the opera to hear his latest work and that "from the overture to the last choir there was no piece that didn't elicit a bravo or bello out of him." Salieri would later be employed by Mozart's widow to teach music to their son. Sadly, this picture of cordiality is chronically blurred by Salieri's apparent deathbed confession to poisoning Mozart, but in fact the Austrian probably died of rheumatic fever, Salieri quickly recanted and the whole affair can probably be blamed on delirium. The best evidence of good relations between the two is a cantata for voice and piano, *Per la ricuperata salute di Ophelia*, that they composed jointly in 1785 to mark English soprano Nancy Storace's return to the stage. Sadly no copy has survived, but should one ever turn up, it might serve as a retort to those who believe only in the silver-screen Salieri.

BEST OF ENEMIES
Main picture:
*Wolfgang Amadeus
Mozart as painted by
Johann Nepomuk della
Croce around 1780/81.*
Inset: *Mozart's
sometimes friend
and occasional arch
rival, Antonio Salieri,
depicted in a portrait
by Joseph Willibrod
Mähler.*

The Great Mogul Diamond

WHAT IT IS A giant among gemstones
WHY YOU WON'T FIND IT After disappearing centuries ago, it was probably cut down

The largest diamond ever to be mined in India, the Great Mogul had a varied if all too brief known life span. After its last recorded owner was murdered in the first half of the 18th century, the stone disappeared and has never been recovered. Speculation is rife as to what became of it. Could it still exist in all its glory today, or was it cut down into several lesser gems?

The first owner of the diamond was Emir Jemla, the right-hand man of the king of Golconda in Southern India. A military general and wily politician, Emir Jemla built up a vast personal fortune by plundering the region's diamond mines under an assumed name. The Great Mogul was probably brought up from the famous Kollur mine around 1650.

The Mogul emperor of the day, Shah Jahan, had sent his quarreling sons to various corners of the empire to stop them attacking him or each other. One of these sons, Aurangzeb, fell into dispute with the king of Golconda at the behest of Emir Jemla. It was while immersing himself in these dynastic games that the emir presented his fabulous gem to Shah Jahan, probably in 1655. The emperor had the stone cut by a certain Ortensio Borgio, an Italian lapidary, who by all accounts did such a clumsy job that he almost lost his head for it. Nevertheless, the Great Mogul retained such beauty and grand proportions that it enraptured all who saw it. The jewel was soon passed onto Dara, Shah Jahan's oldest

son and stated successor, but Aurangzeb had other ideas. After defeating Dara in battle in 1658, he deposed his father and seized control of both the throne and the Great Mogul. He proudly showed it off to visiting French diamond merchant Jean-Baptiste Tavernier, in 1665, who provides us with the last known record of it.

Thereafter, the fate of this natural wonder is a mystery, though it is widely supposed that it was looted by the Persian king Nadir Shah during his 1739 invasion of India (see page 170). Some have suggested that the Great Mogul later "reappeared" as the Koh-i-Noor diamond, though this is impossible since Shah Jahan already owned the Koh-i-Noor before Emir Jemla made his gift. Others claim that the blue-tinged Orlov Diamond (now in the Kremlin) was its reincarnation, though this is also widely disputed by experts. The most likely fate is that the Great Mogul was cut into many smaller diamonds to raise revenue without attracting undue attention. But just perhaps it's still out there somewhere, in all its original pomp.

Lost Dutchman's Gold Mine

WHAT IT IS A purported gold mine in the USA
WHY YOU WON'T FIND IT The "Dutchman" died in the 1890s without revealing its precise location

The Lost Dutchman's Gold Mine still tempts treasure-hunters with the promise of unfeasible riches. Its exact location is a matter of conjecture, though legend has it that it lies somewhere in the Superstition Mountains of Arizona. Rarely can there have been a more appropriately named location for a place engulfed in such myth and mystery.

So who exactly was the Dutchman? Well, he was Jacob Waltz—not Dutch at all, in fact, but German (a *Deutsch*-man, as it were). Whether the story of his mine is true or merely an urban legend is much debated. It has been pointed out by those who suspect it is folklore that several variants of the tale have circulated over the years, placing the mine as far afield as California, Colorado, and even Mexico.

What we do know is that a Jacob Waltz, born in 1810 in Germany, did come to America in 1839, arriving in New Orleans before finding work in the goldfields of North Carolina and Georgia. After becoming a naturalized US citizen in 1861, he turned up in Arizona in 1863, and between 1868 and 1886 is thought to have made regular scouting missions into the Superstition Mountains to the east of Apache Junction. He died in October 1891, nursed in his last days by one Julia Thomas, and a short while later Thomas led a party into the mountains in search of the mine. Just what Waltz did or didn't tell her, we can only speculate, but she certainly found no gold—in fact, she started a small business selling treasure maps (replete with inaccuracies) in a bid to cover some of the costs of the failed mission.

By 1895, the story of the Dutchman's lost mine had taken on a life of its own, partly as a result of the flamboyant writings of one P.C. Bicknell, who had paid Thomas for an interview. As the story became more elaborate, there was talk of a curse on the mine. There was also a series of enigmatic clues credited to Waltz, such as "No miner will find my mine," "To find my mine you must pass a cow barn," and "The rays of the setting sun shine into the entrance of my mine." Many have died in search of it, including a certain Adolph Ruth who went missing in 1931 and whose skull was discovered five years later, complete with two bullet holes. Geology suggests that the presence of gold in the Superstition Mountains is unlikely, but there are notable gold fields scattered about Arizona. Did the Dutchman's mine really exist? Until there is conclusive proof against the fact, plenty will continue to believe so.

MINE ALL MINE *The Lost Dutchman's Gold Mine has lured plenty of adventurers and speculators to the Superstition Mountains, and several of them have paid a heavy price. Even if the mine were to exist, it would take a brave soul to excavate it after all this time.*

Final panels of the Bayeux Tapestry

WHAT THEY ARE Artistic interpretations of the historic events of 1066
WHY YOU WON'T FIND THEM They have probably rotted away

Recognizable to pretty much anyone who has studied history at school, the Bayeux Tapestry is not only a formidable piece of embroidery, but a fascinating historical document as well. It details the build up to the Norman invasion of England by William the Conqueror, and the demise of King Harold at the Battle of Hastings. There's only one problem ... the end is missing.

Across some 230 foot (70 m), the tapestry depicts dozens of scenes from the historic year of 1066, from the death of the English king, Edward the Confessor in January, through to William of Normandy's victory over Harold Godwinson at Hastings in October. It ends today with the Anglo-Saxon troops in disarray, but it almost certainly contained a further two panels depicting the victorious William's coronation at Westminster Abbey on Christmas Day. Modern research suggests it was the brainchild of Odo, William's brother and the Bishop of Bayeux, and was very probably embroidered in England.

So what happened to the "big finale"? Difficult though it is to believe now, for much of its existence the Bayeux Tapestry was not hugely famous. The first recorded mention of it comes from the 15th century, some 400 years after its creation, when it was mentioned in the inventory of Bayeux Cathedral. And it was not until the 18th century that it really started to garner attention after academics "rediscovered" it during annual public displays. So precisely when the missing panels disappeared is thus unknown, but there is no record of them by the time the artwork first attracted interest. Nor does the rather ragged final panel that we have today suggest a clean cut of the final section, which tends to rule out the idea of theft. In fact, the way the tapestry currently finishes indicates that William's crowning glory simply rotted away. Considering that it was regularly moved in and out of storage in an era when temperature and moisture control were simply not considered, this would seem the most logical and likely scenario.

There have been several subsequent attempts to give the tapestry a suitable finish, though these are inevitably reliant on contemporary imagination rather than historic authenticity. For instance, in 2013 some 350 residents of Alderney, a Channel Island that was once part of the Duchy of Normandy, completed their version of the coronation. On viewing it, the deputy mayor of Bayeux declared it was "marvelously well done."

KFC's original recipe

WHAT IT IS The recipe that makes KFC chicken so "finger-lickin" good'
WHY YOU WON'T FIND IT It is one of the most heavily guarded trade secrets in the world

Kentucky Fried Chicken is one of the planet's fast food giants, with some 17,000 restaurants spread across well over 100 countries. Its success has been underpinned by its Original Recipe chicken, covered in a secret blend of 11 herbs and spices. As such, it is a recipe worth billions and so it is little surprise that its secrets are so tightly guarded.

The mix was developed some time around 1939–40 by Colonel Harland Sanders. Having founded his original restaurant, the Sanders Court & Café, a decade earlier in North Corbin, Kentucky, he is said to have kept the recipe only in his head for many years, sharing it with just his wife Claudia, and his business partner Jack C. Massey. "In those days, I hand-mixed the spices like mixing cement on a specially cleaned concrete floor on my back porch ..." the Colonel would later recall, depicting a scene unlikely to satisfy the food standards officers of today.

Massey led a consortium in 1964 that bought the American franchise from Sanders for US$2 million. It was probably at this stage that the recipe was finally committed to paper, and it is this document, signed by Sanders, that resides today in a high-security vault at the headquarters of KFC's holding company, Yum! Brands Inc., at Louisville, Kentucky. Alongside the precious listing, the vault also houses 11 vials of the specific herbs and spices.

Only two high-ranking executives, neither of whom are publicly identified, are said to know the complete recipe at any one time. They are not allowed to travel together as a security precaution, and are contractually obliged to maintain their silence. When it comes to manufacturing, one company blends half the recipe while another does the other half, and a third computer-operated facility blends the two halves together. This eliminates the risks of reverse engineering and industrial espionage.

In 2008, the recipe was briefly moved while the Louisville vault was upgraded. It was returned in February 2009, nestled in a computerized safe with a steel door 0.5 inches (1.25 cm) thick. To open it, two different keys and two different pin numbers are required, with no single person having access to all of them. The vault in which the safe sits is under 24-hour surveillance. Any security breach triggers a silent alarm and the room can be filled with security guards (no doubt beefed-up by regular KFC bargain buckets) within half a minute.

SANDERS CAFE

KFC

drive thru
7PC VALUE MEAL
$9.99

THIS IS A SMOKE FREE FACILITY

COMMONWEALTH OF KENTUCKY
UNITED WE STAND
DIVIDED WE FALL

BIRTHPLACE OF
KENTUCKY FRIED CHICKEN

In 1932 Colonel Harland Sanders bought the small restaurant near this site. Here he combined good cooking, hard work and showmanship to build regional fame for his fine food. His restaurant and a motel, now gone, flourished. To serve his patrons better Sanders constantly experimented with new recipes and cooking methods. Here he created, developed and perfected his world famous Kentucky Fried Chicken recipe. In 1956 plans were announced for a Federal highway to by-pass Corbin. Threatened with the traffic loss, Sanders, then 66, and undaunted, sold the restaurant and started travelling America selling seasoning, and his recipe for fried chicken to other restaurants. His success in this effort began the world's largest commercial food service system and made Kentucky a household word around the world.

Presented by the innumerable friends of Kentucky's greatest goodwill ambassador

35 HMS *Hussar*

WHAT IT IS A treasure-laden British ship that sank in New York in 1780
WHY YOU WON'T FIND IT Scouring the waters of a modern metropolis is no picnic

HMS *Hussar* was a 28-gun Royal Navy frigate launched in 1763, which sank off New York in 1780 during the American War of Independence, allegedly while carrying a large military payroll. The British government quickly rejected the notion, but plenty of treasure-hunters have been unconvinced by their denials.

Launched in 1763, the *Hussar* served around Ireland and Portugal before being called into action in North America. The War of Independence had started in 1775, and by 1780 the British knew that their authority in New York was under serious threat from combined French and Revolutionary forces. A decision was taken to move the military payroll out of the city—the last thing the British forces needed were unhappy, unpaid troops—so a large store of gold was loaded onto a ship assumed to be the *Hussar* (despite later government denials) for transfer to either the eastern tip of Long Island, or further north to Rhode Island on November 23, 1780.

For reasons best known to himself, however, Captain Charles Pole ignored a local pilot to sail through the ominously named Hell Gate, a treacherous stretch of the East River between Long Island and Manhattan. Here, the *Hussar* struck a reef called Pot Rock. Attempts to run aground failed thanks to powerful currents that pulled her into Long Island Sound where she sank.

Rumors immediately began to circulate that there had been a valuable cargo on board, an idea that Captain Pole would later officially deny. Skeptics suspected this was misinformation to put locals off the scent, and this theory was given extra credibility when the British did indeed launch several salvage expeditions in the years that followed.

No less a figure than Thomas Jefferson—third president of the USA and one of its Founding Fathers—funded an early private search, while another mission launched in 1856 failed to find the treasure, but did recover bones that seemed to support allegations that dozens of manacled American prisoners on board the ship had been left to drown.

The chances of success were considerably reduced in 1876, though, when the US Army Corps of Engineers blasted Hell Gate with some 28 tons of dynamite in a bid to make the area more navigable. As a result, there is every chance that the *Hussar* and her treasure were shot to kingdom come.

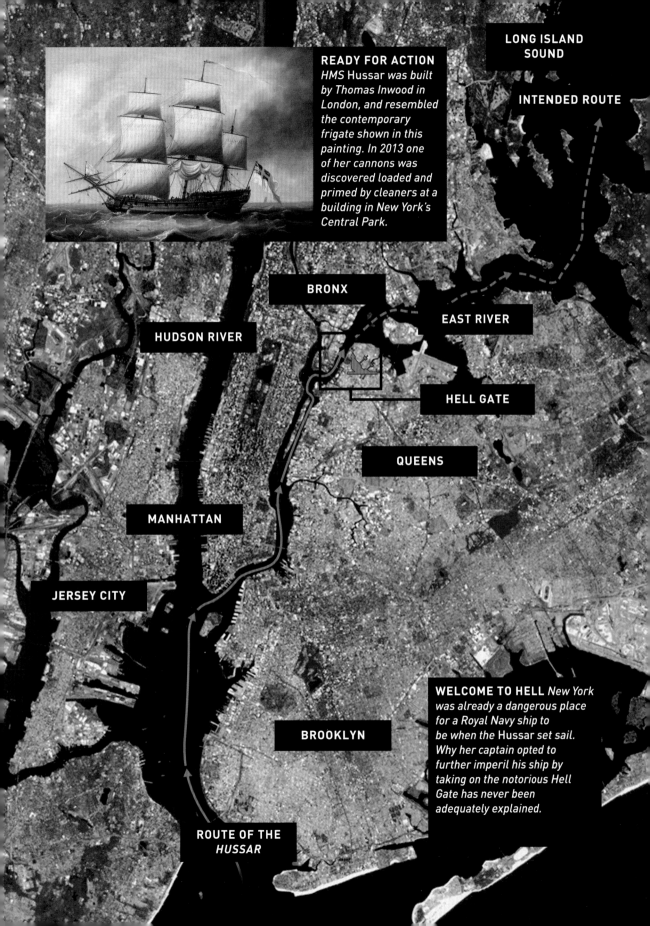

LONG ISLAND
SOUND

INTENDED ROUTE

READY FOR ACTION
HMS Hussar *was built
by Thomas Inwood in
London, and resembled
the contemporary
frigate shown in this
painting. In 2013 one
of her cannons was
discovered loaded and
primed by cleaners at a
building in New York's
Central Park.*

BRONX

EAST RIVER

HUDSON RIVER

HELL GATE

QUEENS

MANHATTAN

JERSEY CITY

BROOKLYN

WELCOME TO HELL *New York
was already a dangerous place
for a Royal Navy ship to
be when the Hussar set sail.
Why her captain opted to
further imperil his ship by
taking on the notorious Hell
Gate has never been
adequately explained.*

**ROUTE OF THE
*HUSSAR***

36 Treasure of the *Awa Maru*

WHAT IT IS A valuable hoard of gold and gems rumored to have been aboard a Japanese warship
WHY YOU WON'T FIND IT Was it ever on board?

Saying something enough times does not, of course, make it so. But that is exactly what seems to have happened in the case of the Japanese ship *Awa Maru*, sunk during the Second World War. Almost immediately, rumor spread that it had been carrying great riches. Decades later the Chinese government would spend millions on trying to recover it. But was it ever there?

The *Awa Maru* was launched in 1942 as a liner, but before the ship could begin commercial operations, she was requisitioned by a Japanese Navy desperate to swell its ranks as the Second World War raged. By 1945, she was serving as a Red Cross ship, free from the threat of Allied attack under the terms of an international agreement.

On March 28, 1945, after off-loading a cargo of medical supplies in Singapore, the *Awa Maru* was ready to make the return trip to Japan. As she steamed out of Singapore that evening, the 2,004 people aboard included merchant seamen and civilians who had become stranded on the island, along with a cargo that is believed to have included nickel and rubber. Three days later, she was sailing in the Taiwan Strait headed for Japan. A US naval submarine, USS *Queenfish*, was also in the area, fully aware that Red Cross ships were off limits. However, the American captain somehow misidentified the *Awa Maru* as a destroyer and ordered a fatal torpedo attack for which he would later be court-

martialed. The liner went down with the loss of all but one of those on board.

Before long, tales began to circulate that the *Awa Maru* had been carrying tons of looted gold, platinum, and precious stones. It has even been suggested that the fossils of Peking Man (see page 201) may have been aboard. After the war, Japan made a compensation claim of over US$50 million against Washington, though most of this was deemed to cover the loss of human life. No mention of the alleged treasure was ever made.

Nevertheless, the story clearly lingered in China's national memory and in 1977 the Chinese government located the wreck. Over the next five years, it is thought to have spent somewhere between US$20 million and US$100 million on salvage operations before calling off the search for booty having found nothing but human remains and personal effects. In 1981 newly declassified US records of wartime intercepts seemed to confirm that no treasure was ever aboard the *Awa Maru*.

CHINA

STRAIT OF
TAIWAN

TAIWAN

HAINAN

VIETNAM

PHILIPPINES

ROUTE OF THE
AWA MARU

MALAYSIA

TREASURE SHIP *An aerial view of the* Awa Maru. *The second ship owned by the Nippon Yusen Kaisha company to carry the name, she saw great drama in her short naval service, and had narrowly avoided sinking after being torpedoed in August 1944.*

37 Wright Brothers' patent for a flying machine

WHAT IT IS The patent that ushered in the age of the airplane

WHY YOU WON'T FIND IT It is missing from its home in the US National Archives

If pushed to identify the pivotal moment in aviation history, it is hard to look past the Wright Brothers' first prolonged, controlled, heavier-than-air flight on December 17, 1903. And yet the patent they were awarded for their groundbreaking engineering system, one of the most profitable in US history, has been missing since sometime around 1980.

Born in 1867 and 1871 respectively, Wilbur and Orville Wright initially worked together in publishing and printing before moving into the booming bicycle business in the 1890s. From there, it was a relatively natural progression into experiments with aviation. They built a series of gliders before, in 1902, making their historic first powered flight in an aircraft known as the Wright Flyer I. Taking off from a base in North Carolina, they undertook two flights each, the longest of which lasted for 59 seconds and covered 853 feet (260 m). The secret behind their success was a "three-axis control" system that allowed them

to steer the plane while maintaining balance. The principles behind this system were to underpin the future of all fixed-wing aircraft.

Widely regarded as heroes, the brothers were also well aware of their work's commercial potential. They applied for a patent in March 1903, vowing that "they verily believe themselves to be the original, first, and joint inventors of improvements in flying machines." Nevertheless, their application was at first rejected. They employed a specialist attorney to redraft it the following year, and this time it was accepted as US Patent 821,393 on May 22, 1906.

Once they had their patent, the brothers proceeded to defend it with the ferocity of commercial sharks, pursuing rivals for license fees that saw their bank balances bulge but did little to endear them to fellow aviators or, indeed, the public at large. They were even accused of holding back the development of the entire industry in America and, come the First World War, legislation was introduced to ensure greater sharing of patents between engineers and designers.

By the time that Orville died in 1948 (Wilbur had succumbed to typhoid fever in 1912), Patent 821,393 was safely filed in the National Archives. From 1969 it was passed between several archive offices and also had a spell at the National Air and Space Museum. It finally returned to the National Archive in 1979 and an employee claims to have seen it there in 1980. But when staff came to retrieve it in 2003 for use in centenary celebrations, it was gone. Few doubt that it was stolen, perhaps for sale on an online auction website.

Hope of securing its return has not died, though. A Recovery Team revealed in 2012 that they were continuing to investigate the disappearance (one of several thefts from the institution). Their tactics include direct appeals to enthusiasts who may have come across the lost document or even been offered it for sale. Just maybe it will be winging its way back home some day soon.

Buddhas of Bamiyan

WHAT THEY ARE Two giant statues of Buddha that were much revered cultural monuments
WHY YOU WON'T FIND THEM They were willfully destroyed by the Afghan Taliban in 2001

Until 2001, the Bamiyan Valley of central Afghanistan was graced by two giant statues of Buddha that had survived for almost 1,500 years overlooking the ancient Silk Road between East and West. Then the fundamentalist Taliban regime decreed they should be destroyed in one of the most wretched cases of cultural vandalism in modern times.

Bamiyan was a thriving center of Buddhism between the second and seventh centuries, and the area around it was adorned with numerous important examples of statuary and frescoes, but nothing rivaled the fame of the two giant Buddhas. Both were carved directly out of a cliff face, the smaller of the two (some 115 foot or 35 m tall) in the second half of the sixth century and the larger (174 foot or 53 m tall) a century later. Detailing was added using stucco and they were brightly painted, though the colors faded long ago. It is possible that they were also decorated with gold and gems. They were, until 2001, the largest standing Buddhas in the world.

The statues survived many near misses over the centuries. They were spared by Genghis Khan's army in the 1220s, though the rest of the valley was pillaged. Some suspect the Mogul emperor Aurangzeb attacked them with artillery in the late 17th or early 18th century. Then a few decades later, the Persian king Nader Afshar pointed his cannons at them. Through it all, they endured, but they would not be so lucky against the Islamic fundamentalist Taliban, who came to power in the 1990s. In March 2001 their supreme leader, Mullah Muhammad Omar, ordered the destruction of the statues, proclaiming them "the gods of the infidels." Troops then set about the ancient giants with a variety of small arms, hand tools, and explosives.

The order was met with uproar around the world, but to no avail. Koichiro Matsuura, Director General of UNESCO, called the Taliban's actions a "... crime against culture. It is abominable to witness the cold and calculated destruction of cultural properties which were the heritage of the Afghan people, and, indeed, of the whole of humanity." Yet one unexpected good came from the episode—the destruction uncovered hidden caves containing wall paintings of scenes from the Buddha's life. Dating from the fifth to the ninth centuries, they are believed to be the oldest known oil paintings in the world. Meanwhile, plans are afoot to one day restore the Buddhas to their former glory.

Library of Alexandria

WHAT IT IS Antiquity's equivalent of the British Library or the Library of Congress
WHY YOU WON'T FIND IT It was destroyed by fire in mysterious circumstances

The Great or Royal Library of Alexandria was perhaps the greatest seat of learning in the ancient world. It was founded by either Pharaoh Ptolemy I Soter or his successor, Ptolemy II, in the third century BC, and subsequently destroyed at some stage in the ensuing centuries. But just when, and by whom? There are a few key suspects, but this lost ancient wonder still refuses to offer up its secrets.

The great Macedonian conqueror Alexander the Great founded Alexandria as a center for Hellenic culture in Egypt shortly after his conquest of the ancient land in 331 BC. In little more than a decade, it had risen to become Egypt's capital, while the dynasty established by his general Ptolemy, ensured the city's status as the world's leading intellectual hub. The famous Library was part of a huge museum complex in the city's Brucheion (or Palace) quarter. It contained at least 40,000 scrolls and perhaps as many as 400,000, including the works of all the great thinkers of antiquity. According to an inscription said to have been written above its many shelves, the Library was: "The place of the cure of the soul."

Frustratingly, we do not have a record of just where the building stood, nor precisely when it was destroyed. All the potential culprits for this crime against culture were identified years afterward, and each accusation comes burdened with political baggage, but let's consider the three chief suspects in turn.

Suspect 1 is the great Roman general, Julius Caesar. Around 47 BC, Caesar's armed dispute with his own senate came to a head in the vicinity of Alexandria, and he subsequently became involved in Egypt's own dynastic conflict, backing Cleopatra VII's claim to the throne over that of her brother Ptolemy XII. Besieged by Ptolemy's forces from land and sea, Caesar set light to his own ships in order to break free, but the conflagration, it is said, soon spread onto land, raging through dockside buildings and eventually taking grip in the Library.

Suspect 2 is Theophilus, the Christian Patriarch of Alexandria. In AD 391 he is said to have sought permission from the devout Emperor Theodosius to attack the city's impressive pagan temple devoted to the god Serapis. This Serapeum was said to incorporate a library historically attached to the Great Library, and when the mob was let loose on the building, tens of thousands of scrolls were set alight in the streets. This, it has been argued, marked the real end of the Great Library.

PAST ITS SHELF LIFE *A romantic but sadly inaccurate 19th-century engraving depicts the ruins of the Great Library in Alexandria. After the Library's disappearnace, it became a focus for local folklore and wider regret at an enormous cultural loss.*

Finally, Suspect 3 is Caliph Omar, ruler of Egypt following the Muslim invasion of the seventh century. Although the caliph's rule was largely tolerant, he was said to have been unnerved by the idea of a vast library housing centuries' worth of knowledge. If these books were in line with the teaching of the Qu'ran, he concluded, there was no need for them in addition to the Qu'ran. Alternatively, if they disagreed with the Qu'ran, they were heresy and needed to be destroyed. According to legend, the texts were burned as fuel in the city's bath houses for the next six months.

But which narrative to believe? We can reasonably acquit Suspect 3 for the lack of any corroborating evidence. It is likely that Omar was blamed by later Christians keen to discredit Muslim rule. Theophilus, meanwhile, is almost certainly innocent, too, the accusation

seemingly not emerging until Edward Gibbon's *Decline and Fall of the Roman Empire* in the 18th century. Gibbon's argument may been inspired at least in part by his distrust of organized religion.

So we are left with Caesar. He himself made no mention of the destruction of the Library in his memoirs, but then it's hardly the sort of accident for which you'd rush to claim credit. What's more, the Greek scholar Strabo, who visited Alexandria in 20 BC, wrote extensively of the museum but made no reference to a library, which is certainly suggestive.

The truth about the Great Library, however, remains elusive. As a result of a succession of natural disasters in the Middle Ages, the Brucheion quarter was badly damaged and now lies mostly under water. Yet there is a glimmer of hope. In 2004, archaeologists working in Brucheion discovered the remains of a series of lecture halls capable of accommodating up to 5,000 students. This discovery, it was reported, might just indicate the exact location of this legendary store of knowledge.

The victims of Korean Air Lines Flight 007

WHO THEY ARE The 269 people who died when their passenger jet was shot down
WHY YOU WON'T FIND THEM They became pawns in a game of Cold War intrigue

On September 1, 1983, Korean Air Lines Flight 007 set off from New York for Seoul in South Korea via Anchorage, Alaska. Tragically, it crashed over the USSR with the loss of all 269 passengers and crew. It had been shot down by a Soviet Air Force jet, ramping up tensions between the Cold War superpowers. The wreck today lies beneath the sea—but nearly all the bodies mysteriously disappeared.

The Boeing-747 passenger jet was on the last leg of its journey when for reasons that are still unclear, it veered from its intended course into Soviet airspace. As it flew over the Kamchatka Peninsula in the Russian Far East, it was crossing an area home to several sensitive military bases. Moscow scrambled fighter jets to intercept the airliner and, after unsuccessful attempts to make contact, shot it down over the Sea of Japan. Of the 269 victims, 105 were South Korean and the next biggest contingent, totaling 62, came from the US—including a congressman, Lawrence Macdonald. Washington responded with horror to the incident, with President Reagan describing it as a massacre. After initially stonewalling, the Kremlin admitted several days later that they had shot down the passenger jet, but claimed the aircraft was unidentified at the time of the attack. Meanwhile, military figures claimed the Korean jet had been involved in espionage.

In truth, the incident was probably the result of a set of tragic coincidences.

The airliner's unexplained diversion (most likely through technical failure of the navigation systems) brought it into an area where US spy planes were known to operate. The Soviets then failed to accurately identify the jet and assumed that any foreign plane flying in that area was likely to have hostile intentions.

Unsurprisingly, the process of searching for and recovering the jet did not go smoothly, and the situation was not made any easier by the complications in establishing jurisdiction in international waters. At the time, Moscow claimed not to know the exact point where the plane fell, although documentation released after the collapse of the Soviet Union suggests that at least two search-and-rescue missions were sent to an area around Moneron Island. The race was onto find the aircraft's flight recorders, which it was assumed would reveal the truth of what had happened. If the craft was in Soviet waters, Moscow could claim them. Otherwise, the US could

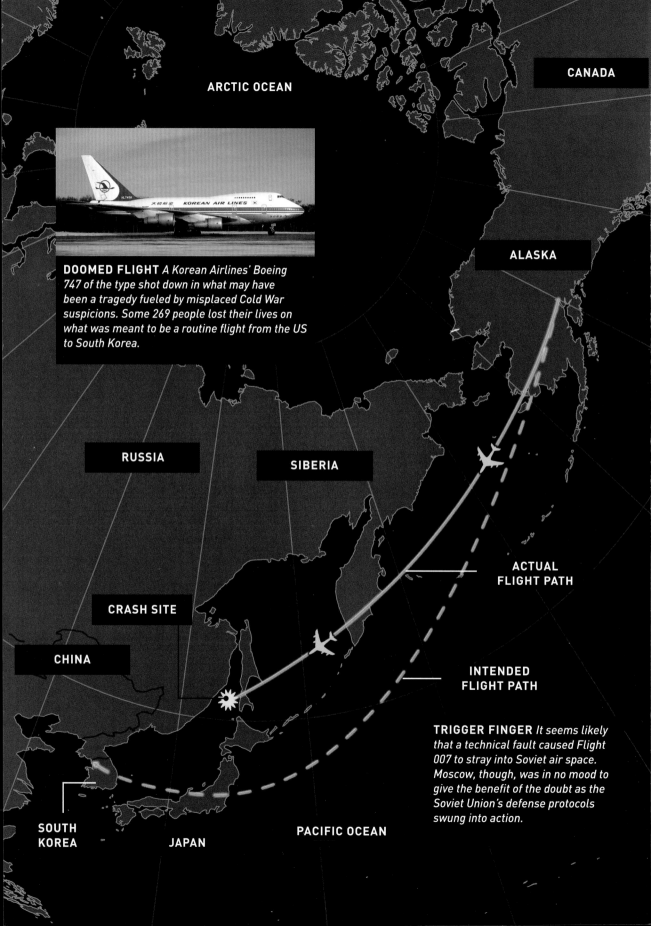

ARCTIC OCEAN

CANADA

ALASKA

DOOMED FLIGHT *A Korean Airlines' Boeing 747 of the type shot down in what may have been a tragedy fueled by misplaced Cold War suspicions. Some 269 people lost their lives on what was meant to be a routine flight from the US to South Korea.*

RUSSIA

SIBERIA

ACTUAL FLIGHT PATH

CRASH SITE

CHINA

INTENDED FLIGHT PATH

TRIGGER FINGER *It seems likely that a technical fault caused Flight 007 to stray into Soviet air space. Moscow, though, was in no mood to give the benefit of the doubt as the Soviet Union's defense protocols swung into action.*

SOUTH KOREA

JAPAN

PACIFIC OCEAN

but none of them could be conclusively linked to specific passengers.

In 1991, Russian media revealed that the Soviets had in fact located the wreck in September 1983. Civilian divers had searched it later in the month, but found neither bodies, nor any luggage. The immediate assumption was that the military had got there first and cleared out the scene. In 1992, Boris Yeltsin, Russia's first post-Soviet president, revealed that his Moscow predecessors had also recovered the flight recorders but kept them secret when they failed to back up claims of Western espionage.

Yet what happened to the bodies of 250 innocent victims remains unresolved. One theory posits that the nose and tail were blown off the jet, creating a wind-tunnel that scattered corpses far and wide across the ocean. However, this doesn't offer an explanation for why none of them were subsequently recovered. Even less credibly, it has been suggested that there were no corpses because the airliner was indeed a spy plane after all.

Some in the Kremlin did, however, make the ridiculous claim that the bodies may have been consumed by vast numbers of crabs present in those waters. But surely the most probable scenario was that Soviet military divers located the wreck within a few days of the initial incident and stripped out the incriminating evidence. Where those people and their property ended up is a mystery that may or may not have its answers in the closed files of the Russian archives.

claim precedence, having struck a deal with South Korea.

With large numbers of vessels from the Soviet Union, the US, Japan, and South Korea all searching the likely accident area, there were regular complaints of obstruction from the Soviet side. The International Civil Aviation Organization would ultimately report that a lack of cooperation from Moscow had scuppered hopes of recovering the wreck. The Soviets did, though, hand over large numbers of shoes and other items of dress that were found floating in the water. Just over a week after the tragedy, some human remains washed up on Japan's Hokkaido Island, brought on the tide from around Sakhalin Island. They came, it was concluded, from 13 of the crash victims,

The second book of Aristotle's *Poetics*

WHAT IT IS A classical treatise on the nature of comedy
WHY YOU WON'T FIND IT While evidence points to its existence, no copy has ever been found

Along with Plato and Socrates, Aristotle arguably makes up the grand triumvirate of ancient Greek philosophy. Born in 384 BC and dying in 322 BC, his works spanned areas as diverse as physics, rhetoric, and zoology. His *Poetics* is considered by many to be the founding text of literary theory—yet it seems likely that we have only ever seen half of his work on the subject.

The *Poetics*, written around 335 BC, deals not merely with poetry as we understand it today, but with drama in general. To the best of our knowledge, it was the first work to approach the subject in a theoretical and philosophical way. In the text that has come down to us today (principally through Latin and Arabic translations of the Middle Ages), Aristotle identities two key dramatic genres— tragedy and comedy—and strives to analyze the content of each, and the way in which they effect certain responses in their audience. For instance, how does tragedy bring about catharsis—that is to say, the release or purgation of strong and often repressed emotion?

But something soon becomes evident to anybody reading the *Poetics* today: Aristotle has much to say about tragedy, but precious little about comedy. A second part dealing with that discipline is clearly missing—most uncathartic!

Plenty of fine minds have attempted to reconstruct the missing material, pondering just what conclusions the great Greek philosopher might have drawn. Umberto Eco, for instance, made the lost second book a central feature in his own modern masterpiece, *The Name of the Rose*. Yet according to some, Aristotle's take on comedy may have come down to us after all. At the National Library in France is a tenth-century manuscript designated *Tractatus Coislinianus 120*. It previously resided at a monastery on Mount Athos in Greece and was largely forgotten before being republished in 1839 at the behest of classicist A.J. Cramer, who considered it likely to be a commentary on the lost volume of the *Poetics*—an argument that has gained support in recent years.

The *Poetics* does not provide us with all the answers about the nature of tragedy but it provides an extraordinary basis for debate, which is surely the ultimate point of philosophy. That Aristotle might have provided us with a similar platform for the discussion of comedy is a delicious thought, and the *Tractatus Coislinianus* may be the closest we will ever get to his original text.

The *San Miguel*

WHAT IT IS One of the lost ships from a Spanish treasure fleet
WHY YOU WON'T FIND IT It sank during a storm off the Florida coast in 1715

El Señor San Miguel was one of a dozen ships forming a Spanish treasure fleet that set off from Cuba in 1715, laden with awesome volumes of gold, silver, and other valuables. Within seven days, all but one of the vessels had been sunk in a storm. Today, seven of these wrecks have been identified—but not the *San Miguel*, believed by some to have been the richest of all the fleet.

The War of the Spanish Succession that started in 1701 made the trade routes between the Old and New Worlds dangerous, but by 1714 a tentative peace was in place and Philip V was ensconced on the Spanish throne, having given up his additional claim to France. Now he needed to restock his coffers—not least to pay a dowry for his marriage to Elizabeth Farnese, duchess of Parma.

Treasure had been accumulating in Spain's American colonies as treasure fleets had become a rarity during the war, so Philip ordered a fleet comprising 11 Spanish vessels and a French merchant ship, *Griffon*, to bring new supplies of booty from the Americas. The ships were soon overflowing with gold bars, worked silver, gold, and silver coins, emeralds, pearls, jewelry, porcelain, and countless other exotic wares. The value of the cargo today would certainly have been in the hundreds of millions of US dollars, if not more. By July 1715, after repeated delays, the fleet was moored at Havana in Cuba and the pressure was on to get

going. The hurricane season had started, but there was thought to be less risk of encountering pirates and privateers, so at last, on the morning of July 24, the treasure fleet began its journey.

The first few days were relatively incident-free, as the various captains picked their way through the potentially treacherous reefs and shoals off the Florida coast. However, by July 29 the winds were picking up, and experienced heads sensed a big storm in the offing. In the early hours of July 31, the elements pummeled the fleet, driving it inextricably toward land. By dawn, all bar one of the ships had been smashed to pieces—only the *Griffon* survived. Some 40 percent of the combined 2,500 crew perished, while the rest were stranded in what was then dangerous and unforgiving territory. Many more died either from injuries or illness, exposure, thirst, and hunger in the following days, but it was the middle of August before word of the disaster made it back to Havana and a rescue mission was sent. In a remarkable feat

FACE VALUE *An ancient Peruvian mask crafted from gold. If legend is to be believed, this is just the sort of priceless artefact that might have gone down with the doomed* San Miguel.

of salvage, about half the cargo was recovered over the next few months, despite the vessels perishing often miles apart.

Valuable flotsam and jetsam washed up on the Florida shores over the subsequent decades and centuries, while mariners with long memories cast their nets in the area in the hope of pulling in something precious. Yet the story had all but faded from collective memory by the mid-20th century. Then building contractor Kip Wagner had his interest piqued by a coin he found washed up on a beach. After intensive research, he located one of the wrecks and established his own company to salvage it. In the decades since, other

operations have used ever-improving technology to locate and plunder seven of the wrecks, while amateur enthusiasts have continued to play a role. In 2010, for instance, an 87-year-old woman and her daughter turned up a 22-carat solid gold bird figure while diving. Yet four of the fleet remain lost: the *Maria Galante*, *El Cievro*, *Nuestra Señora de la Concepción*, and *El Señor San Miguel*.

The *San Miguel* was probably the fastest of all the vessels in the fleet. Speeding ahead, it had become separated from the other ships on July 30. On such a voyage where the ability to outpace both the elements and pirates was vital, it seems logical that the *San Miguel* would have carried the most valuable cargo. Because of this, it is widely thought that she may be among the richest wrecks in all history. It is a shame, therefore, that no one knows where she lies. A shame— but perhaps also an opportunity …

Official files on the Rendlesham Forest Incident

WHAT THEY ARE Records of an alleged UFO encounter **WHY YOU WON'T FIND THEM** Papers were discovered missing almost two decades after the original incident

In December 1980, a number of military personnel reported seeing mysterious lights and, according to some, a glowing object near two US military bases located in the British countryside. The UK Ministry of Defence (MoD) insisted that these events were not a danger to national security. But are there still secret files on what has become known as Britain's "Roswell Incident"?

Rendlesham Forest is not far from the town of Woodbridge in the English county of Suffolk. The US Air Force at the time had personnel at the nearby twin Royal Air Force bases of Woodbridge and Bentwater. The undisputed facts of the Rendlesham Incident are relatively sparse and soon give way to speculation, contradiction, claim, and counterclaim. However, here are the basics.

In the early hours of December 26, 1980, a security patrol close to the East Gate of RAF Woodbridge saw flashing, colored lights over Rendlesham Forest that were strange enough for them to report. They described a triangular-shaped, glowing, metallic object. The deputy base commander, Lieutenant Colonel Charles Halt, led a party to investigate, and a note was sent to the local police saying: "We have a sighting of some unusual lights in the sky, we have sent some unarmed troops to investigate, we are terming it as a UFO at present." (It's worth noting at this point that the term unidentified flying object, does not necessarily imply an extraterrestrial spacecraft.)

Some of the servicemen reported seeing the UFO hovering on legs and then passing through the trees as they approached. Animals in the surrounding area were described as "in a frenzy." Several hours later another party went back into the forest to inspect an area of ground that showed three indentations, possibly indicating something had landed there. Nearby trees exhibited burn marks and broken boughs. On December 28, Halt returned to the area with specialist equipment and reported unusually high levels of radiation around the indentations and in some of the surrounding foliage. More flashing lights were also reported.

It was not until October 1983 that the story became public, prompting much interest and excitement. By that stage, the MoD had determined that national security was not at risk, but others did not see it in quite the same light. For instance, one of the USAF servicemen, Sgt. Jim Penniston, would in due course claim that he had got close enough to examine a "craft of unknown origin" for

TRICK OF THE LIGHT? *Orford Ness Lighthouse on the Suffolk coast began operating in 1792. The light from its 100-foot (30-m) tower could be seen many miles away until it was decommissioned in 2013, leading some to believe that it may have played a key role in what became known as the Rendlesham Forest incident.*

accounts were inconsistent and some changed over time. The so-called "landing marks" in the forest were probably debris created by burrowing rabbits, they suggest, while the "burn marks" were actually axe indentations inflicted by foresters. Doubt has also been cast on the validity of the radiation readings. As for what the men saw, some have speculated it was a Soviet satellite that broke up as it reentered the atmosphere, while others suggest a passing meteor. Most compellingly, close to the forest is the Orford Ness Lighthouse, whose pulsing light when seen in particular circumstances can play tricks on the eye.

Alternatively, the whole thing may have been a hoax. In 2003, a US security man once based at Rendlesham claimed to have achieved the effect by flashing the lights of his patrol car, though he later partially rescinded his confession. In a bid to head off claims that Britain had hosted an alien spacecraft, the MoD released the relevant official papers to the public. They seemed to back up the Ministry's stance that it was not deemed a particularly serious incident. However, this position was somewhat undermined in 2011 when it came to light that civil servants discovered in 2000 that large numbers of papers had "gone missing," leaving a "huge" gap in the official records. All of this led to inevitable accusations of a cover-up.

45 minutes, even making notes about its look and feel. No one else, however, corroborated his story, and it did not tally with his own earlier statements.

Conspiracy theorists received a boost in 2010 when Halt swore an affidavit saying: "I believe the objects that I saw at close quarter were extraterrestrial in origin and that the security services of both the United States and the United Kingdom have attempted—both then and now—to subvert the significance of what occurred at Rendlesham Forest and RAF Bentwaters by the use of well-practiced methods of disinformation."

However, most independent investigators reached conclusions in line with the MoD. They pointed out that eyewitness

Baron Hill-Norton, a member of the House of Lords and one-time Chief of the Defence Staff, had this to say about the affair: "Either large numbers of people were hallucinating (and for an American Air Force nuclear base this is extremely dangerous), or what they say happened did happen, and in either of those circumstances there can only be one answer, and that is, that [the incident] was of extreme defense interest."

Log of Columbus's first voyage

WHAT IT IS The record of Christopher Columbus's landmark voyage to the New World
WHY YOU WON'T FIND IT The original and its copy were both lost in the 16th century

As we all know, in 1492 Christopher Columbus sailed the ocean blue and discovered the Americas—we even have a record of some of the voyage in his own words. But what we do not have is his original log—that was lost long ago, so that today we must rely on a secondhand abstract based on his manuscript.

The first of Columbus's four voyages to the Americas set out from the Spanish town of Palos de Frontera on August 3, 1492. The three ships in his fleet—the *Pinta*, *Niña*, and *Santa María*—were about to sail into history. The trip was not, however, without hitches. Needless to say, Columbus did not intend to discover a new land—his purpose was instead to find a new trade route to Asia. But after ten difficult weeks at sea, with a crew on the brink of mutiny, he spied land. The island he named San Salvador would eventually become part of the Bahamas, and before heading back to Spain, he also explored part of Cuba and the island of Hispaniola. So the West started its adventures in the New World.

Columbus returned to a hero's welcome in Barcelona in March 1493, convinced he had actually reached Asia. He gave the log of his trip to the Spanish royal family, and Queen Isabella promptly had it copied, presenting Columbus with this new version (known as the Barcelona Copy). The original was never seen again. Columbus kept the Barcelona

Copy until his death in 1506, after which it passed to his son, Fernando, who used it as a primary source in his biography of his father. The copy itself disappeared in 1554, but fortunately for us, sometime around 1530 a Dominican monk and historian called Bartolomé de las Casas had also seen the log and wrote an abstract of it as part of his multivolume *History of the Indies*. So assuming he was accurate in his work, we can still read some of Columbus's own words about this world-changing trip. Among other things, we learn that Columbus played fast and loose when it came to telling his crew how far they had sailed—providing his unsettled men with doctored figures in a bid to appease fears that they had veered vastly off course.

The log was crammed full of information about the logistics of the voyage, shipboard life, and the sights the sailors saw. We are blessed to have at least a taste of this material, but it is frustrating to think of all those entries that have been lost to us. It is to be hoped that by some miracle they will be found again.

FLORIDA

ATLANTIC OCEAN

BAHAMAS

APPROXIMATE ROUTE OF
COLUMBUS'S VOYAGE

CUBA

TURKS AND CAICOS
ISLANDS

JAMAICA

HISPANIOLA

NEW WORLD ORDER *An engraving depicts Columbus and his crew landing on the island of Hispaniola on December 6, 1492, where they were greeted by Arawak Indians. These exploratory voyages ultimately paved the way for later European colonization of the Americas.*

CARIBBEAN SEA

45 Flight 19

WHAT IT IS A training flight consisting of five US Naval aircraft
WHY YOU WON'T FIND IT The aircraft and their crew, plus another search-and-rescue sea plane, disappeared without trace in the Atlantic

Thanks to the curious circumstances surrounding its disappearance somewhere over the Atlantic Ocean at the dawn of the Cold War, Flight 19 has become one of the most mythologized air disasters in history. The lack of material evidence as to its resting place has only deepened the sense of mystery, and it has become one of the key pieces of evidence for the so-called "Bermuda Triangle."

At 2.10 p.m. on December 5, 1945, the five TBM Avenger torpedo bombers making up Flight 19 left Naval Air Station Fort Lauderdale in Florida. They were to undertake a routine training exercise that should have seen them safely back to base in around two hours. The crew totaled 14 men, led by Lt. Charles Carroll Taylor, a man with several thousand hours of flight experience.

Each of the aircraft was given a thorough check before setting off, and all were in good working order and fully fueled. The mission proceeded entirely normally and the aircraft completed their glide bombing practice on schedule before turning around to make for home. However, at around a quarter of four, Fort Lauderdale received a panicked message from Taylor. "Cannot see land," he told them. "We seem to be off course."

Amid frequent periods of lost contact, the best efforts of the control tower to guide the flight back to safety were to no avail. "It looks like we are entering white water ... We're completely lost," relayed

one of the pilots (not Taylor). They were the last words ever heard from Flight 19.

Two PBM Mariner flying boats were sent out to search for the planes and their men. Tragically, one of the Mariners and its complement of 13 crew was never to be seen or heard of again either. The navy orchestrated a huge manhunt that lasted for several days, employing ships and aircraft to scour some 115,000 square miles (300,000 square kilometers) of the Atlantic and the Gulf of Mexico. Yet nothing was recovered. Subsequently, an official Navy Board of Inquiry concluded: "We are not even able to make a good guess as to what happened."

Inevitably, imaginations went into overdrive. One conspiracy theory held that Flight 19 had fallen victim to the Bermuda Triangle. Though not officially recognized by any government or maritime authority, this legendary region broadly comprises an area with Bermuda, Miami, and San Juan, Puerto Rico, at its apexes. Since the early 19th century a great many ships (and later,

FORMATION FLYING
The Grumman Avenger first saw action in 1942 at the Battle of Midway in the Pacific Ocean. Pictured here is a squadron of Avengers flying over Norfolk, Virginia, in September of that year.

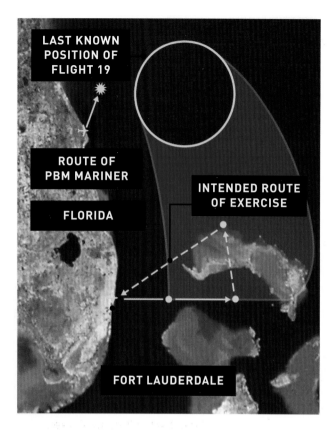

LAST KNOWN
POSITION OF
FLIGHT 19

ROUTE OF
PBM MARINER

INTENDED ROUTE
OF EXERCISE

FLORIDA

FORT LAUDERDALE

WATERY GRAVE *Flight 19's doomed trip began in Florida and ended with a fruitless search of a vast stretch of ocean. Does the fabled Bermuda Triangle hold the answers to the fate of the aircraft and those flying in them?*

good yarn, but none went far to providing a credible explanation. Later evidence that Lt. Taylor had arrived late for the exercise and had unsuccessfully tried to find a stand-in increased the confusion.

However, another theory seems to fit all the evidence and is no less tragic for being rooted in the real world. Taylor had told the control tower that both his onboard compasses were out. Nor did he have a working clock. Unaware of his precise position or the accurate time, it seems likely that he believed he was flying over the Florida Keys, when he was actually passing above the Bahamas. Having made this wrong assumption, he led his students over what he no doubt believed was the Gulf of Mexico en route to Fort Lauderdale. In fact, he was taking them out further over the Atlantic. At some point, the terrible error was surely realized but by then the aircraft had too little fuel to get home. The crewmen perhaps ditched into what was now a rough squall of a sea, never to be seen again. Their aircraft were most likely destroyed on impact with the water, with whatever debris there may have been sinking to the bottom of the ocean.

As for the lost Mariner, the evidence strongly points to a purely coincidental midair explosion. A tanker, the SS *Gaines Mills*, reported seeing a huge ball of flames crash into the sea at the relevant time and position, though its subsequent search of the area recovered neither survivors nor wreckage. Debris from several Avengers was discovered in the waters off Florida in the decades that followed the accident but tests proved that none of it originated from Flight 19. The conclusive evidence of what happened that day may well still be lying beneath the waves but it seems unlikely that the sea will ever yield its secrets.

airplanes) were lost without trace in this part of the ocean, leading to claims of unknown forces at work. In reality, the high number of tragedies attached to the area is more a reflection of the parlous natural conditions that prevail there. In addition, the Gulf Stream is quick to erase evidence of disaster, so leaving perplexing questions unanswered.

Other theories were equally outlandish. Some claimed alien abduction, others that the planes had fallen through a gap in the space-time continuum. Another theory suggested the nefarious involvement of the Soviets. All made for a

Hanging Gardens of Babylon

WHAT THEY ARE The finest gardens in antiquity
WHY YOU WON'T FIND THEM Shrouded in mystery, they were probably destroyed in the second century BC

One of the Seven Wonders of the Ancient World, the Hanging Gardens have traditionally been attributed to the reign of Nebuchadnezzar II, who ruled over the city-state of Babylon in modern-day Iraq from 605 BC until 562 BC. However, the exact location of the gardens remains a mystery, and no archaeological evidence for them has ever been uncovered.

Although they are most commonly dated to Nebuchadnezzar's reign, some have argued that the gardens predate him, having perhaps been built by the Assyrian Queen Semiramis around 800 BC. Other ancient historians speak only in vague terms of a "Syrian king" as architect. As for what they looked like, the gardens did not hang as such, but spanned a grand series of raised terraces, supported by huge pillars and rising perhaps tens of feet into the air. The effect was undoubtedly spectacular. In the first century AD, Roman historian Quintus Curtius Rufus (drawing on the fourth century BC writings of Cleitarchus) described them as "a wonder celebrated by the fables of the Greeks," while Strabo, writing around the same time, said they were "called one of the Seven Wonders of the World":

The first known reference to the Hanging Gardens is from a priest called Berossus, writing around 290 BC. His work was used as a key source by first-century AD Romano-Jewish historian, Josephus, who was the first to credit their creation to Nebuchadnezzar: "In this palace he erected very high walks, supported by stone pillars; and by planting what was called a pensile paradise, and replenishing it with all sorts of trees, he rendered the prospect an exact resemblance of a mountainous country."

In this story, Nebuchadnezzar created them for his wife, Amyitis, "because she had been brought up in Media [an area in Western Iran], and was fond of a mountainous situation." The king built extensive palaces, temples, and fortifications throughout his realm, but the gardens posed a unique problem: how could elevated gardens be watered in an area of notable dryness? The answer was apparently a vast irrigation project to divert water from the nearby Euphrates River. From a large pool at the bottom of the gardens, water was then raised to the highest terrace either by a system of chain pumps (in which a chain and two wheels raise and lower a series of buckets), or perhaps by screw pumps that would have predated Archimedes' famous invention by 300 years.

AQUEDUCTS CARRY WATER DOWN FROM THE MOUNTAINS

PLANTED TERRACES

ARTIFICIAL LAKE

IRRIGATION USING ARCHIMEDES' SCREW

SUPPORTING ARCHES AND TOWERS

ANCIENT WONDER *The Hanging Gardens were a true miracle of engineering, stunning visitors not only with their technical magnificence but with their aesthetic beauty too. But have we been searching for them in the wrong place?*

THE OTHER BABYLON? *Recent academic research suggests the Gardens may have been located in the city of Nineveh. Shown here is a stone relief from the ancient city once ruled by King Sennacherib, who prided himself on his garden design.*

The eventual fate of the gardens is not recorded—many historians believe they were destroyed by an earthquake sometime in the second century AD, but no physical evidence of their site has ever been found. Furthermore, records of Nebuchadnezzar's achievements written close to the time of his reign make no reference to the gardens. The great Greek historian Herodotus, for instance, wrote in the mid-fifth century BC that Babylon "surpasses in splendor any city in the known world" but did not mention a garden. These curious omissions have led some academics to conclude that they were nothing more than a myth.

Then in 2013 an alternative explanation was offered up by Dr. Stephanie Dalley of Oxford University's Oriental Institute. In her book on the mystery, she elaborates on a theory developed over two decades, arguing that the gardens were never in Babylon, but were actually at Nineveh,

300 miles (500 kilometers) to the north. As such, they would have been watered by the Tigris rather than the Euphrates.

In evidence, she cites a bas-relief discovered in the mid-19th century but lost shortly afterward. A drawing made at the time shows a garden complex similar to the one supposedly in Babylon. The gardens were created, she suggests, at the behest of the Assyrian King Sennacherib, who is known to have built palace gardens around 700 BC that he himself described as "a wonder for all the peoples." In addition, he is known to have ordered the construction of a huge system of canals and aqueducts bringing water from up to 50 miles (80 kilometers) away, and to have technology of the sort required to keep the gardens watered.

As for the question of why we remember the Hanging Gardens of Babylon and not Nineveh, Dalley suggests that Babylon became a sort of generic name used in reference to a number of cities in the region. If she is right about all this, then we may yet find the remains of these fabulous structures.

Reimerswaal

WHAT IT IS A lost Dutch city in the province of Zeeland
WHY YOU WON'T FIND IT It was abandoned in the 17th century after a series of devastating floods

Reimerswaal was a once-proud city in the Zeeland region of the Netherlands, somewhere near the eastern end of the Oosterschelde River. After it was gradually rendered uninhabitable by a succession of floods in the 16th century, the last citizens abandoned the town in the 1630s. Today, its name lives on in a new municipality, but the original site has long been lost.

Reimerswaal was granted city status in 1374 and over time grew to be the third largest city in the Zeeland region that covers the southwestern tip of the Netherlands. However, life changed in Reimerswaal forever on November 5, 1530—the festival day of St. Felix.

An epic storm caused the river to burst its banks, its waters utterly ravaging the surrounding area. This natural disaster came to be known as the St. Felix Flood. The list of villages and hamlets that disappeared altogether was lengthy—Assemansbroek, Nieuwkerke,

FLOOD WARNING *This engraving shows the town of Reimerswaal in 1570, by which time it had suffered several devastating floods but had not yet lost the battle altogether. It would be deserted for good within a few decades.*

Ouderdinge, and St. Jooskapel, to name but a few. Many more towns were seriously affected and when, a mere two years later, they faced another deluge, several were unable to cope. Among the swathe of settlements lost forever in 1532 were Broecke, Duvenee, Kapeldorp, Kouwerve, Kreke, Lodijke, Looketers, Nieuwlande, Schoudee, Steelvlet, Tolsende, Yersekeroord, and Zwartewale.

Reimerswaal, meanwhile, sat on slightly higher ground and so managed to survive. However, its population faced life on what was effectively now an island. Attempts to dam the surrounding area were successful in the short term, but proved no match for several further storms and floods that took their toll over the course of the next hundred years. Eventually, only a handful of citizens remained, the last of whom left Reimerswaal for good in 1634.

While it is clearly unfair to blame the loss of an entire city on any one individual, experts have suggested that the Lord of Lodijke contributed to the wider area's vulnerability by refusing to address a growing tidal creek on his land. Today, the district where Reimerswaal once stood is called *Verdronken Land van Reimerswaal* ("the Drowned Land of Reimerswaal"). One consolation, though, is that the freshwater beds that the floods produced have become an ideal environment for culturing shellfish!

Even though the town of Reimerswaal died, its name proved more enduring. In 1970 a new municipality named in honor of the ancient city was established south of the Oosterschelde. By 2004 it boasted a population of over 20,000. It is centered around Yerseke, a village with roots in the Middle Ages, which today has a reputation for high-quality mussels and oysters.

Zeeland, meanwhile, remains prone to flooding, with the majority of its territory lying below sea level. The North Sea flood of 1953 killed more than 1,800 people in the Netherlands, most of them in this province—a reminder, if it were needed, that water remains as powerful a foe in the modern age as it was in the 16th century.

The thylacine

WHAT IT IS An extinct mammal native to Australia

WHY YOU WON'T FIND IT The last one was seen in the 1930s—but a band of believers are convinced that the species survives

The thylacine or Tasmanian tiger was—or perhaps is—a meat-eating marsupial that roamed Australia and New Guinea for some 4 million years. By the time Europeans arrived in the 17th century, it had long since died out from these larger islands, though a significant population remained in Tasmania. Soon, though, European settlers would set about about wiping these survivors from existence.

When Abel Tasman first landed on the island that today bears his name in 1642, members of his crew reported tracking footprints of "wild beasts having claws like a Tyger." Yet it was not until the start of the 19th century that the animal was scientifically described. The thylacine resembled a large yellow-brown dog with a long, stiff tail and distinctive stripes across its back. A nocturnal hunter with a diet of small birds and mammals, adults could grow to weigh 70 pounds (32 kg).

The reasons for the thylacine's decline were manifold, but included habitat degradation, imported illnesses, and falling availability of prey. Perhaps most devastatingly of all, however, the animal got a reputation for stalking sheep. From 1830 the authorities ran a bounty system with a reward for every thylacine killed, which accounted for the deaths of many thousands of animals. By the 1920s, the situation had become critical, and the last known shooting of a thylacine in the wild occurred in 1930. Some lingered on in captivity until 1936, when the last of all died at Hobart Zoo. A few weeks later, and much too late, the species was finally given official protection.

After a long wait with no more thylacines forthcoming, the species was declared extinct by the International Union for the Conservation of Nature in 1982. Tasmania's state government followed suit four years later, and that should be the end of the story—except for the fact that since the 1930s, there have been at least several hundred (and possibly as many as 4,000) reported sightings of the thylacine. Discounting hoaxes, that still leaves a lot of sightings to explain, many from trained scientists and naturalists and some backed up with (admittedly, inconclusive) photographic evidence.

So it might just be possible to see an extinct animal in the wild—a rare inversion of the usual story of species destruction—but the chances of proving it are thin. In the meantime, there have been attempts to extract living DNA from preserved specimens, in the hope that the Tasmanian tiger may one day be regenerated in the science lab.

LAST REFUGE *The temperate rainforests of western Tasmania hosted the thylacine for millions of years but could not sustain the species once humanity became involved. The last wild specimen was seen in 1930.*

END OF THE LINE *Beaumaris Zoo opened in Hobart, Tasmania's capital, in 1895. It was home to the last verified thylacine, which died on site in 1936. The zoo itself closed down the following year.*

Hemingway's lost manuscripts

WHAT THEY ARE The early output of Ernest Hemingway
WHY YOU WON'T FIND THEM They were stolen from a train in 1922

The ultimate voice of modern American masculinity, Ernest Hemingway won the Nobel Prize in Literature in 1954 and is responsible for such classics as *A Farewell to Arms* and *For Whom the Bell Tolls*. He was married three times, first to Hadley Richardson in 1921. It was she who would accidentally deny us a great swathe of his early work.

Shortly after their marriage, the couple moved to Paris, where Hemingway was employed as a foreign correspondent by the *Toronto Star*. In December 1922 he was sent to Lausanne in Switzerland to cover the peace conference that was being held in the city. While there he met a fellow American, journalist, and book editor Lincoln Steffens, who declared his admiration for Hemingway's work and asked if he might be able to see some more. Hadley swung into action as the dutiful wife and searched their Paris apartment high and low for every bit of her husband's output. She put all the materials in a suitcase, headed to the Gare de Lyon, bought a ticket to Switzerland, and stowed her luggage.

She then went to buy a bottle of water but on her return found the suitcase had disappeared. Despite a comprehensive search by Hadley and the train staff, it was nowhere to be found. We can only imagine the horror she must have felt as the train rattled on its way to her reunion with Hemingway. He would later write in his memoirs, *A Moveable Feast*:

"I had never seen anyone hurt by a thing other than death or unbearable suffering except Hadley when she told me about the things being gone. She had cried and cried and could not tell me."

Among the lost manuscripts were some 18 short stories and the draft of a prospective novel. Only two stories from this period of his life escaped the cull—one fortunately hidden in the bottom of a drawer and the other in the possession of a magazine editor at the vital moment. These two short works—*Up in Michigan* and *My Old Man*—would appear in his first book, *Three Stories and Ten Poems*, which came out in 1923.

The fate of the suitcase is unknown, and unless the thief had a particularly strong critical eye, it is unlikely he would have realized that his swag was worth a potential fortune. The chances are that the manuscripts were destroyed, though there is, perhaps, the slimmest of chances that they survive, doubtless unrecognized as the work of one of the truly great men of American letters.

50 Oliver Cromwell's head

WHAT IT IS The head of the man who beheaded a king

WHY YOU WON'T FIND IT While its location in Cambridge is a closely guarded secret, some doubt if the head is there at all

Execution is a nasty fate at the best of times, but it really is adding insult to injury when your corpse is dug up to undergo the indignity after a natural death. This was the unusual fate of England's 17th-century regicide and Lord Protector, Oliver Cromwell. Today, his head is thought buried at a secret location in the grounds of Sydney College at the University of Cambridge—or is it ...?

Cromwell was the leading figure on the parliamentarian "Roundhead" side of the English Civil War that ravaged the country in the 1640s. In 1649, he became one of the regicides—signatories to the order that saw King Charles I beheaded. Thereafter, he became head of the new republican Commonwealth established in 1651, styling himself Lord Protector. But in seven years of rule, he was little less autocratic than Charles at his worst.

Cromwell died on September 3, 1658 in London, and so began the incredible tale of his body's adventures postmortem. After a period lying in state, he was buried in Westminster Abbey with all the pomp and ceremony of a royal funeral. There, his corpse might have been set to rest in eternal peace—had it not been for the brief, disastrous rule of Cromwell's son and successor as Lord Protector, Richard. Amid public clamor for the end of the Commonwealth, the monarchy was restored in 1660 under Charles II, son of the previous king. Understandably peeved by his father's fate, Charles was keen to get some form of redress. He

announced that Cromwell's body and those of two other regicides should be exhumed from their graves and transported to Tyburn in London. There the corpses were hanged, cut down, and decapitated. The bodies were then cast into a pit, while the heads were set on spikes and displayed outside Westminster Hall as a warning to any other proto-republicans.

Thus was Cromwell's head displayed from early 1661 until at least the mid-1680s. However, his head was said to have eventually blown to the ground in a storm, probably in 1688. It was spotted by an alert guard who promptly took possession of it, hiding it beneath his cloak until he was able to lodge it in the chimney of his house for safekeeping.

The head then went through numerous private hands, and was displayed in the 18th century to the paying public, no longer so much a grisly admonition as a macabre historical curiosity. During this period, its historical provenance became hazy, and its owners largely

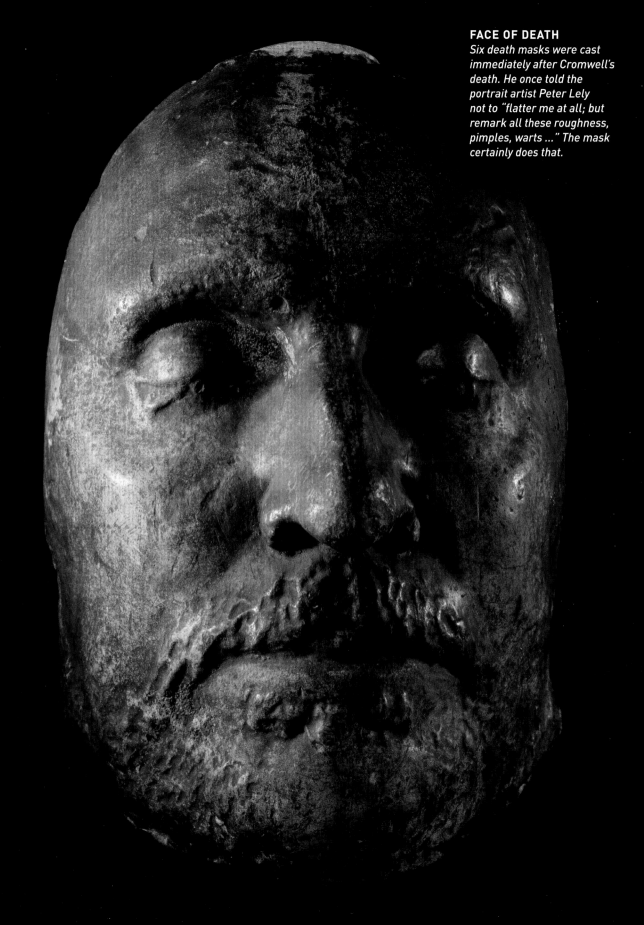

FACE OF DEATH
Six death masks were cast immediately after Cromwell's death. He once told the portrait artist Peter Lely not to "flatter me at all; but remark all these roughness, pimples, warts ..." The mask certainly does that.

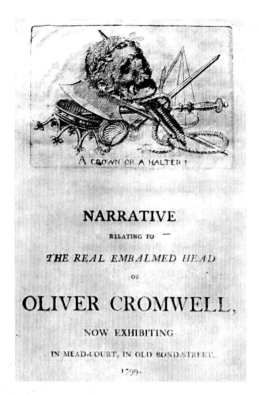

A CROWN OR A HALTER?

NARRATIVE

RELATING TO

THE REAL EMBALMED HEAD

OF

OLIVER CROMWELL,

NOW EXHIBITING

IN MEAD-COURT, IN OLD BOND-STREET.

1799.

purchased it on trust. In 1815, it was bought by Josiah Henry Wilkinson after he had been convinced of its authenticity, although that great historian and man of letters, Thomas Carlyle, cast doubt on its provenance by describing it as "fraudulent moonshine." The head subsequently passed down through the Wilkinson line until 1960, when Horace Wilkinson reached an agreement that the head should be finally laid to rest in the grounds of Cromwell's *alma mater*, Sydney College, Cambridge.

So runs the generally accepted history of Cromwell's head—but it is certainly a story with some enormous gaps. In fact, from virtually the moment of his death, we lose track of Cromwell's body. It was certainly embalmed, but there is strong evidence to suggest that it was then buried quickly and privately (the body that lay in state and was processed around London in a coffin was almost certainly a mannequin with

a wax head). There are also plentiful theories that Cromwell was never really buried in Westminster, where his friends feared potential desecration by his enemies (rightly, as it turned out). Among the most prominent in a plethora of alternative final resting places are Holborn in London, and Naseby, the scene of one of his greatest Civil War victories. If such stories are true, the head at Sydney College clearly never belonged to the Lord Protector.

Nevertheless, there is also evidence in favor of the head's authenticity. In the 1930s Drs. Karl Pearson and G.M. Morant undertook the most thorough scientific testing of the relic and agreed that it was indeed that of a man dating to the correct period, who had been embalmed and posthumously beheaded. Furthermore, the skullcap had been removed, as we know Cromwell's was after his death. The chances of there being another individual who coincidentally had his skullcap removed after death and was then embalmed and later beheaded pushes the bounds of credibility. Pearson and Morant concluded with "a moral certainty drawn from circumstantial evidence" that this was indeed Cromwell's head.

Yet even if we accept their findings at face value, we cannot view its last resting place. In the interests of finally letting Cromwell have his peace, the exact location of the head's burial is a secret tightly guarded by the college authorities. They have also stated their reluctance to approve any further scientific analysis in search of its true identity.

The Fifth Man

WHO HE IS The last unidentified member of a notorious Cold War spy network

WHY YOU WON'T FIND HIM In the world of intelligence and counterintelligence, the truth is hard to pinpoint

Emerging out of the illustrious university in the 1930s, the "Cambridge Five" was a spy ring whose members rose to positions of power and influence in British society while simultaneously passing national secrets to the Soviet Union until at least the 1950s. Across a period of several more decades, four of the Five were unmasked, but the identity of the ring's infamous "fifth man" has never been confirmed.

British intelligence first became aware of the ring of five spies, all of whom studied at Trinity College, Cambridge, when a KGB defector by the name of Anatoliy Golitsyn alerted them in 1961. Two of the five, Guy Burgess and Donald Maclean, had already defected to Russia. After graduating, Burgess had spent several years working for the BBC, concurrently serving MI5 (the UK's internal Security Service) from the 1940s. Later on, he took up an appointment with the Foreign Office and was sent to Washington.

Meanwhile, Maclean—the son of a cabinet minister—studied modern languages before joining the diplomatic service. Also posted to Washington during the Second World War, he passed secrets concerning the US nuclear program to Moscow. Despite erratic behavior, he held a series of other important diplomatic roles, eventually becoming chief of the Foreign Office's American Department. By 1950, he was under investigation for espionage, but both he and Burgess fled to Russia before they could be apprehended.

Burgess and Maclean had been tipped off about the investigation by Kim Philby— "the third man." Philby had worked as a journalist before joining MI6 (the Secret Intelligence Service, focused on overseas operations) in 1940. Eventually, and ironically, he rose to become head of its anti-Soviet section, and would later serve as the UK's highest-ranking intelligence officer in the USA—all the while supplying the Kremlin with sensitive information. Maclean and Burgess's flight brought Philby under extreme scrutiny and he quit MI6, though he was officially exonerated of any involvement in the affair. In 1956, he gave up spying for good and moved to Beirut, working as a foreign correspondent. However, Golitsyn's revelations refocused attention on him and in 1963 Philby fled to the USSR.

With the "third man" thus unmasked, it would be a further 16 years until the next member of the gang was publicly unveiled. There was widespread astonishment at the unmasking of Sir Anthony Blunt, not only a knight of the realm, but the director of the Courtauld

SPY RING *Clockwise from top left: Anthony Blunt, Guy Burgess, Donald Maclean, and Kim Philby. The heady mixture of Cold War espionage, English academe, and personal frailties continues to fascinate us—but who was the Fifth Man?*

Institute of Art and Surveyor of the Queen's Pictures. At Cambridge he had "talent-spotted" potential Kremlin spies among the ranks of undergraduates. In the Second World War, he became an MI5 agent but evidence of his double life came to light after Philby's defection. In return for a full confession, Blunt was allowed to continue life as an esteemed art historian. However, when Andrew Boyle's 1979 book, *Climate of Treason*, cast the spotlight on him, Prime Minister Margaret Thatcher confirmed suspicions about Blunt's past. Ultimately, he was stripped of both his knighthood and his academic titles, though he was never prosecuted and remained in Britain, living a largely secluded life until his death from a heart attack in 1983.

But what of the "fifth man"? Many look no further than John Cairncross, a contemporary of the other four at Trinity who admitted to passing on information when a note of his was found at Burgess's flat shortly after Burgess's flight. Another KGB defector, Oleg Gordievsky, pinpointed him in 1990, but others continue to point the finger elsewhere. Suspects include:
• Goronwy Rees—a Welsh journalist who was actually educated at Oxford, but had contact with Philby and admitted in the late 1970s to having spied for the USSR.
• Guy Liddell—a senior MI5 agent who took early retirement following an investigation into his links with Philby, and was subsequently accused by Rees.
• The 3rd Baron Rothschild—a wartime MI5 agent, he was identified as the culprit in a 1994 book, though Rothschild fervently rejected the claim during his lifetime.
• Andrew Gow—a one-time tutor of George Orwell and Cambridge academic who died in 1978. He was accused by Brian Sewell, a renowned art critic and friend of Blunt.

But in a world of smoke and mirrors no one has yet been able to produce the irrefutable evidence as to the mysterious Fifth Man's identity.

The maharaja's lost treasure

WHAT IT IS Valuables that once belonged to the Maharaja of Kapurthala
WHY YOU WON'T FIND IT They were lost at sea during the First World War

Shortly after Christmas 1915, the passenger liner SS *Persia* was sunk by a German torpedo in the Mediterranean Sea en route to India. More than 300 people died in the incident, and rumors soon abounded that the ship had been carrying a rich cargo belonging to an Indian Maharaja. His treasure, though, has never been recovered.

The *Persia*, built in 1900, was one of the finest liners owned by the Peninsular and Oriental Steam Navigation Company (today better known as simply P&O). Nevertheless, passengers who boarded her in December 1915 knew that their journey would be an anxious one. The First World War was in full swing and submarine warfare had made sea travel a perilous undertaking. On December 30, 1915, the *Persia* was sailing some way off Crete, headed for Port Said in Egypt. Just before lunchtime, she was spotted by a German U-boat, whose captain promptly ordered a devastating attack without warning and in contravention of international law. The liner sank in just five minutes.

One passenger who should have been aboard had made the fortuitous decision not to get on at Marseille a week or so earlier, opting instead to take a later sailing on another vessel. He was Maharaja Jagatjit Singh, the hugely wealthy rluer of Kapurthala, a princely state in the Punjab. Jagatjit Singh was a colorful character who liked to spend at least half the year away from India, mostly in Europe where he became renowned as a Francophile. A spectacular palace and gardens he had built in Kapurthala was based on Louis XIV's Palace of Versailles.

In March 1915, Singh had sailed from Bombay to Paris, and he had spent the rest of his year traveling between Europe and North America. In Britain he had been entertained by King George V and Queen Mary, who wished to express their thanks to him for his contributions to the war effort. In October he had even made a visit to the front line in France to witness the horror of the fighting at first hand. After planning to join the *Persia* for his trip back home on Christmas Day, he changed his plans at the last minute.

However, one of his most trusted companions, Inder Singh, took his place on the ship, accompanied by much of the maharaja's luggage. This, it is thought, contained gold, silver, and exquisite jewelry that he had accumulated during

GLOBE TROTTER *A portrait of Jagatjit Singh made when he was around 21 years of age. He was a man of refined tastes and gloried in picking up treasures as he traveled the world. Having narrowly escaped disaster aboard the SS Persia, he died in 1949 aged 76.*

for decades. However, in 2003 British company Deep Tek—specialists in complex underwater engineering projects—undertook the world's deepest salvage operation, working some 10,000 feet (3,000 m) beneath the surface of the Mediterranean.

The operation called for specially designed equipment and used cutting-edge video technology to assist engineers cutting through five decks of the *Persia* to gain access to her strong room—the presumed location of the maharaja's booty. But to their surprise and disappointment, there was no sign of the mooted hoard of gold and silver. Instead, the winches brought up artefacts of undeniable historical value but limited economic worth. There was, for instance, plentiful flatware and crockery, as well as spectacles, pipes, newspapers, and even unopened bottles of vintage champagne. Finally, on the last day according to Moya Crawford of Deep Tek, they salvaged more than 200 rubies and other precious stones, some as big as 2 carats. Crawford went on to say: "We did not find the gold—someone will have to go back for that—but the real value lies in showing that no part of the seabed is now beyond reach."

that year's travels. The maharaja was by then five-times married (although one of his wives had died several years earlier) and many of these valuable were destined for his surviving spouses—though they would never receive them.

The treasure trove was valued at as much as $1.6 million in 1915 (more than US$90 million at today's prices) but there was so much confusion over the exact location of the wreck site that no attempt was made to retrieve it

After the war, the captain of the U-boat that sank the *Persia* was indicted for war crimes, though he was never convicted. Compared to the hundreds of lives that were lost, the value of the maharaja's treasure rather pales. But assuming that it was stowed on the ship as is widely believed, its absence from the strongroom is an intriguing mystery. The sea has kept its fate secret for a century but perhaps developments in salvage technology could provide us with answers sooner rather than later.

53 Shergar

WHO HE IS One of history's greatest racehorses
WHY YOU WON'T FIND HIM He was kidnapped and apparently died while being held captive

Shergar was a once-in-a-generation racehorse, valued at $16 million when he disappeared. Owned at the time by a syndicate headed by the Aga Khan, Shergar was at stud in the Republic of Ireland when he was kidnapped. It has long been believed that the militant Irish Republican Army (IRA) was responsible, though no one was convicted for the crime and the unfortunate horse has never been found.

With a white flash across his face, four distinctive white "socks," and a tendency to run with his tongue hanging out one side of his mouth, Shergar cut a highly recognizable figure. His greatest day came in 1981 when he romped to victory in the Epsom Derby, winning by a record ten lengths. Further successes came at the Irish Derby and in the King George Stakes. He retired a hero in 1982, with breeders paying up to $13,3264 for him to sire a foal. In his single season at stud in County Kildare in Ireland, he helped produce 35 mini-Shergars.

But on the evening of February 8, 1983, the fairy tale came to an abrupt and violent end. At 8.30 p.m. masked gunmen arrived at the Ballymany Stud. "We have come for Shergar," they said. "We want £2 million for him," Then they forced the head groom, Jim Fitzgerald, to load his prize asset into the back of a horse box while they held his young family at gunpoint. The assailants drove both Fitzgerald and the horse into the night, eventually dumping the unharmed Fitzgerald several miles from home.

The groom first called his brother, and the crime was soon reported to both Ireland's finance and justice ministers. However, for reasons that remain unclear, the Garda police force were not contacted until 4 a.m. the next morning. By that point, they were playing a game of catch-up they stood little chance of winning. Confidence in their ability to recover Shergar was not increased after it was reported that psychics and mediums had been asked to help with the search.

It was not long before the criminal gang made contact with a representative of the Aga Khan, identifying themselves through a series of codewords. Unfortunately, they were under the misapprehension that the Aga Khan was Shergar's sole owner, when in fact, he was just one of 35 members in a syndicate. As a result, he was unable to make any decisions without consulting his fellow owners, and so the process of negotiating for Shergar's release quickly became complex and laborious.

According to O'Callaghan, Shergar was killed not long after being stolen—shot after suffering a leg injury while in a panicked frenzy. He claimed that the kidnappers had originally arranged for a vet to accompany them and keep the horse calm, but the vet had pulled out at the eleventh hour, allegedly after his wife got wind of the crime. Journalists from the *Sunday Telegraph* newspaper reported a variation on this tale in 2008. In their version, the gang soon realized that they were hitting a brick wall in negotiations and sensed that the game was almost up. With Garda swarming across the country in search of their celebrated victim, the gang's leader became convinced it would be impossible to move their hostage safely. He therefore gave the order for the horse to be destroyed—an act that was carried out in the most grisly way possible; Shergar supposedly took several minutes to die after being showered by machine gun fire. As head groom Jim Fitzgerald would note: "... to learn what they did to him. It was a terrible, terrible business."

WONDER HORSE Opposite: *Shergar passes the finishing post to win the Epsom Derby by an outrageous ten lengths in 1981, under Jockey Walter Swinburn.* Above: *The great horse, a popular favorite as well as a sporting hero, on display in the parade ring.*

Meanwhile, all of Ireland was alive with debate over who was responsible. Some claimed it was a branch of the mafia (possibly angered by a horse deal with the Aga Khan that turned bad), while others pointed the finger at the erstwhile Libyan dictator, Colonel Gaddafi. Many, however, believed it had all the hallmarks of an IRA heist designed to raise funds for arms. This theory was seemingly verified by Sean O'Callaghan, a former IRA member, who gave details of the plot in his 1999 memoirs.

What happened to the body remains a mystery—it is possible that Shergar was driven to the coast and dumped into the sea. However, it is more likely that he was buried on the mainland. County Leitrim has regularly been identified as his most likely final resting place—a sparsely populated region, parts of which were effectively bandit country during the Irish "Troubles." In the meantime, a great many lives continue to be blighted by the incident, not least those of the co-owners who lost vast amounts of money because their insurance would not pay out without a corpse to prove Shergar had been killed. Thankfully, though, the wonder horse's cruel end does little to diminish his remarkable achievements in life.

54

D.B. Cooper

D.B. Cooper's march into infamy began on the afternoon of November 24, 1971 when, carrying a black attaché case, he bought a ticket in the name of Dan Cooper. The flight from Portland, Oregon to Seattle aboard a Northwest Orient Airline's Boeing 727 should have been a short hop of little more than 30 minutes—but the mysterious Mr. Cooper had other plans.

Shortly after takeoff, Cooper passed a note to one of the flight attendants stating that he had a bomb in his case and that she should take a seat next to him. Having shown her what appeared to be an explosive device, he told her he wanted US$200,000, four parachutes, and a tanker on hand at Seattle to refuel the plane. As she went to the cockpit to communicate his demands, he put on a pair of sunglasses.

The hijacker was notably calm and polite throughout, and the airline soon decided to meet his demands. The plane landed just before 5.40 p.m. and the money and parachutes were delivered. At that stage, Cooper agreed to release all 36 passengers and two of the six crew. He then told the pilot that the plane was to fly low and slow to Mexico, stopping en route at Reno, Nevada for a further refuel. The rear exit door was to be kept open. The onward journey commenced at around 7.40 p.m., with the remaining crew locked in the cockpit. A little before 8:15 p.m., the crew became aware of a disturbance in the cabin, and when they landed at Reno, they found that Cooper had vanished. He had seemingly parachuted out of the cabin somewhere over Washington State, undetected by three military jets shadowing the plane. Investigators quickly concluded that Cooper could not have survived a jump into the dark in such testing weather conditions.

One of the first tasks for the police was to rule out a low-level Oregon criminal called D.B. Cooper. He proved to be entirely innocent, but a journalistic miscommunication resulted in Dan becoming known to the public as D.B. instead. Years passed without serious progress in the investigation, although in 1980 an eight-year-old boy discovered some of the ransom on the banks of the Columbia River. Whether it had floated there or been purposely buried was not clear. Numerous suspects were subsequently accused or offered up confessions. None is considered credible by the FBI but if Cooper did die during his attempted escape, then where is his corpse? The case remains open.

A BULLETIN FROM THE F.B.I.

Following is an artist's conception of the hijacker who extorted
$200,000 from Northwest Airlines on November 24, 1971

MAN OF MYSTERY Above: *An FBI bulletin issued in the hope of tracking down the unknown hijacker.* Below: *A Northwest Orient 727 similar to the one Cooper so infamously disrupted.*

55

A complete dodo skeleton

WHAT IT IS A land-bound bird that once thrived on the island of Mauritius **WHY YOU WON'T FIND IT** Contact with humans saw it extinct within a century

There is perhaps no sadder symbol of mankind's unfortunate ability to do damage to other species than the dear old dodo. Having survived millions of years on Earth out of the way of humans, it found itself in the wrong place at the wrong time at the end of the 16th century. Now we do not even have a complete skeleton to serve as a monument to our brutality.

The dodo was indigenous to the island of Mauritius in the Indian Ocean, where it had proved highly resilient despite a slightly ungainly appearance. There was no soaring like an eagle for the dodo—in fact, flight was off the cards altogether. Adults had a gray plumage, grew up to 3 feet (90 cm) in length and weighed up to 44 pounds (20 kg). Stubby wings left them rooted on terra firma, but this was no hardship as they fed on forest-floor fruits and seeds, and had no predators to fear.

At least, that was the case until 1598, when Dutch sailors landed on the island. Since the bird resembled a waddling turkey, it was not long before the new arrivals decided to hunt them. Their meat, though, was tough, and the taste so disagreeable that the dodo earned the nickname *walckvogel*, or "disgusting bird." In fact, the cats, dogs, pigs, and rats that the Dutch introduced onto the island proved far more dangerous than the dining table. So devastating was this invasion and the ensuing environmental damage that the last bird died in 1680.

It took less than 100 years for man to destroy a species that had lived long before humans even existed. A few preserved examples were traded by European collectors, but today the most complete soft-tissue remains—at the Museum of Natural History at Oxford University—consist of only a mummified head and foot. Meanwhile, what few skeletal remains we have are either incomplete or composed of bones from several different birds. Nonetheless, there was a ray of hope in 2007 when the most complete skeleton so far was found in a cave in Mauritius.

But the truth is that the dodo's extinction was considered so inconsequential that no one even made the effort to preserve a decent example for future generations. Had Lewis Carroll not immortalized the creature in *Alice's Adventures in Wonderland*, it might have dropped out of the popular recollection altogether. Today the Nicobar pigeon is the closest living relative of the dodo, and in case we feel too smug about our own conservation efforts, that species, too, is under threat.

NOT SO COMPLETE *Although dodo "skeletons" are displayed in many natural history museums around the world, most are either cast replicas, or at best, patchworks cobbled together from several different sources.*

56

Formula for WD-40

WHAT IT IS An essential household product
WHY YOU WON'T FIND IT It is a closely guarded trade secret

WD-40 is one of those products that comes to the rescue in countless domestic crises—the company that makes it lists more than 2,000 uses from preventing rusts and loosening stuck parts to separating Lego pieces and softening leather. Today, it sells in 187 countries and territories around the world, yet its formula has remained a closely guarded secret since it first hit the shelves in 1958.

In 1953, industrial chemist Norm Larsen founded the Rocket Chemical Company in San Diego, California. With a small team of scientists, he set out to perfect a range of antirust solvents and degreasers for use in the aerospace industry. Legend has it that these intrepid researchers got the formula right at the 40th attempt, hence WD-40 (the "WD" stands for "Water Displacement"). After five years of successful industrial use, Larsen decided it was time to sell to domestic consumers. In 1969, the decision was taken to rename the business after its one and only product line.

Amazingly, the company never applied for a patent on the basis that if it did, it would have to make a full disclosure of its production process. Needless to say, commercial rivals (as well as the merely curious) are constantly trying to reverse engineer the product to discover its composition. However, the company's website insists: "Any information that you may encounter alleging the disclosure of the 'secret sauce' is inaccurate."

Nevertheless, we can safely make a few assumptions. We know, for instance, that it comprises: a stable, viscous oil that sits on the surface of a material to lubricate and displace moisture; a volatile hydrocarbon that gets the substance into all those tiny gaps; and a propellant to force it out of the can in the first place. The company has disclosed that more than 50 percent of WD-40 is mineral spirits, produced by distilling petroleum, and carbon dioxide is the propellant of choice these days. The formula is also believed to contain a number of different "alkane" hydrocarbons, including decane (which helps WD-40 stay liquid in cold temperatures), nonane (vital in repelling water) and undecane (derived from the pheromones of cockroaches and ants!).

Anyone who doubts WD-40's usefulness need only consider the story of the Asian bus driver who used it to dislodge a snake from his vehicle's undercarriage, or the policeman who used it to release a naked thief from an air vent. Just don't expect to make a batch of it yourself.

ROCKET SCIENCE *Originally developed for use on US Atlas missiles, WD-40 is a spray that acts to both lubricate and protect all sorts of materials. Its success and ubiquity are undoubtedly beyond the wildest dreams of its creator, Norm Larsen.*

Book of the Wars of the Lord

WHAT IT IS A book referenced in the Bible
WHY YOU WON'T FIND IT Theologians have failed to track it down for centuries

The biblical book of *Numbers* mentions an intriguing chronicle that supposedly describes crucial events in the early history of the Israelites. But not only is there no known copy of it, we are not even sure what form it took—the academic consensus is that it was probably a collection of songs, but others favor a prose history. Were it to be found, it would rival the Dead Sea Scrolls for theological importance.

Our only clue to this mysterious book's existence comes from *Numbers*, chapter 21, verses 13–15: "Wherefore it is said in the book of the wars of the Lord, What he did in the Red sea, and in the brooks of Arnon, And at the stream of the brooks that goeth down to the dwelling of Ar, and lieth upon the border of Moab." Most scholars agree that the book described a series of military campaigns, possibly including the victories of Moses, Joshua, and the Israelites. Its importance, though, goes beyond mere historical knowledge—for believers, it would be an extraordinary addition to the Old Testament Scriptures, important to followers of all three great Abrahamic faiths, Christianity, Islam, and Judaism.

In the search for an extant copy, there is little to go on. Some hope that it may yet be discovered by some grand stroke of luck, just as the Dead Seas Scrolls were found in a cave by a wandering shepherd in the 1940s. It is even suggested that those scrolls may yet provide a clue as to what happened to the *Book of the Wars of the Lord*. Others wonder if a version resides, long forgotten, in some Middle Eastern library of ancient manuscripts. Most, though, suspect this particular item of Scripture is gone forever.

In fact, it is just one of several works mentioned in the Bible that have not come down to us. They include the books of Gad the Seer, Nathan the Prophet, and Samuel the Seer (all mentioned in 1 *Chronicles*, 29: 29) and the *History of the Kings of Judah* (1 Kings, 14: 29). There is also the *Book of Jasher*, which is mentioned twice in the Bible (*Joshua*, 10: 12–13 and 2 *Samuel*, 1: 18–27). Also known as the *Book of the Upright One* or the *Book of the Just Ones*, it was likely a collection of verse celebrating Israelite victories—something it might well have had in common with the *Book of the Wars of the Lord*. It has occasionally been proposed that they may indeed be one and the same work, though most experts agree this is likely not the case. With so many lost Scriptures to be rediscovered, anyone fortunate enough to turn up the *Book of the Wars of the Lord* need not look far for another challenge.

ANCIENT LAND *Pictured is one of the "brooks of Arnon," with the Dead Sea in the background. Arnon, a deep gorge in Jordan, is today known as Wadi Mujib and lies about 60 miles (100 km) from the capital city, Ammam. Military campaigns fought in this area probably formed the subject matter of the Book of the Wars of the Lord.*

58 Vineta

WHAT IT IS A lost city on the Baltic coast
WHY YOU WON'T FIND IT It is said to have been submerged as a punishment for its population's dissolute lifestyle

Around the tenth century, Vineta was a highly prosperous town somewhere on the Baltic coast, but at some point during the late 12th century it disappeared beneath the water. There is a sharp split between those who believe the story is mere myth and those convinced Vineta was a real locality—several possible sites have been suggested, but so far the ancient city has eluded rediscovery.

Legend has it that Vineta was a hub for traders from across the known world, with Vikings, Jewish traders from Spain, Slavs, Saxons, and assorted Baltic locals coming here to do business.

According to some, the city boasted a population of 50,000 or more and was richer even than Constantinople. Even the pigs, it was said, ate from troughs made of gold. Alas, such wealth brought

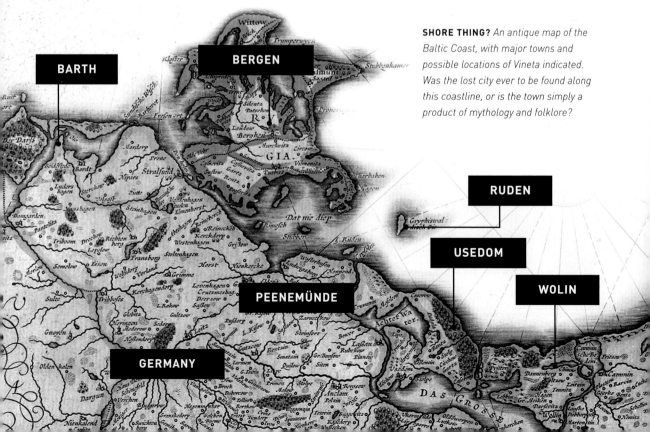

SHORE THING? *An antique map of the Baltic Coast, with major towns and possible locations of Vineta indicated. Was the lost city ever to be found along this coastline, or is the town simply a product of mythology and folklore?*

BARTH

BERGEN

RUDEN

USEDOM

PEENEMÜNDE

WOLIN

GERMANY

with it greed, avarice, pride, and moral decrepitude. After ignoring omens of disaster (including strange lights in the sky and even the appearance of a wailing mermaid), the city was deluged in 1170 and disappeared into the Baltic forever. This was considered by some as a just punishment for immorality.

As time passed, tales sprang up that the city reappeared on certain days of the year, or that its church bells could be heard on special occasions. Some academics have looked beyond the myth-making and concluded that there may well be memories of a real city, and a real disaster, at its heart. So where might Vineta have stood?

Wolin, an island off the Polish Baltic coast, is among the most regularly touted sites. Archaeological excavations here have revealed evidence of a major Viking Age trading settlement, but no "smoking gun" to link it firmly to Vineta. Other researchers favor an island called Usedom, located in the Baltic between Germany and Poland and nicknamed the Sunshine Island. However, there is scant evidence of Slavic habitation in the area.

An alternative school of thought argues instead for the nearby German island of Ruden, now a nature reserve. Marked as the site of the city on several 17th-century maps, Ruden was in the path of the devastating All Saints' Flood of 1304, which might go some way to explaining the association.

Finally, there is Barth, a medieval town on a lagoon in northeastern Germany. Its case has been strongly argued by archaeologist Klaus Goldman and journalist Günter Wermusch, but without strong physical evidence the debate will continue as to whether Vineta was ever more than a city fit for a parable.

USTKA

BALTIC SEA

POLAND

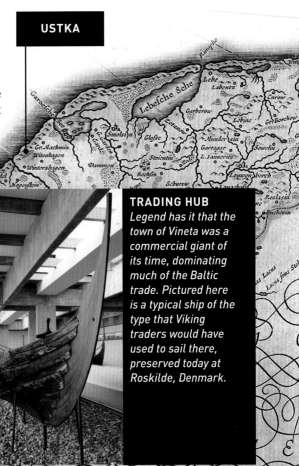

TRADING HUB
Legend has it that the town of Vineta was a commercial giant of its time, dominating much of the Baltic trade. Pictured here is a typical ship of the type that Viking traders would have used to sail there, preserved today at Roskilde, Denmark.

Tomb of Nefertiti

WHAT IT IS The last resting place of the legendary Egyptian queen
WHY YOU WON'T FIND IT We know little of the circumstances of her death and burial

Of all the queens of Ancient Egypt, Nefertiti's fame is only eclipsed by that of Cleopatra. Yet our knowledge of her life is patchy and we know even less about her death. Was she buried in el-Amarna, the capital that she and her husband founded? Or was her body subsequently moved to the Valley of the Kings or the Valley of the Queens? It is a puzzle that has foxed Egyptologists through the ages.

Like Cleopatra, Nefertiti owes much of her fame to a reputation for almost unearthly beauty—indeed, her very name translates as "the beautiful one is come." Her elegance is fixed in the modern imagination by a bust discovered in 1912 and now on display in Berlin's Neues Museum. However, this queen of Egypt was much more than just a pretty face.

Nefertiti was born around 1370 BC, in the time of the 18th Dynasty. She married the Pharaoh Amenhotep IV, who revolutionized Egyptian life by turning his back on the traditional worship of multiple gods to found a monotheistic religion centered on Aten, the sun disk. Five years into his reign, Amenhotep changed his name to Akhenaten ("living spirit of Aten"). Confronted by widespread opposition to his religious reformation, he deserted the old capital city of Thebes to found a new one further north called Akhetaten (today known as el-Amarna).

During her husband's reign, Nefertiti was immensely powerful, and when he died at some point in the mid-1330s BC,

she may even have briefly ruled alone. She was the mother of six daughters, though the oft-quoted theory that she was also the mother to Tutankhamen is less certain—latest evidence points to Akhenaten and one of his sisters or cousins as the Boy King's parents.

Nefertiti outlived her husband by several years, but the exact circumstances of her death are not known. It is thought that she was initially buried with other members of her family in the vicinity of Akhetaten. But after Tutankhamen became pharaoh around 1332 BC, reverting to the old religion and moving the capital back to Thebes, it is possible that her loyal officials brought her mummy with them to the city, rather than leave it at risk of pillage at Akhetaten. Hence, the widely held suspicion among Egyptologists that she is now somewhere in the Valley of the Kings or the Valley of the Queens.

There has been much debate as to whether Nefertiti may be one of several mummies discovered inside a tomb

HAPPY FAMILIES *This highly stylized "house altar" dating from around 1350 BC shows Queen Nefertiti, her husband Akhenaten, and three of their children in happier days. But where were the family ultimately buried?*

known as KV35. Discovered in the Valley of the Kings by French archaeologist Victor Loret and opened in 1898, this was originally the tomb of Amenhotep II, who reigned from 1427 to 1401 BC. However, it also contained the mummies of several other royal figures, transferred into a side chamber at a later date. Alongside Thutmose IV, Amenhotep III, Merneptah, Seti II, Siptah, and no fewer than three Ramesses (IV, V, and VI), there were also two unidentified females, nicknamed "The Elder Lady" and "The Younger Lady."

Both have been suggested as Nefertiti. The "Elder Lady" was in her thirties or forties when she died—about the right age for our queen. There is also a degree of similarity between the mummy's face and artistic representations of Nefertiti, but given the highly stylized nature of Egyptian art that can hardly be considered conclusive proof. In fact, the latest thinking suggests this mummy is that of Queen Tiye, Akhenaten's mother.

As for the "Younger Lady" being Nefertiti, the strongest case was made in 2003 by British academic Joann Fletcher. The mummy, dated to the 18th Dynasty, was found to be a good age fit and wore a wig in the distinctive style preferred by Nefertiti. There was also evidence of postmortem facial mutilation, suggesting a controversial figure. However, the evidence was nothing more than circumstantial and some critics commented that it had been molded to fit a conclusion rather than the other way around. Subsequent CT scans, meanwhile, suggest that the mummy may in fact be that of Tutankhamen's unidentified mother.

Conclusively proving any mummy to be Nefertiti will be an immensely difficult task in the absence of solid corroborative DNA evidence. Yet we know that the famously beautiful queen is somewhere out there. Just possibly, though, she wants to be left in peace.

60 Golden Plates of Mormonism

WHAT THEY ARE The engraved plates which Joseph Smith claimed inspired the *Book of Mormon*

WHY YOU WON'T FIND THEM The faithful believe they are no longer in human possession

The Church of Jesus Christ of Latter-Day Saints (also known as the Mormons) was founded by Joseph Smith in 1830. He claimed to have produced the faith's sacred text, the *Book of Mormon*, by translating it directly from a set of golden plates to which he was directed by an angel. After completing his work, and showing the plates to several eyewitnesses, he apparently gave the plates back to the angel.

Born in 1805 in Vermont, Smith had moved with his family to New York by the time he was a teenager. By the early 1820s, he claimed he was experiencing religious visions, and on September 22, 1823 he received a visit from an angel (later identified as Moroni) who told him of a box made of stone, buried in a nearby hill (later known as Cumorah) between the towns of Manchester and Palmyra. Smith tracked down the box and found a series of metallic, pagelike plates inside, but when he attempted to take them out, the angel stopped him and told him to try again in a year. In fact, Smith related, it was not until 1927 that he succeeded in extracting them.

The plates were "golden in appearance" and weighed up to 59 pounds (27 kg), with Smith describing how each "was six inches wide and eight inches long [15 by 20 cm], and not quite so thick as common tin. They were ... bound together in a volume, as the leaves of a book, with three rings running through the whole. The volume was something near six inches in thickness." Each leaf was inscribed on both sides, apparently in a previously unknown language that Smith called "reformed Egyptian."

The plates were, Mormons believe, a record of ancient American settlers known as the Nephite, transcribed onto the plates by a prophet called Mormon. Smith spent several years deciphering them, apparently with the use of "seer stones" kept in the bottom of a hat that he held over his face. These stones were pebbles with apparently mystical powers that Smith was supposed to have used in earlier years to locate lost items and identify hidden treasure (surely useful tools for anyone reading this book!). Blocking out the light by covering his face with the hat, it was said that the meaning of the text became apparent to him symbol by symbol. He published his translation in 1830 as the *Book of Mormon*, which he described as the "most correct of any book on earth, and the keystone of our religion." Within days, he formally established his new religion as the "Church of Christ." The new faith spread rapidly with the

adherents to the faith provided written testimony to the fact, with their signed affidavits appearing at the front of every printed copy of the *Book of Mormon*.

After completing his work, Smith claimed, he returned the plates to Moroni and they were never seen again. So it is that today we have no physical evidence that the plates ever existed. Modern opinion is sharply divided as to their nature. For some devout Mormons, they and the entire story as told by Smith are literally true. Other followers, though, see them in spiritual, rather than literal, terms—just as many modern Christians tend to regard the Creation story outlined in Genesis as allegorical rather than historical. As for the witness testimony, it has been suggested by critics that some or all of these individuals believed they had seen the golden plates, but that in fact they were taken by trickery or perhaps even hypnosis. Alternatively, Smith has been accused of manufacturing the plates himself.

HOUSE OF GOD Opposite: *An image of the Mormon Tabernacle dating to around 1870. The Tabernacle is on Temple Square in Salt Lake City and was built between 1864 and 1867. Above: A late-19th-century depiction of the angel Moroni appearing to Joseph Smith.*

great migration of settlers toward the American West, though the Mormons would go through many trials and tribulations before their wanderings brought them eventually to their very own "promised land" in Utah.

According to Smith, his access to the golden plates required him to observe several rules outlined by Moroni, including not showing them to anybody else. However, in due course special dispensation was granted so that a total of 11 other people viewed them (the first three shown them by Moroni and the latter eight by Smith). Each of these early

While Smith gave little detail about the return of the plates, other early Mormons related how they accompanied him when he deposited them back within Cumorah hill. Smith would also tell how some of the plates remained sealed (exactly by what means is disputed) and contained a "revelation from God from the beginning of the world to the ending thereof" to be revealed at a future time.

For those who believe in the physical reality of the plates, the closest they can hope to get to them is a visit to Cumorah (also known colloquially as Mormon Hill or Gold Bible Hill). Together with the surrounding area, it was purchased by The Church of Jesus Christ of Latter-Day Saints in the 1920s, and today a statue of Moroni stands at its peak. Whether he is guarding the golden plates is a question best left to personal opinion.

The identity of Beethoven's Immortal Beloved

WHO SHE IS The mysterious muse of Ludwig van Beethoven
WHY YOU WON'T FIND HER The object of a passionate love letter, her identity is a source of much debate

One of the giants of classical music, Beethoven was a man who ultimately turned his back on love in favor of his art. However, he was by no means short of romantic entanglements. On his death, a love letter was found in his possession that he had written to a woman he called "Immortal Beloved." The identity of the Immortal Beloved has provided one of the greatest cultural mysteries of all time.

The letter was written in pencil on July 6–7, 1812, while staying at Teplitz, a spa town in Bohemia (now in the Czech Republic). At the time, Beethoven was in the midst of a creative crisis and the letter, covering some ten pages, is indicative of a tortured soul. Whether he ever sent it is not known, but the fact that he kept it until his death suggests great significance. He began by addressing "My angel, my all, my own self" before asking: "Can you alter the fact that you are not entirely mine, and I am not entirely yours?" Resuming the following day, he wrote the passage that includes the legendary reference: "While still in bed my thoughts turn toward you my Immortal Beloved, now and then happy, then sad again, waiting whether fate might answer us—I can only live either wholly with you or not at all ..."

So just who was this woman who so gripped his heart? One suggestion, made in Bernard Rose's 1994 movie *Immortal Beloved* was Beethoven's sister-in-law, Johanna. That view, however, has found little support in the academic world.

Countess Julia Guicciardi was once considered the most likely candidate—a former pupil to whom the "Moonlight Sonata" is dedicated. Then there is Therese Malfatti, with whom Beethoven was certainly infatuated at one stage (though sadly before 1812). Others have favored one Amalie Sebald, who was in Teplitz at the crucial time, but it is by no means certain that their feelings went beyond a bit of light flirting. The two leading suspects, however, are Austrian Antonie Brentano and a Hungarian aristocrat called Josephine von Brunsvik. Brentano, to whom Beethoven would dedicate his *Diabelli Variations*, was in Bohemia that summer and the two were no doubt close—though Beethoven was also good friends with her husband. The great composer had also sent the recently widowed von Brunsvik a series of impassioned letters in 1805, calling her his "only beloved." Alas, their ardor cooled and in 1810 she married someone else, but that relationship was itself severely strained by 1812. Did Beethoven hope for an opportunity to rekindle their passion?

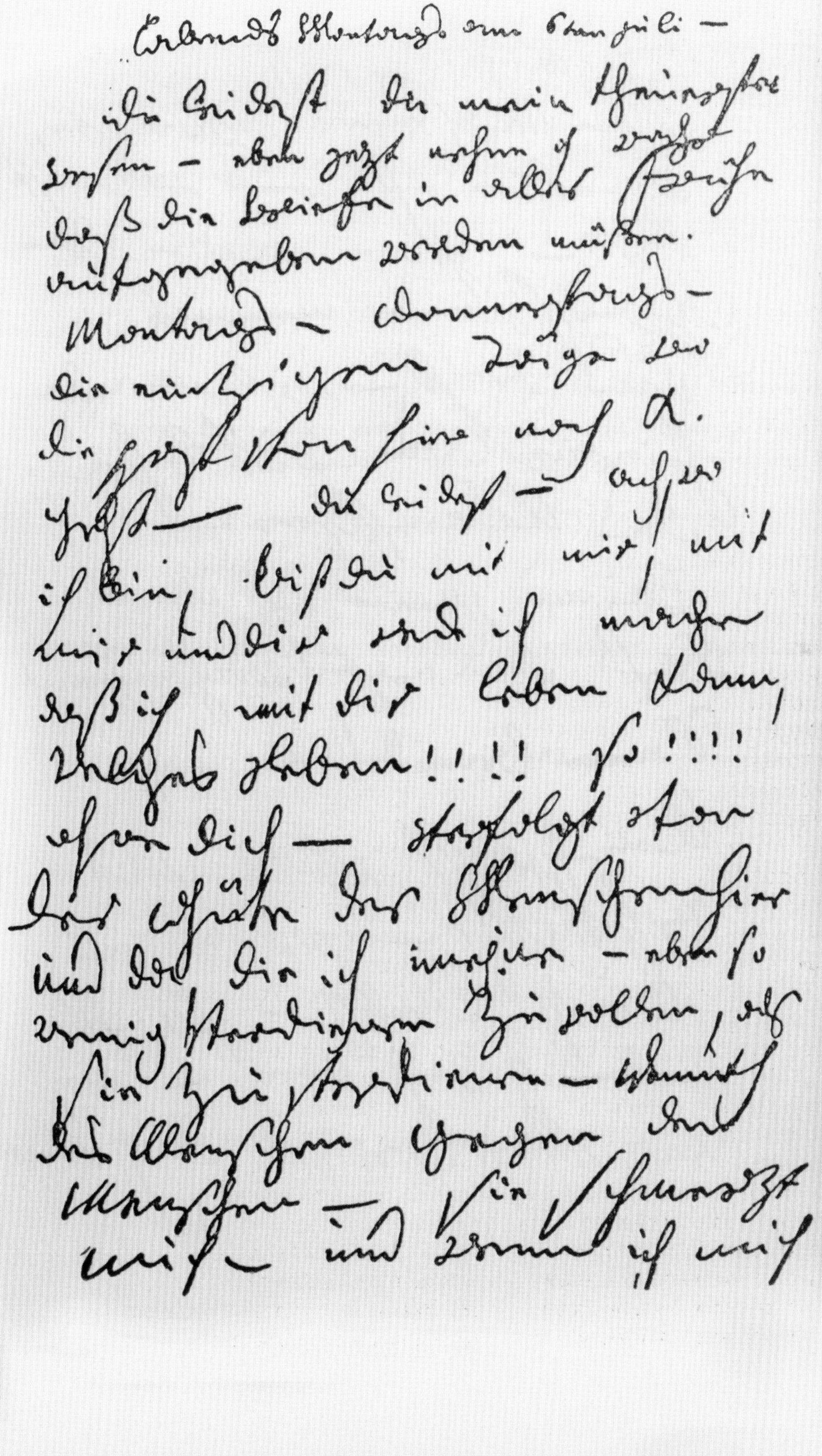
Abends Montags am 6ten Juli —
Du leidest du mein theuerstes
Wesen — eben jezt nehme ich wahr
daß die Briefe in aller Frühe
aufgegeben werden müßen.
Montags — Donnerstags —
die einzigen Täge wo
die Post von hier nach K.
geht — du leidest — Ach, wo
ich bin, bist du mit mir, mit
mir und dir rede ich mache
daß ich mit dir leben kann,
welches Leben!!!! so!!!!
ohne Dich — verfolgt von
der Güte der Menschen hier
und da, die ich meyne — eben so
wenig verdienen zu wollen, als
sie zu verdiene — Demuth
des Menschen gegen den
Menschen — sie schmerzt
mich — und wenn ich mich

HIGH-BORN *Josephine von Brunsvik was born a countess in 1779 and grew up in a castle not far from Budapest, capital of the Hungarian Empire. Beethoven gave her piano lessons while she was a young girl.*

ARTS LOVER *Antonie Brentano was a renowned patron of the arts. Beethoven was great friends with her husband, Franz, with whom she had six children. The idea of an affair between Antonie and the composer gained popularity in the 1970s.*

62 Q Source

WHAT IT IS A notional collection of the sayings of Jesus
WHY YOU WON'T FIND IT There is no certainty that a physical copy ever existed

Scholars of the New Testament gospels have long noted similarities between those of Matthew and Luke. One theory suggests that they both drew upon an earlier common source when writing—one that detailed the teachings of Jesus himself. This source is referred to as the Q Source—but no one has yet proved its existence let alone identified where it might be found.

Three of the gospels—those of Matthew, Mark, and Luke—are sometimes referred to as the synoptic gospels. That is to say, they show broad agreement in the events they depict and sometimes even use the same wording. In other respects, however, they are by no means carbon copies. For academics, this raises a question of how to explain both the similarities, and the marked differences?

It was long thought that Matthew wrote his book first, a view certainly held by the Roman historian Eusebius. However, during the 19th century a counterthesis suggested that in fact Mark's gospel was the oldest. Out of this school of thought, a "two-source" thesis developed in which both Matthew and Luke based their work on the gospel of Mark and a second unidentified source presumed to contain sayings and teachings of Jesus. This is "Q" (a name coined by German theologian Johannes Weiss as an abbreviation for *Quelle*, German for "source"). While Q is currently purely hypothetical, there have been attempts to reconstruct its contents by working out which bits of Matthew and Luke do not derive from Mark. On this basis, adherents argue that Q probably included many of the most important teachings of Jesus, including the Golden Rule ("Do unto others as you would have them do unto you"), various parables, and the Lord's Prayer.

However, opponents of the Q theory ask why the church apparently made no effort to preserve such an important work. Not only is there no extant copy, but there are not even references to it in contemporary historical sources. The most common response is that once the text of Q had been incorporated into the gospels, there was no reason to preserve it. In fact, some argue, Matthew and Luke rephrased some parts to ensure clarity of meaning, after which retaining Q would only have caused confusion.

The mystery of Q represents one of the biggest conundrums of New Testament scholarship. No one realistically expects a copy to be found anytime soon, but mere proof that it existed could prompt a fundamental redefinition of Christianity.

Η ϹΥΝΑΞΙϹ ΤΩΝ ΑΓΙΩΝ ΕΚΑ Δ ΑΠΟϹΤΟΛΩΝ ΠΕΤΡΟ... ΑΝΔΡΕΑϹ ΙΩ...
ΙΩ. ΦΙΛΙΠΠΟϹ ΒΑΡΘΟ... ΑΙ ΘΩΜΑϹ ΜΑΤΘ... ΙΑΚΩΒΟϹ ΟΤΟ...ΦΕΡΑΙ ΘΑΛΛΑΙ...

63 Flor de la Mar treasure

WHAT IT IS
Treasure claimed by the Portuguese during their 16th-century exploits around the Indian Ocean
WHY YOU WON'T FIND IT
It sunk to the bottom of the Malacca Straits during a storm

The *Flor de la Mar* (*Flower of the Sea*) was a 440-ton carrack built in Lisbon in 1502. This formidable vessel patroled the Indian Ocean for the best part of a decade, but in late 1511 she sank on her way back to India, laden with booty after Portugal's conquest of Malacca on the Malay Peninsula. The wreck—thought to be one of the most valuable in history—has never been located.

The *Flor de la Mar* was a formidable vessel for her time, and was involved in many notable skirmishes during a relatively long career. In 1510, she helped Portugal claim Goa in India, but the following year Portuguese attention focused on Malacca, one of the region's most prosperous cities. It soon fell to the superior European forces led by Afonso de Albuquerque, who plundered not only the riches of the sultan of Malacca, but claimed tribute from the king of Siam (modern Thailand) as well.

While the *Flor de la Mar*'s size made her a fearsome opponent at sea, it also rendered her difficult to maneuver and she had a history of springing leaks. Fully laden, she was known to be distinctly unstable. Yet despite this, Albuquerque saw fit to load her with up with what was almost certainly the richest cargo ever assembled by the Portuguese Navy. The hold was filled with some 66 tons of gold, and a reputed 200 chests of diamonds, emeralds, rubies, and other precious stones. Accompanied by several other ships to form a small fleet, the *Flor de la Mar* set off for Malabar in India. However, she was caught in a violent storm in the Strait of Malacca off the northeast coast of Sumatra in November 1511 and quickly broke up. Though Albuquerque and several of his officers jumped to safety, many of the crew perished as the vessel and her cargo sank to the seabed. Albuquerque never properly recovered from the affair, with several of his enemies in Lisbon promptly moving against him. The king eventually replaced him as military commander in the region, and he died some three years later.

As might be expected, treasure-hunters were quick to begin searching for the wreck, but in the six centuries that have passed, so far no one has been able to accurately locate it, let alone excavate the loot. Nonetheless, the ship and its promise of untold riches continues to attract enthusiasts, among them the noted American underwater archaeologist, Robert Marx, who reportedly called the *Flor de la Mar* "the richest vessel ever lost at sea."

SEAWORTHY?
A rare contemporary image of the mighty Portuguese Flor de la Mar. *She was a grand old ship, well used to making long and perilous journeys across the oceans as she transported great wealth from southeast Asia back to her homeland. But was it the weight of one particular bounty that ultimately decided her fate? In the absence of the wreck herself, a replica of the ship can be seen today at the maritime museum in Malacca.*

INDIA

BAY OF BENGAL

THAILAND

CEYLON
(SRI LANKA)

MALAYSIA

INTENDED ROUTE OF THE
FLOR DE LA MAR

SUMATRA

MALACCA
STRAIT

INDIAN OCEAN

64

Lost Tribes of Israel

WHO THEY ARE The constituent tribes of the Northern Kingdom of Israel
WHY YOU WON'T FIND THEM There is no mention of them after they were exiled in the eighth century BC

The Scriptures tell how, around 722 BC, ten of the twelve Tribes of Israel were conquered by the Assyrian king, Shalmaneser V, and exiled to Mesopotamia and Medes (modern-day Iran, Iraq, and Syria). From that moment on, all trace of them is lost. So what might have happened to them? It is a question that dangerously blends historical fact and personal faith.

According to the Old Testament, Jacob had 12 sons, each of whom fathered one of the tribes of Israel. A dynastic dispute in the tenth century BC saw Israel split into a Northern Kingdom (the tribes of Asher, Dan, Ephraim, Gad, Issachar, Levi, Manasseh, Naphtali, Reuben, and Zebulun) and a Southern Kingdom (the tribes of Judah and Benjamin). Those in the Northern Kingdom were exiled after repeated attacks from the Assyrians in the 720s BC. Many historians dispute this version of events, however. Some argue that while significant numbers of people were exiled, it was not the wholesale removal suggested in the Bible. Others point not to a sudden disappearance but rather a gradual assimilation into other communities. Despite these doubts, the reunification of the tribes has been an enduring ambition for many followers of Judeo-Christian faiths through the ages—and one with significant political implications even today.

There have been a great many theories about peoples who may be descended from one or more of the tribes. In the ninth century, a Jewish traveler called Eldad ha-Dani believed he had found the lost Israelites beyond the rivers of Abyssinia. In 1165 a Spaniard, Benjamin of Tuleda, claimed that descendants of the tribes were living in what is now Iran and Saudi Arabia. Fast forward to the 16th century, and Bartholemé de Las Casas became convinced that the Native Americans he met on his trips to the New World originated from ancient Israel —a view shared by the 17th-century Dutch Jewish scholar, Menasseh ben Israel.

Into the 19th century, some historians made the case for the Scythians—who occupied an area from Eastern Europe to Central Asia until the fourth century AD—as both descendants of the Lost Tribes and forefathers of modern Western Europeans. Others even suggested similarities between the Japanese and Hebrew languages. In truth, there are few corners of the world that at one time or another haven't been suggested as a potential home to the Lost Tribes.

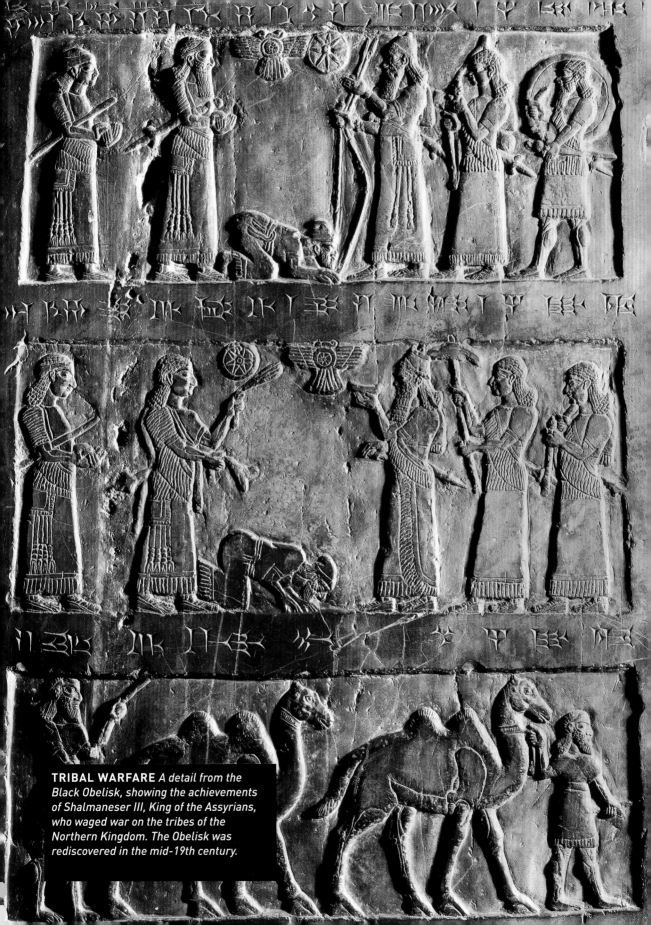

TRIBAL WARFARE *A detail from the Black Obelisk, showing the achievements of Shalmaneser III, King of the Assyrians, who waged war on the tribes of the Northern Kingdom. The Obelisk was rediscovered in the mid-19th century.*

65

USS *Cyclops*

WHAT IT IS A US collier commissioned during the First World War
WHY YOU WON'T FIND IT It sank without trace in 1918, somewhere off the US East Coast

In February 1918, the enormous US Navy collier ship USS *Cyclops* set out on what should have been a routine trip from Brazil to Baltimore carrying vital war supplies. Neither she nor any of her crew were seen again. Then-Secretary of the Navy, Josephus Daniels, would later comment that there was "no more baffling mystery in the annals of the Navy."

Launched at Philadelphia in 1910, *Cyclops* was a veritable beast of a ship, measuring 540 feet (165 meters) long and weighing over 21,000 tons. Her job was to refuel other naval vessels at sea. On that fateful voyage from Bahia in Brazil for Baltimore in Maryland, *Cyclops* set sail with 309 officers and crew and a cargo of some 11,000 tons of manganese ore. In early March, she made an unscheduled stop in Barbados but the captain, Commander George Worley, expected to arrive in Baltimore ten days later. However, neither the vessel nor any of those aboard her would make it and in almost a century since she disappeared, no trace of wreckage has ever been uncovered.

So how does a giant ship disappear without trace? The suggestion that she was dragged to her doom by some great sea monster received understandably short shrift from serious investigators, but for those of a more conspiratorial bent, the answer seemed obvious: *Cyclops* was lost in that notorious graveyard of shipping and air transport, the Bermuda Triangle. Others laid the blame on German U-boats, although German authorities denied involvement both during and after the war.

All of these theories appeal to those seeking a solution with a frisson of danger and mystery. But the answer to this particular puzzle may well turn out to be rather more straightforward. *Cyclops* was aging and, according to some who had sailed on her, not in the best of condition. When she left Barbados, one of her engines was faulty. She was quite possibly overloaded, and what's more, manganese ore is a particularly tricky cargo, prone to moving around. If the *Cyclops* had found herself in a sudden squall, it is highly likely that the manganese shifted, either damaging the ship's integral structure or simply causing her to roll and sink. That is almost certainly the fate that befell her around March 11, 1918, but in the absence of a wreck, we cannot say for sure. As US President Woodrow Wilson, put it: "Only God and the sea know what happened to the great ship."

UNITED STATES

BERMUDA

ATLANTIC OCEAN

FLORIDA

BERMUDA
TRIANGLE

THE BAHAMAS

CUBA

TURKS AND CAICOS
ISLANDS

PUERTO RICO

HISPANIOLA

JAMAICA

FROM THE
DEPTHS
*A water spout
surges from
beneath the
waves. Might
Cyclops have
succumbed to
such a natural
phenomenon?*

BIG BEAST *The USS* Cyclops, *seen here in
the Hudson River in 1911, was never going to
win any beauty contests, but played a vital role
in stocking the ships of the US navy.*

SOUTH AMERICA

Hidden Bourbon treasure

WHAT IT IS The war chest of Louis XVI and Marie Antoinette
WHY YOU WON'T FIND IT It was lost during a failed attempt to escape Paris

In 1791, two years after the beginning of the French Revolution, the Bourbon king, Louis XVI, and his Austrian-born Queen, Marie Antoinette, made an ill-fated attempt to flee Paris. They were soon captured and returned to the capital, but stories emerged of a valuable "war chest," sent over the border into the Austrian Netherlands, that has never been accounted for.

During the royal family's house arrest in the Tuileries Palace, Marie Antoinette kept in regular contact with her brother, the Holy Roman Emperor Leopold II. The outline of a plan emerged in which Louis and Marie would leave Paris and ferment a counterrevolution with Austrian support. Details were worked out by the marquis de Bouillé and the baron de Breteuil, along with the Comte Axel von Fersen, a Swedish aristocrat believed to have been one of Marie's lovers.

The first aim was to get the couple to the relative safety of Montmédy in the northeast of France, close to the border with the Austrian Netherlands. The royal party fled Paris on the evening of June 20, 1791 but soon ran into trouble. Stopping in the town of Sainte-Menehould, Louis was recognized. The party moved onto Varennes, a short way from Montmédy, but here they were arrested by the postmaster general. Humiliated, Louis and his wife were promptly returned to Paris—their actions only increased popular opposition, ultimately leading to their execution at the guillotine in 1793.

Clearly, any plot to lead a counterrevolution would have needed funds, so what of the "war chest" of valuables that they are said to have taken with them in the escape bid? One theory has it that the chest was entrusted to Marie Antoinette's hairdresser, who went on ahead of the main party to deposit it in a safe place. Exactly where is not known, but some suspect the most likely location was the Abbey of Orval (literally "Valley of Gold") in the Ardennes Forest just over the border.

A religious house since 1124, the abbey was razed to the ground in 1793 by French forces in retaliation for its hosting of Austrian troops, and lay abandoned for almost a century until the land was bought by a private family, who later donated it for the establishment of a new monastery. During its years of ruin, there was plenty of opportunity for scavengers to seek out the lost Bourbon treasure, but there is no record that they ever succeeded. If that intrepid hairdresser managed to dispose of the booty here, it presumably still awaits rediscovery.

GOLDEN REPUTATION
A view of the Abbey of Orval. Legend has it that Mathilda of Tuscany (1046–1115) lost her wedding ring here only to have her prayers for its return answered when a trout emerged from a spring with the ring in its mouth.

Lost city of Z

Manuscript 512 in Rio de Janeiro's National Library offers an account of a Portuguese expedition into the Brazilian rainforest in search of gold and silver mines. The explorers, it claims, came upon a wondrous city, but unfortunately the author failed to give much clue as to where it was located. Manuscript 512 remains at the center of a mystery that has claimed many victims, and continues to the present day.

Early in the 20th century, famed British explorer, archaeologist, and cartographer Colonel Percy Fawcett heard about this mysterious Amazonian settlement and was immediately intrigued. Fawcett was a remarkable character, widely believed to have helped inspire Sir Arthur Conan Doyle's Professor Challenger. He began to study records of the lost city in detail, undertaking preliminary archaeological studies and talking extensively to local tribes. One of these, the Botocudo, described a city "enormously rich in gold—so much so as to blaze like a fire." After concluding that the city—which he nicknamed "Z" for reasons unknown— was located in the Mato Grosso region of western Brazil, he was preparing an expedition when his plans were stalled by the onset of the First World War.

Fawcett finally set off into the jungle in 1925, accompanied by his 21-year-old son Jack, and Jack's friend Raleigh Rimell. For five months, native runners brought dispatches from Fawcett, before an abrupt silence. The disappearance made headlines around the world and prompted a host of other adventurers to go in search of both him and Z. Their quest was made doubly difficult because Fawcett, who had once been a spy, never shared his planned route with anybody and made many of his notes in code. A good many of those who tried to find him disappeared themselves, succumbing to hunger, disease, or occasionally, attacks from indigenous people. In the 1950s, members of the Kalapalos tribe apparently admitted killing Fawcett and his friends, though exactly what happened remains uncertain.

Meanwhile, the desire to locate Z continued to excite archaeologists and explorers. One of them, Michael Heckenberger, has in recent years discovered a network of 20 ancient settlements in the general area where Fawcett was searching. Each had a population of between 2,000 and 5,000, with a developed infrastructure including straight roads, bridges, moats, and causeways. Was this, as has been suggested, Z? It's certainly possible, though the jury remains out.

ZED-HEAD *Colonel Percy Fawcett pictured in 1911. He was a genuine British eccentric whose remarkable character and experiences are said to have inspired several works of fiction, most notably Conan Doyle's* The Lost World, *in which he provided the prototype for Professor Challenger.*

LOST LANDS *An aerial shot of one of the settlements that archaeologist and anthropologist Michael Heckenberger has uncovered in the Amazon. They have given credence to the tales of a lost city that so obsessed Fawcett.*

68 Peacock Throne

WHAT IT IS The spectacular throne of the Mughal emperors
WHY YOU WON'T FIND IT It disappeared in 1836 and was probably subsequently dismantled

The Mogul Emperor Shah Jahan is best known today for his creation of the Taj Mahal, an architectural declaration of love to his dead wife. Yet incredibly the building of that wonder of the world was not the most expensive project he undertook. That accolade rests with the Peacock Throne—constructed from gold and inlaid with jewels, it cost twice as much as the Taj.

When Shah Jahan succeeded his father in 1628 as ruler of a large part of the Indian subcontinent, he inherited an extraordinarily rich imperial jewel house. Keen to make the big statement, he decided to use the finest gems to adorn his throne. The Peacock Throne was created by the emperor's finest craftsmen from more than a ton of gold and almost a quarter-ton of precious stones. The finished item was more like a bed than a chair, measuring 6 feet by 4 feet (1.8 m by 1.2 m) and resting on four legs of gold. Twelve columns supported a canopy perhaps 15 feet (4.5 m) above the ground, and the throne got its name from pairs of peacocks—their tails open and encrusted with jewels—that topped each column.

The variety and quality of stones was beyond compare—diamonds, emeralds, garnets, pearls, rubies, and sapphires were inlaid by the handful. There were four diamonds of over 80 carats each, including the legendary Koh-i-Noor that was once the world's largest and now forms part of the British Crown Jewels.

Work on the throne was completed in 1635, and Shah Jahan sat upon it for the first time on March 12. It remained the property of the Mogul emperors for just over a century, until the Persian Emperor Nadir Shah seized it from Delhi in 1739. When he was assassinated by one of his own officers eight years later, his empire collapsed and the Peacock Throne went missing in the ensuing chaos.

Some believe the throne was dismantled by Turkish tribesmen Nadir Shah had been about to attack, with its jewels divided and dispersed across Asia and the Middle East (the Koh-i-Noor, for instance, fell into the hands of one of Nadir Shah's generals in Afghanistan). Others said it was gifted to the Ottoman emperor, while a third theory suggests that parts were incorporated into the Sun Throne, built for the Persian king Muhammad Shah Qajar in 1836. Today, we lack even an authentic image of what was once the greatest treasure in the world. But based on historical accounts, its modern value has been conservatively valued at around a billion US dollars.

SITTING COMFORTABLY *Shah Jahan depicted here sitting upon the legendary Peacock Throne sometime around 1635. Whether the artist worked from imagination or had access to the Emperor and the artefact itself is unclear.*

The real King Arthur

69

WHO HE IS The legendary king of the Britons
WHY YOU WON'T FIND HIM Separating legend from fact can be tough

Among all the richness of British history, King Arthur holds a unique place. Pivotal in the formation of a British identity, he is the ultimate enigma. Was he a real man, a myth, or a conflation of two or more historical figures? And just how well do the many claims from specific locations for links with the historical Arthur stack up?

Arthur is said to have been a warrior king of the Britons in the late fifth and early sixth centuries AD, earning hero status by fighting off Saxon invaders in 12 mighty battles. Yet there is no mention of Arthur in the historical record until AD 830, and even then he is described as a "commander" rather than a king.

The waters were muddied further when Arthur became the figurehead of a Celtic renaissance after the Norman invasion of England in 1066. Most famously, he was depicted in Geoffrey of Monmouth's quasi-historical *History of the Kings of Britain* (supposedly based on an ancient Celtic manuscript to which only Geoffrey had access). It is here that many well-known elements of Arthurian legend make their debut, including a supposed birthplace at Tintagel Castle in Cornwall, the sword Excalibur (or Caliburn, as Geoffrey called it), Queen Guinevere, and Merlin the sage. Geoffrey also described Arthur's burial at the mysterious Avalon.

In the late 12th century, French writer Chrétien de Troyes hijacked the legend to promote ideals of courtly love and the chivalric code. He told how Arthur led his knights on a quest for the Holy Grail, and was also the first to make mention of Camelot. The Round Table around which Arthur and his knights sat, meanwhile, was recorded in the poet Wace's 1155 Norman reworking of Geoffrey's *History*. However, Arthur's recreation as a mythical figure was perhaps most fully realized in Thomas Mallory's *Le Morte d'Arthur*, which in the 15th century brought together all the strands from previous versions of the story. After several centuries out of favor, Arthur made a strong comeback at the height of the British empire in the 19th century. By now, unpicking the legend from the reality was a complex process.

For some, the quest for a historical Arthur is pointless. The British historian and archaeologist, Nowell Myres, for instance, noted that "no figure on the borderline of history and mythology has wasted more of the historian's time." Yet just because artists and propagandists have taken over Arthur's life, does

KNIGHTS OF THE ROUND TABLE *The Winchester Round Table is thought to have been commissioned by King Edward I, a renowned Arthurian enthusiast, in the late 13th century. It is just one of countless artefacts and stories that have muddied the waters in the search for a historic King Arthur.*

that mean he has no basis in fact? Not according to some. In 1998, a slate was discovered at Tintagel, close to a spot traditionally known as Merlin's Cave, adorned with engravings dating from the sixth century. Translated, its Latin inscription reads: "Artognou, father of a descendant of Coll, has had this built." Some were quick to make the link between this Artognou and Arthur.

Several locations have also been claimed as the historic Camelot, including Colchester (known to its Roman founders as Camulodunum), Winchester (which even has a Round Table on display in its castle), and Cadbury Castle in Somerset (first identified as Camelot in 1542, and subject to archaeological digs in the 1960s that uncovered evidence of an extensive fifth/sixth-century fort).

Then there is Glastonbury, often cited as Arthur's burial place. At the end of the 12th century, monks are said to have uncovered the ancient skeleton of a large man who bore the scars of battle, buried with a woman who some have claimed was Guinevere. Alongside

them was a cross apparently inscribed: "Here lies King Arthur buried in Avalon." Alas, if the story is to be believed, both cross and the corpses were lost forever around the time of the Dissolution of the Monasteries under Henry VIII.

So if there was a real Arthur, who was he? The Artognou of Tintagel is just one of many contenders. The 2004 movie *King Arthur* opted for a Roman military commander, Lucius Artorius Castus. Others suggest Arthur is an incarnation of Magnus Maximus, emperor of the Western Roman Empire in the 380s, who spent much of his career in Britain. Another popular contender is the late fifth-century Roman commander of Britain, Ambrosius Aurelianus. There is a strong body of support for Riothamus, listed in several contemporary sources as a fifth-century king of the Britons with an impressive military record. Or perhaps it was Artúr mac Áedáin, the son of a Celtic king who, though never king himself, led the military and was killed in battle around 582. Finding the real Arthur is a tall order, but there is no shortage of candidates!

70

Leonardo's *Battle of Anghiari*

WHAT IT IS A flawed Renaissance masterpiece
WHY YOU WON'T FIND IT If it was not destroyed, it lies beneath a later fresco

Painted in the early 16th century by the immortal Leonardo da Vinci, *The Battle of Anghiari* is one of the legendary artworks of the Renaissance period, depicting a scene from the eponymous battle of 1440. There is evidence that the work still exists, hidden beneath another, later painting, but attempts to reveal it were brought to a halt in late 2012.

Leonardo was commissioned to paint the picture—a fresco or mural painted on wet plaster—in 1504 by a senior Florentine public official, Piero Soderini. It was to adorn one wall of the Salone dei Cinquecento (Hall of Five Hundred) in Florence's monumental town hall, the Palazzo Vecchio. The room had been built in the 1490s at the behest of the firebrand Tuscan preacher, Girolamo Savonarola. In a stellar bit of commissioning, Leonardo was hired along with Michelangelo to be chief interior decorators of the hall. Michelangelo was to create a work for the wall opposite Leonardo's, a scene depicting the Battle of Cascina. However, before he was able to complete his labors, he was summoned to Rome to work on the tomb of Pope Julius II.

Leonardo's *The Battle of Anghiari*, meanwhile, was the largest work he would ever undertake. The battle itself had seen the papal forces (headed by the Florentines) defeating those of the rival city-state of Milan. For his scene, Leonardo chose to depict four horsemen battling to claim a standard. He even had a bespoke folding scaffold built so that he might cope with the scale of the work. Judging from the preparatory cartoons, the fresco was set to be an astonishing achievement, wrought with tension, violence, struggle, and heroism—a truly visceral work far removed from the serenity we are used to from works such as the *Mona Lisa*.

However, its creation was beset with problems from the outset. Leonardo had already struggled with the fresco form during his work on *The Last Supper*, so this time he took the unprecedented decision to use oil paints directly on the wall. Alas, unfavorable climatic conditions meant that the colors dripped into each other. He used heaters in a bid to hasten the drying process, but only the lower portions emerged relatively unscathed. No doubt utterly distraught, he abandoned the project in 1506. The reality was that rather than two unimpeachable masterpieces adorning the hall, there was a half-done Michelangelo (soon allegedly defaced

LOST MASTERPIECE Opposite: *A detail from Peter Paul Rubens's copy of Leonardo's* Battle of Anghiari *is a brilliant work in itself, and hints at what we have lost.* Above: *Part of* The Battle of Marciano, *the work created by Vasari as part of his "redecorating" commission.*

by an embittered rival, Bartolommeo Bandinelli) and one highly compromised and incomplete Leonardo.

And there things stood for half a century, until the authorities commissioned Giorgio Vasari (probably better known as the author of the landmark *Lives of the Artists* than as an artist in his own right) to redecorate the hall. Both Leonardo's and Michelangelo's works garnered legendary status in the decades and centuries that followed. Today, the closest we can get to Leonardo's original is an early 17th-century work by Peter Paul Rubens, *The Battle of the Standard*, itself based on a mid-16th-century engraving of Leonardo's work by Lorenzo Zacchia. However, more recently, cutting-edge science combined with an artistic flourish by Vasari have brought new hope of rediscovering Leonardo's fresco.

In the 1970s, Italian art historian Maurizio Seracini began to ponder if *The Battle of Anghiari* might still lie hidden within the hall. First, he found it

difficult to believe that Vasari would have simply done away with an epic work by Leonardo, a man for whom he had the utmost respect. Secondly, he noticed that Vasari had included in his own work, *The Battle of Marciano*, a soldier holding a flag that bears the words: *"Cerca, trova"* or "He who seeks, finds." Was this a message to future generations to look a little more closely at the fresco?

Infrared imaging allowed Seracini to look at the foundation layers of Vasari's painting, confirming that it had not simply been painted over the top of the previous work, but little more was done until the year 2000, when a variety of red tape was cleared up and Seracini's team received a grant from the Guiness family. With a variety of noninvasive techniques, they undertook a survey to reconstruct the first layout of the hall—and discovered a gap between the building's original stone wall and the one on which Vasari had painted. Had the great chronicler of Renaissance art preserved one of its greatest works for posterity by bricking it up?

In 2011, amid controversy over fears that Vasari's work would be compromised, Seracini received permission to drill a series of small holes through previously restored sections. Endoscopic cameras were then inserted to see what lay beneath, revealing tantalizing fragments of paint, and pigment samples were retrieved that match well with those used on other Leonardo paintings. Seracini now planned to use a technique in which the painting would be bombarded with neutron particles to map its large-scale composition, but in 2012, in a politically charged atmosphere, the decision was taken to put his project on hold for the foreseeable future. So one of the greatest art mysteries remains unsolved and a masterpiece perhaps remains tantalizingly hidden from view.

King Solomon's Mines

71

WHAT THEY ARE The Old Testament king's legendary mines at Ophir

WHY YOU WON'T FIND THEM No one knows where Ophir was

King Solomon, the tenth-century BC king of Israel and son of David and Bathsheba, was famed for his wisdom and for his extravagant riches. The Old Testament's unrivaled "king of bling" drank from golden cups, had armor crafted from gold, and sat upon a throne hewn from gold and ivory. Much of his wealth, the Scriptures tell us, originated in mines located in a mysterious region known as Ophir.

Though the Bible (and specifically the First Book of Kings) is somewhat vague on details when it comes to Ophir, Solomon seems to have worked with Hiram, king of the Phoenicians, to send fleets there and load up with riches. The Phoenicians were renowned as the greatest explorers, mariners, and traders of the ancient world, so it would have been a thoroughly logical alliance.

Interest in the location of Solomon's mines received a great fillip in the 1880s when H. Rider Haggard's novel, *King Solomon's Mines*, promoted the idea that they could be found somewhere in Africa. It was just the latest theory in a long line formulated by some of the greatest minds throughout history. In the second century AD, for instance, the classical scholar Ptolemy concluded that the mines were somewhere in modern-day Pakistan, or else in the vicinity of Malaysia or Indonesia. John Milton, by contrast, foreshadowed Rider Haggard when he suggested in *Paradise Lost* that they could be found in what is now Mozambique in southern Africa.

Christopher Columbus, discoverer of the New World, for a time favored Haiti, and in 1568 the Spanish explorer Álvaro de Mendaña discovered an island chain that he named the Solomons in the belief (or at least hope) that they were home to Ophir. Indeed, there is scarcely a corner of the globe that hasn't at some time been put forward as the site of Solomon's mines, from China and India to South America and Australia, via Ethiopia, Zimbabwe, and Sierra Leone. Today, academic consensus favors the Indian subcontinent or southwest Arabia, with Yemen regularly cited.

There is the possibility that modern archaeology may already have solved at least part of the conundrum. In 2008 in Jordan, a complex of holes and tunnels, covering some 24 acres and topped with large slag heaps, was excavated and carbon-dated to Solomon's era. These may well have supplied valuable copper to the king of Israel, but where he dug up all the other, really precious stuff remains a question no one has so far been able to answer.

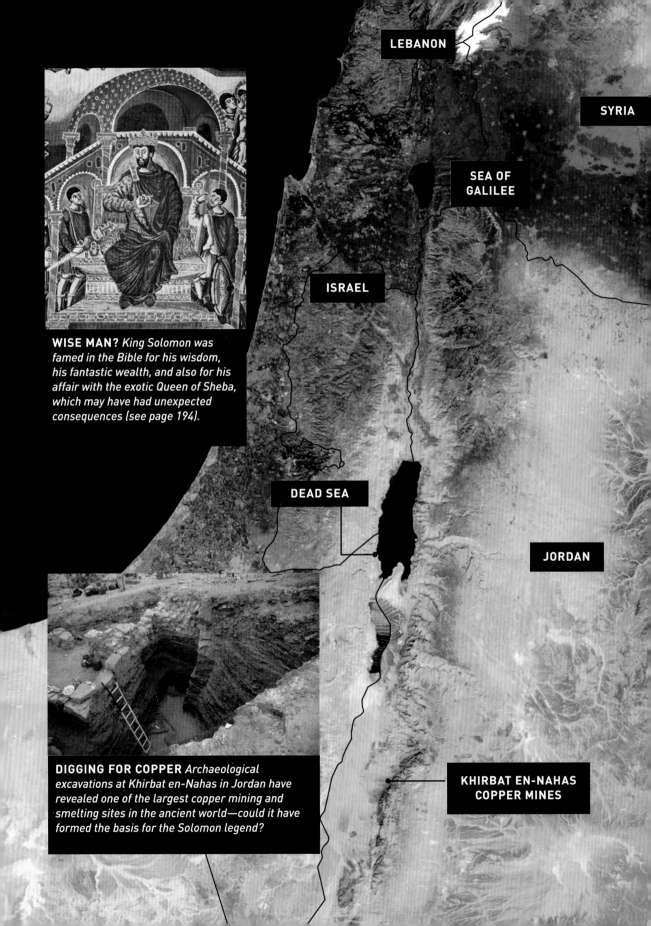

LEBANON

SYRIA

SEA OF
GALILEE

ISRAEL

DEAD SEA

JORDAN

WISE MAN? *King Solomon was famed in the Bible for his wisdom, his fantastic wealth, and also for his affair with the exotic Queen of Sheba, which may have had unexpected consequences (see page 194).*

DIGGING FOR COPPER *Archaeological excavations at Khirbat en-Nahas in Jordan have revealed one of the largest copper mining and smelting sites in the ancient world—could it have formed the basis for the Solomon legend?*

KHIRBAT EN-NAHAS
COPPER MINES

72

Kruger's millions

WHAT IT IS An alleged treasure trove hidden on the orders of the former president of the Transvaal, Paul Kruger

WHY YOU WON'T FIND IT It is not known for certain that it even exists

Known as "Uncle Paul" to his followers, Paul Kruger was the president of the independent South African Republic (also known as the Transvaal Republic) during the Second Boer War. When British military forces were about to seize its capital, Pretoria, in 1900, Kruger fled. He is said to have taken a vast supply of gold with him—a fortune that some believe has never been accounted for.

Born in 1825 into a farming background, Kruger became leader of the resistance movement that sprang up after Britain annexed the Transvaal in 1877. He was a key figure in the First Boer War (1880–81) and later elected president of the Transvaal Republic. While the subsequent discovery of gold brought wealth to the region, it also prompted renewed British interest. With troops massing on his borders, Kruger issued an ultimatum for them to leave on October 9, 1899. Their refusal provoked the Second Boer War, and by May 1900 the advantage was with the British. As troops under the command of Lord Roberts bore down on Pretoria, Kruger made the decision to flee. After several months in Eastern Transvaal (now Mpumalanga) he crossed the border to Mozambique and boarded a Dutch warship to Europe. Once there, he traveled about the continent before settling in Switzerland, where he died in 1904.

Viscount Milner, appointed administrator of the Transvaal in 1901, soon reported that more than $2.5 million in gold had been removed from banks, mines, and mints in the months before the British took power. Attempts to locate it yielded nothing, and rumors that the treasure had been buried on Kruger's orders received a boost in 1905 when petty criminal John Holtzhausen claimed he had been ordered to hide a supply of gold and diamonds at a location north of Leydsdorp in the latter-day Limpopo province. His two alleged accomplices were, conveniently, dead by then, and no one has ever been able to verify his story.

Others claim that Kruger successfully got the booty as far as Europe, though this is not well supported by historical evidence. For many years it was also suspected that the trove lay in the wreck of the *Dorothea*, a ship that sank off modern-day KwaZulu-Natal, but this story has subsequently been debunked. Some suspect it was simply all used up in paying for the war effort. But, every few years, stories emerge that someone somewhere in the Transvaal has been digging on the farm or in the backyard and uncovered handfuls of gold coins.

73

Gene Roddenberry's ashes

A hero to generations of sci-fi fanatics, Gene Roddenberry was the man who devised the original series of *Star Trek* and followed it up with the long-running *Star Trek: The Next Generation* for good measure. After he died in 1991, his ashes were sent into space—a fitting "final frontier" for the creator of the USS *Enterprise*.

Roddenberry, born in 1921 in El Paso, Texas, crammed plenty of earthbound adventures into his 70 years on the planet. He was an Air Force pilot in the Second World War and a commercial pilot afterward. Later on he worked for the Los Angeles Police Department, all the while honing his skills as a writer. In 1964 his life changed forever when his idea for a sci-fi drama was picked up— *Star Trek* hit screens two years later, and ran for an initial three seasons, by the end of which it was a cult phenomenon.

An animated version followed in the 1970s, and in 1979, the original crew migrated to the silver screen. In 1985, Roddenberry became the first television writer to receive a star on Hollywood's Walk of Fame, and from 1987, he masterminded a new take on the brand, creating *Star Trek: The Next Generation*. With a new cast and characters, it ran until 1994, chronicling the voyages of a new starship *Enterprise* a century after the original series in 178 episodes. Alas, in 1991, Roddenberry died in California from heart failure. In terms of belief, he had for many years identified himself as a humanist. Rather than a traditional religious burial, therefore, his widow, Majel Barrett Roddenberry (who had played Christine Chapel in the original *Star Trek*), decided to help him in his long-held ambition to go into space. In 2002, a proportion of his ashes were taken on one of Space Shuttle *Columbia's* missions, officially classified among the personal effects of one of the astronauts!

Five years later, he took another trip, this time aboard a Pegasus XL rocket owned by Celestis—a pioneering company in the field of "space burial." Roddenberry and 22 others blasted off from near the Canary Islands. On May 20, 2002, a little over five years after launch, the spacecraft disintegrated and the ashes of those on board disappeared into the ether forever. In 2008, Majel also passed away—her ashes (along with more of Roddenberry's, as well as those of James Doohan, who found fame as Scotty in the original series) will join a Celestis flight scheduled for late 2014. May their spirits live long and prosper.

74

The production process for Damascus steel

WHAT IT IS The means to manufacture a metal highly prized for weaponry
WHY YOU WON'T FIND IT It died out in the 18th century

Damascus steel was a particularly resilient form of steel commonly used in knife and sword blades in medieval India and the Middle East, and encountered by the European Crusaders from the 11th century onward. A Damascus steel blade was enough to strike fear into even the most doughty warrior, but the secrets of its manufacture disappeared sometime in the 18th century.

Damascus steel got its name because it was widely marketed in that great city, although it was manufactured in several other locations throughout the region from around the fourth century AD. Displaying a distinctive "watery" finish, blades remained devastatingly sharp and tough through battle after battle. It was even said that they could slice a hair in half in midair.

The metal was derived from *wootz*, a type of steel originating in India that is unusually rich in carbon and historically contained other impurities—such as manganese, phosphorus, silicon, sulfur, tungsten, and vanadium—that assisted in the manufacturing process. Heated and then rapidly cooled or "quenched," the metal was then folded multiple times and welded into a blade, which was finally "etched" with acid.

Many have tried to replicate Damascus steel, reverse engineering extant examples. Indeed, some have managed to produce a metal that mirrors its appearance and qualities, but they have relied on ultramodern technologies to do so. In 2006, a research team from the Dresden Technical University discovered that the material contains strong and pliable "nanostructures" never previously found in steel. These, they concluded, are key to understanding its unique properties. That blacksmiths hundreds of years ago could work the metal to create these tiny structures is both a remarkable and a humbling thought.

Yet by 1750, the method of production was lost to the world. Quite why is a mystery, though it was most likely due to a combination of factors. By this time firearms had supplanted swords in warfare so there was naturally less demand for the metal. It may be that the pool of people versed in its secrets simply grew too small. It is also possible that the trade routes supplying *wootz* from India were disrupted, or that supplies of the raw material no longer had the same essential characteristics. Whatever the reasons, a magnificent art and cutting-edge technology was lost to humankind forever.

TO THE POINT *An 18th-century Persian curved-blade dagger. Damascus steel was not only a remarkable feat of engineering but it was a thing of aesthetic beauty too. Examples of the craft remain highly prized and exchange hands for large sums.*

Sindia treasure

In 1901, the Anglo-American Oil Company's four-masted barque *Sindia* ran aground off Ocean City, New Jersey. Listed as carrying a varied commercial cargo, gossip soon began to report that she also contained treasures looted during clashes in China between locals and foreigners. If indeed she did, the booty has lain undiscovered, caked in decades' worth of accumulated sand.

On July 8, 1901, the *Sindia* left the port of Kobe in Japan, heading for New York with a cargo that included silks, porcelain, and camphor. Under Captain Allan MacKenzie, she made her way across the Pacific Ocean and around Cape Horn. By December 11, she was making her way up the US East Coast when she was caught in a savage storm.

For four days, the *Sindia* was battered by waves and wind, before finally being driven toward Peck's Beach near Ocean City. Stuck fast, her hull gave way, and her hold began to fill. MacKenzie put out an SOS and eventually he and all of his 32 crew were rescued amid rumors that they had got into the festive spirit a few weeks too early. A naval court subsequently suspended the captain's certification for six months. Attempts to salvage the cargo were only partially successful, as the lower hold was quickly engulfed in sand.

Before long, rumors were circulating that the ship had carried goods not listed on her manifest. The Boxer Rebellion, a violent antiforeigner campaign, had been raging in China, many overseas powers fought back, and looting had been commonplace. Some said that the *Sindia* had been loaded with treasures taken from Buddhist temples, including golden and jade statues among countless other valuables.

At the center of the conspiracy theory were 200 crates of manganese ore listed as ballast on the ship's manifest. Why, people asked, was manganese ore being brought halfway across the world when the US produced plenty of its own? It has also been noted that the crates were to be delivered to the "B. Ellis Co." No such company appears to have existed, but a B. Ellis had worked for the American Consul-General in Shanghai who had ordered the "ore" to be loaded onto the ship. Was all not quite as it seemed? Plenty of treasure-hunters have thought so, and a few have recovered curios and antiques that were not officially recorded among the cargo. Such finds have fired suspicions that there is much more left to be discovered.

ON THE OCEAN WAVE *Built in 1887 in Northern Ireland, the four-masted Sindia cut a fine figure on the water. She proved there was still a role for sail in the age of steam.*

MYSTICAL EAST *A view over the Japanese port city of Kobe, dating to around 1900. This was the starting point for the Sindia on her last doomed voyage—but was her cargo all that it was claimed to be?*

76

Atlantis

WHAT IT IS A great ancient civilization that disappeared over the course of a day and night
WHY YOU WON'T FIND IT Was it a real place, or simply a literary device employed by Plato?

The most famous "lost civilization" of them all, Atlantis was first mentioned by Plato in 360 BC in his dialogue on government, *Timaeus*. Ever since that time, there has been a split between those who consider it fictional and those who believe it was a real place. For believers, the search for this great lost empire continues even today, in disparate corners of the globe.

Atlantis was described by Plato as located in front of "the Pillars of Hercules" (that is to say, at the entrance to the Strait of Gibraltar). It was apparently "larger than Libya and Asia together" and "there existed a confederation of kings, of great and marvelous power, which held sway over all the island, and over many other islands also and parts of the continent."

The story is picked up again in another dialogue, *Critias*, which tells of how Atlantis had been ruled by Poseidon, who built a palace for his great love, Cleito, in the mountain where she lived. Atlantis was subsequently divided between the ten sons she bore him. The Atlanteans were a highly developed civilization who undertook major engineering works, building bridges, docks, moats, gates, and towers. Their city walls were built in multicolored stone quarried from the moats, and adorned with both precious and nonprecious metals.

As time passed, the Atlanteans extended their rule abroad as far as Libya and Egypt in Africa, and to Tyrrhenia (west-central Italy) in Europe, enslaving those they conquered. Resistance inevitably grew to this once Utopian land, culminating in a war dated at around 9600 BC between Atlantis and the Athenians. The Athenians triumphed and liberated the occupied lands. Atlantis's ultimate decline, the focus of later legends, is described only briefly:

"*But at a later time there occurred portentous earthquakes and floods, and one grievous day and night befell them, when the whole body of your warriors was swallowed up by the earth, and the island of Atlantis in like manner was swallowed up by the sea and vanished; wherefore also the ocean at that spot has now become impassable and unsearchable, being blocked up by the shoal mud which the island created as it settled down.*"

Almost as soon as Plato had written his dialogues, debate began about whether Atlantis was real or simply a fictional setting for a parable about governance. Plato wrote in that he had based his

WINDOW ON THE PAST *A wall painting from Akrotiri, the Minoan settlement on the island of Thera (now known as Santorini), reveals an advanced maritime culture. Is it to the Minoans that we should look for the origins of Atlantis?*

TURKEY

GREECE

AEGEAN SEA

PELOPENNESE

THERA/SANTORINI

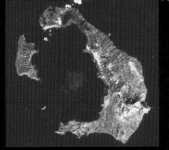

THERE SHE BLOWS *A view of the Thera/Santorini volcanic caldera. Was Atlantis' fate connected to an eruption here?*

CRETE

MEDITERRANEAN SEA

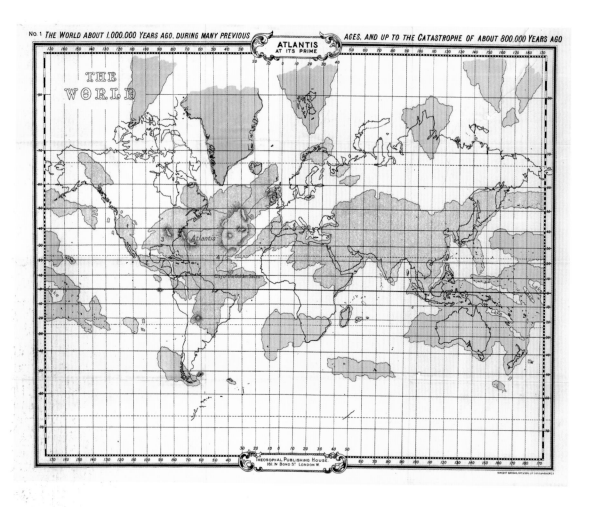

ON THE MAP *This map was created in the Victorian era at the height of the "Atlantis craze," spearheaded by the likes of American Ignatius Donnelly. It shows an imagined version of the Atlantean empire, based on a huge island in the middle of the Atlantic Ocean.*

account on that of Solon, an Athenian poet and statesman who had visited Egypt some three centuries earlier. Solon was said to have met a priest who had translated the story of Atlantis from ancient hieroglyphic texts.

Crantor—a Greek philosopher who studied under Xenocrates, who himself had been a student of Plato—appears to have taken the entire story at face value in a lost commentary on, and according to some interpretations may even have made his own trip to Egypt to confirm

the story. But it was only in more recent times that the movement to actually *find* this lost ancient land really began to gain momentum.

The discovery of the New World provided much of the impetus, with some seeing echoes of Atlantis in the pre-Columbian Mayan culture. In 1882, American politician Ignatius Donnelly published, and introduced a generation to the idea that Atlantis was a real and incredibly advanced civilization with links to all the other great cultures of antiquity. He concluded that it was home to the Garden of Eden, had been destroyed in the biblical great flood and was situated in the Atlantic Ocean—though our modern knowledge of plate tectonics would seem to argue against this last fact at least.

Countless rival theories about Atlantis and its fate have spread since then, most paying scant regard to Plato's own guidance on its geography. It has been put as far afield as northwest Africa, off the coast of India, in the Caribbean, in the Andes, and even in Antarctica. In 2007, a Swedish research team cited Dogger Bank in the North Sea as the genuine location, describing how the area was submerged during the Bronze Age. And in 2011 a team in Spain used cutting-edge radar and mapping equipment to make the case for an area just north of Cádiz. But most outrageous of all is the idea expounded by a few that the Atlanteans were a race of advanced extraterrestrials who invented airplanes millennia before the Wright Brothers!

For those who are convinced that Atlantis did exist, perhaps the most credible theory describes it as lying in the Mediterranean close to Crete. This thesis argues for a mistranslation by Plato so that Atlantis was destroyed not 9,000 years before Solon's visit to Egypt (long before the founding of Athens), but just years before. This would place its destruction around 1500 BC, coinciding with the volcanic eruption of Thera (now Santorini) in the Aegean Sea. This natural disaster caused tsunamis and resulted in widespread devastation, including the collapse of the Minoan settlement of Akrotiri. For some, then, Akrotiri was "the real Atlantis."

UNDERWATER WORLD *A Victorian engraving by Henri Theophile Hildibrand for an edition of Jules Verne's 1870 novel* 20,000 Leagues Under the Sea. *In the book, Captain Nemo takes his submarine, Nautilus, on a trip to Atlantis.*

77

The missing Apollo 11 tapes

WHAT THEY ARE The tapes containing the original footage of the first moon landing
WHY YOU WON'T FIND THEM It seems NASA recorded over them

On July 21, 1969, NASA's Apollo 11 mission put a man on the moon for the first time. Video evidence of this "giant leap for mankind" was broadcast live on television to a global audience of 600 million people (about one-sixth of the world's population at the time). It was the sort of event you'd definitely save for posterity—except NASA managed to lose its highest-quality footage.

Anyone who has seen the footage of Neil Armstrong on the moon will know that the pictures are "of their time," are no match for today's high-definition images. The footage was captured by a single camera on the lunar module, recording in a format known as slow-scan television (SSTV). However, while SSTV was as good as recording got in 1969, it was incompatible with commercial broadcast systems. So the footage was beamed to one of three tracking stations—Goldstone in California (run by NASA), and the Honeysuckle Creek and Parkes Observatories in Australia—where it was reformatted for the TV networks.

It was soon apparent that the stream from Goldstone had a fault, so the Honeysuckle Creak footage was what the world at large saw. However, as digital technology developed, it was hoped that it would be possible to take the original SSTV recordings and upgrade them to provide better images of the momentous event than we had ever seen before. That was when it became clear that NASA had somehow lost track of the tapes.

A dedicated Apollo 11 Tape Search and Restoration Team was set up in 2003, but by 2006 was forced to admit that the hunt had proved fruitless. Not only had NASA's own tapes disappeared, but so had the backups sent from Australia. According to a statement: "After an exhaustive search, we were sad to conclude that all the tapes were shipped back to the US after the mission and were reused, probably in the early 1980s. No one had ever expected to access the slow-scan TV, and so those few tapes weren't singled out to be preserved."

The next best option for the Restoration Team was to take the best converted recordings and upgrade those instead. Over the next three years, tapes were gathered from around the world and restored. The new, improved footage was shown at the 2010 Australian Geographic Society Awards, with Buzz Aldrin (the second man on the moon) as guest of honor. No doubt the bosses at NASA secretly hope that the priceless SSTV tapes may yet turn up to provide us with even more dramatic images.

78

Ark of the Covenant

WHAT IT IS The repository that held the Ten Commandments
WHY YOU WON'T FIND IT It disappeared from Jerusalem many centuries ago

According to the Old Testament Book of Exodus, the Ark of the Covenant is the chest used to store the stone tablets inscribed with the Ten Commandments, brought down from Mount Sinai by Moses. Yet despite its prominent place in Christianity, Judaism, and Islamic traditions, it has been missing since around 600 BC.

Said to have been made in accordance with instructions from God, the Ark apparently measured a little over 40 inches (1 m) long and 28 inches (70 cm) wide and high, and was manufactured from acacia wood decorated with gold. Two long rods of acacia and gold were used to carry it, while two cherubim figures on the lid were said to keep watch on it. As the Old Testament tells, the Ark was carried out of Egypt, covered in skins and cloths so that none could set eyes on it, during the exodus of the Israelites. The Book of Joshua describes its pivotal part in the fall of Jericho. Later, it was seized by the Philistines as Solomon worshipped before it, but later still, it found its way back to Jerusalem. However, its fate after the Babylonian siege of the city in 597 BC is unknown.

Some conclude that the Ark was taken to Babylon by victorious raiders but other sources—namely, the Second Book of Maccabees, written in the second century BC—suggest that it was removed from the city after a divine warning of the coming attack. Some have claimed it was then buried at Mount Nebo in Jordan. An alternative theory is that it was buried for beneath the First Temple in Jerusalem. Since that site is now home to the Dome of the Rock, modern excavation to test this hypothesis is all but impossible. Nonetheless, this theory feeds into the idea that it later fell into the possession of the Knights Templar (see page 53), who operated on the Temple Mount, and eventually found its way to mainland Europe or a location in Ireland or Britain. It has also been suggested that the Ark was stored in Rome at the Basilica of St. John Lateran, but perished when the church burned in the 14th century.

However, the location with perhaps the strongest claim is Axum in Ethiopia. According to the nation's royal chronicles, it came to Ethiopia in the tenth century BC with Menelik I, alleged son of King Solomon and the Queen of Sheba. A forgery of the Ark, meanwhile, was left back in Jerusalem. Today, the purported relic is housed in a treasury next to the Church of St. Mary of Zion, with only one priest permitted access.

GOLDEN CASKET *A modern replica of the Ark of the Covenant on display at Timnah Valley Park in Arabah, southern Israel. This modern-day Ark sits within a reconstruction of the tabernacle—the portable temple used by Moses during the Exodus from Egypt.*

79

Lost army of Cambyses

WHO THEY ARE The army of Cambyses II, an ancient king of Persia
WHY YOU WON'T FIND THEM There's a lot of sand to sift through in Egypt's Western Desert where they disappeared

Fifty thousand men can't just go missing, can they? Well, according to ancient historical sources, they can. The Persian troops, under the command of King Cambyses II, were sent out from Thebes (modern-day Luxor) in Egypt, but went missing on their march through the part of the Sahara known as the Western, or Libyan, Desert. Truth or fable? Experts remain divided to this day.

Cambyses II reigned from 530 BC to 522 BC. His father, Cyrus the Great, had expanded Persia's empire in the Near East and Central Asia, and Cambyses made great inroads into Egypt, ultimately defeating Pharoah Psamtik III, at the Battle of Pelusium in 525 BC. Famously, the famed oracle of Ammon located at the Siwa Oasis (not far from the modern Libyan border), had predicted Cambyses' demise, and thinking the prophecy disproven, the enraged king now set out to take his revenge the oracle. Some 75 years later, the Greek historian Herodotus, recorded what happened next in Book VI of his *History*:

"The men sent to attack the Ammonians, started from Thebes, having guides with them, and may be clearly traced as far as the city Oasis ... seven days' journey across the sand ... But thenceforth nothing is to be heard of them ... It is certain they neither reached the Ammonians, nor even came back to Egypt. Further than this, the Ammonians relate as follows: That the Persians set forth from Oasis across the sand, and had reached about halfway between that place and themselves when, as they were at their midday meal, a wind arose from the south, strong and deadly, bringing with it vast columns of whirling sand, which entirely covered up the troops and caused them wholly to disappear."

Over time, many came to see the story as little more than a myth. Others, however, kept faith in its accuracy. British explorer Major-General Orde Wingate made an unsuccessful search in the early 1930s, while in the mid-1980s an American expedition backed by Harvard University and the National Geographic Society proved similarly fruitless.

Then in 2009 Italian brothers Angelo and Alfredo Castiglioni claimed to have found artefacts and human remains close to Siwa Oasis that they said offered archaeological evidence for Herodotus's story. The Egyptian Supreme Council of Antiquities, however, claimed that their work was not authorized and that their claims could thus not be verified. And so the search for the lost army goes on.

80

Captain Kidd's treasure

WHAT IT IS The booty of one of history's most infamous pirates
WHY YOU WON'T FIND IT No one knows which "X" marks this particular spot

The inspiration for a thousand fictional pirates from Long John Silver to Captain Jack Sparrow, William Kidd's own life ended ingloriously hanging from a gibbet by the River Thames. In more recent times, some historians have argued that he has been much maligned. Regardless of his character, he claimed to have buried a vast stash of booty captured on the high seas.

Born in Scotland in 1645, William Kidd settled across the Atlantic in New York. By middle age he was a noted buccaneer, active in the West Indies and around the coasts of New York and Massachusetts. In 1695, he was commissioned in London as a privateer—that is to say, as the captain of a private ship commissioned by a government to carry out armed warfare on its behalf. He was to hunt down enemy French and pirate ships that were hindering the passage of East India Company vessels in the Indian Ocean and the Red Sea.

Kidd's mission had auspicious backers, including four leading British Whig politicians—the earl of Orford, the baron of Romney, the duke of Shrewsbury, and Sir John Somers. Kidd also received a letter of marque from King William III himself which secured 10 percent of any booty for the crown. Kidd set sail in a new vessel, the *Adventure Galley*, in early 1696, stopping in New York to find a suitable crew. By summer, he was ready to make for the Cape of Good Hope, but the voyage was not a happy

one. There was a dearth of suitable ships to plunder and the crew fell victim to bouts of scurvy and cholera. Sailing onto Madagascar, the ship was in bad shape and supplies were running low. Fearing mutiny, Kidd determined to capture some booty, whether legally or not.

Yet even then, he does not seem to have immediately become the ruthless pirate of legend. In October 1697, for instance, he got into a fight with one of his gunners, William Moore, after Kidd refused to attack a Dutch ship that had been spied. As King William was Dutch-born this was a politically astute decision, but the spat resulted in Moore's death from a fractured skull after Kidd threw a bucket at him. It was an incident that would come back to haunt him.

In January 1698, Kidd won his biggest prize off the tip of India—the *Quedah Merchant*, carrying a rich cargo including calico, silks, sugar, opium, and precious metals. Kidd took over the captured ship, renamed her the *Adventure Prize*, and sailed on to Anguilla. The *Quedah*

STORYBOOK PIRATE *Famed for inspiring adventure tales such as Treasure Island, Captain William Kidd actually met an inglorious end, hanged at Wapping in East London after being abandoned by his political allies.*

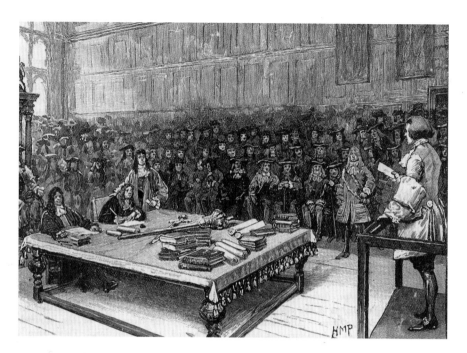

Merchant had been under French protection, so Kidd could claim it as fair game, but alas for him, attitudes to piracy had hardened in the two years since he had left London and he discovered he was now a marked man, regarded as a maverick endangering Britain's legitimate trading activities.

He determined to make for New York, where he hoped old friends might come to his aid. After selling the *Adventure Prize*'s cargo he scuppered the ship and took the captaincy of another, the *Saint Antonio*, instead. Nevertheless, on arrival in America he was arrested and sent for questioning in England. He refused to cooperate with his interrogators, presumably believing his original aristocratic backers would come to the rescue. But they were considerably less powerful than they had been in 1698, and left him to his fate. He was thrown into Newgate Prison, from where he wrote to the Speaker of the House of Commons promising to reveal the location of some $166,850 worth of booty in return for clemency. It did no good—he was convicted of piracy and murder (relating to Moore) and was hanged on May 23, 1701 at Execution Dock, Wapping, in East London. His corpse was hung in a cage downriver for three years as a macabre warning to other would-be buccaneers.

If Kidd really left vast stores of treasure buried, he took their secret with him. He certainly left a relatively modest hoard on Gardiners Island off Long Island on his trip back to New York, but this was recovered and used as evidence at his trial. There is also speculation that he deposited treasure on Block Island (part of Rhode Island), in 1699. Others have identified potential locations as disparate as New Jersey, Connecticut, Japan, Vietnam, and assorted spots in the Indian Ocean. Perhaps the best chance of tracking any hidden booty lies in a series of maps that turned up in the 1920s and 1930s, supposedly found secreted in furniture that sailed with Kidd on his final voyage to the UK. However, experts are divided as to their veracity. Just as with so much of Kidd's story, discerning where the truth lies is no easy job.

The bones of the Peking Man

WHAT THEY ARE Fossils that open a window onto human history
WHY YOU WON'T FIND THEM They disappeared in 1941 amid the chaos of Japan's invasion of China

When they were discovered close to Beijing, China, in the 1920s, the fossilized remains that became popularly known as Peking Man rewrote the history books and provided paleontologists with a rare glimpse of an early ancestor of modern man. But when the Second World War descended upon the region, these ancient bones were lost in the upheaval. Even today, scientists remain desperate to recover them.

In 1921, a team led by Swedish scientist Johan Gunnar Andersson took their search for prehistoric fossils to China's Zhoukoudian cave complex, close to the city then known as Peking. The area had a reputation for rich archaeology, and locals directed them to a site called Dragon Bone Hill. Over the next few years they uncovered plentiful evidence, including fossilized teeth, of previously unknown ancient humans.

From 1927, Canadian researcher Davidson Black undertook his own work in the area. Within a year, he uncovered more teeth, as well as skull fragments. Over the next decade, a total of 200 fossils from perhaps 40 individuals were found, including several almost complete skullcaps and a number of jaw bones. Studies revealed that these bones belonged to a human species that lived around 750,000 years ago. Given the scientific name *Homo erectus pekinensis*, "Peking Man" quickly became a household name. With his heavy brow and broad nose, he was an early user of tools, and may even have harnessed fire.

After Black died in 1934, his work was continued firstly by Pierre Teilhard de Chardin and then Franz Weidenreich. However, excavations ceased in 1937 following Japan's invasion of China. The fossil samples were sent for safety to the US-run Peking Union Medical College. Yet by 1941 fears were growing that the fossils would not be secure even there. In September 1941, therefore, the skulls were careful packed into crates, which were to be taken by train to a nearby port (probably Tientsin), and loaded onto a ship to America. They never got there.

So what might have happened to these scientific treasures? Given the turmoil at the time there is a strong suspicion that plans changed late on. One theory had them sent to the US Legation in Peking, and some believe they are still buried somewhere in the grounds. Alternatively, perhaps they were simply misplaced somewhere en route to Tientsin, perhaps after their train was intercepted by Japanese troops. In a worst-case scenario, they could have been cast aside by people who had no idea how precious

Opposite: *One of the casts of Peking Man made in the 1930s under the direction of Franz Weidenreich. Had he not been so conscientious, we may have been entirely robbed of the knowledge that Peking Man has given us in recent years.*
Right: *A few of the surviving teeth fragments discovered with the plethora of jawbones that researchers uncovered.*

they were, or perhaps fell into the hands of enterprising locals who ground them up for use in traditional medicines. Some suspect they were smuggled out of Peking after all, and subsequently hidden elsewhere in China or even in the USA. Others argue that they were seized by the Japanese who put them aboard a ship that may or may not have then sunk.

One oft-repeated tale has Peking Man last seen at a US military base, Camp Holcomb, destined for the nearby port city of Qinhuangdao. The story goes that the ship meant to pick up the fossils never made it to port. Former US Marine Richard Bowen has credibly claimed that while stationed at Camp Holcomb in 1947, he dug up and reburied a box full of bones, but the land where the camp once stood is now filled with warehouses and car lots. So even if the bones were indeed here, and survived subsequent building developments, it is difficult to

imagine permission being granted for the speculative excavations that would be needed to find them.

Fortunately, Weidenreich had previously insisted on making plaster-casts of all the bone samples and these, along with copious descriptive notes, have allowed scientists to continue studies of Peking Man. But the absence of the bones themselves has been a huge hindrance, especially when modern scientific analysis of a few small fragments could tell us so much more than we can learn from copies. If the original discovery of Peking Man helped us fill a gap in our knowledge of mankind's origins, their rediscovery would no doubt let us fill many more. If we never get them back, their loss must rate—as American paleoanthropologists Noel Boaz and Russell Ciochon wrote in 2004—as "the single greatest loss of original data in the history of paleontology."

Montezuma's treasure

WHAT IT IS Booty associated with the great Aztec emperor

WHY YOU WON'T FIND IT It was hidden during the war with the Conquistadors

Montezuma (or Moctezuma) was the Aztec ruler whose life and reign ended in violence after his capital city Tenochtitlán (located in modern-day Mexico) was invaded by Spanish Conquistadors under the leadership of Hernán Cortés. Amid the bloody fighting, a colossal volume of gold and precious treasure was said to have been looted from the city. Yet after centuries of searching, it has never been found.

Hernán Cortés was born in Spain in 1485, and set off for the New World while a young man, settling for some years in Cuba. In 1519, he led a party of about 600 Conquistadors onto the mainland, accumulating lands and booty by a strategy of befriending certain local peoples and promoting enmity against their neighbors. Cortés soon heard rumors of the vast wealth possessed by Montezuma II, leader of the Aztecs. Montezuma for his part was not keen to engage with the foreign interlopers, so sent envoys bearing gifts in return for the Spaniards' departure. This only heightened their hunger for riches, however, and in November 1519 the Conquistadors arrived at Tenochtitlán. Some of Cortés's men found a concealed treasury that was described by one Bernal Díaz del Castillo:

"When it was opened Cortés and some of his Captains went in first, and they saw such a number of jewels and slabs and plates of gold (...) and other great riches, that they were carried away and did not know what to say about such wealth ...

When I saw it I marveled, and as at that time I was a youth and had never seen such riches as those in my life before, I took it for certain that there could not be another such store of wealth in the whole world."

The Conquistadors kept Montezuma as a virtual prisoner in his own city, but in 1520 Cortés was forced to lead his troops out of the city toward the Mexican coast to head off a small army that had been dispatched after the Spanish governor of Cuba had grown nervous of Cortés's activities. Pedro de Alvarado was left in charge of Tenochtitlán but, suspecting the Aztecs of plotting a coup, ordered a massacre. Its effect was to consolidate opposition to the Spanish and by the time Cortés returned, the situation was desperate. The Conquistadors' leader decided he had no option but to retreat from the city and he sent Montezuma before his people to attempt to negotiate safe passage. What happened next is unclear but the result is not: Montezuma was killed. Whether he died at the hands of Aztecs who considered him now as merely a puppet of the Spanish

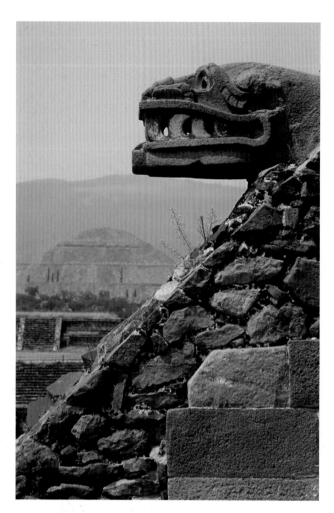

GODLIKE *A close-up of a temple dedicated to Quetzalcoatl, a Mesoamerican deity who took the form of a feathered serpent, in the temple city of Teotihuacan near modern-day Mexico City. It has long been argued that Montezuma believed the conquistador Hernán Cortés was in fact an incarnation of Quetzalcoatl.*

or whether the Spanish themselves slaughtered him has never been proven.

On June 30, 1520, Cortés led his men out of the city in the dead of night, loaded with as much Aztec treasure as they could carry. But thus burdened, they were slow to make their escape and before long the Aztecs were upon them, killing many and reclaiming the looted riches. This battle, known as *La Noche Triste* ("the sorrowful night") turned out to be the first real battle in a much longer conflict, and in 1521 Cortés returned to Tenochtitlán and seized control. By then, however, the treasure that had once resided within the city

walls was gone. One of Montezuma's successors had ordered it to be moved to a place of safety, a job rumored to have been carried out by no less than 2,000 porters.

So began one of the most enduring treasure hunts in the history of the New World. Dozens of locations in Mexico and the American Southwest have been put forward as possible hiding places. Many believe it was taken north to Aztlan, the fabled homeland of the Aztec civilization. Alas, no one actually knows where Aztlan was. Others point instead to Kanab in Utah, based largely on a story popularized in a magazine article of the 1940s about a prospector called Freddie Crystal. In 1920 he turned up with what he claimed to be a 400-year-old treasure map he had found in a monastery. He and a hopeful band of followers spent the next several years using it to search for Montezuma's wealth. They bored into a local landmark, White Mountain, supposedly uncovering several hidden chambers but, sadly, no booty. A similar lack of success has been encountered at sites throughout Mexico, California, Colorado, Texas, and beyond.

There are those that suspect there is a perfectly good reason that Montezuma's treasure remains unfound. The tale of the treasure and its relocation, they believe, is nothing more than a myth to add to many others about the Aztecs and the Conquistadors.

The solution to the Beale Ciphers

WHAT THEY ARE The key to solving the whereabouts of a long-lost treasure
WHY YOU WON'T FIND THEM Many believe the ciphers are merely a mischievous joke

In 1885, a three-part cipher was published, apparently revealing details of a treasure hoard somewhere in Virginia. Only the second segment of the code had been decoded, while no one had identified the cipher key (that is to say, the key to unlock the code) for the first and third parts. Could the whole enterprise have been nothing more than a hoax anyway?

As told, the story begins at the inn of one William Morriss in 1820s Virginia. One of his guests, Thomas Jefferson Beale, gives him a tin for safekeeping and asks him not to open it for several years unless he fails to return. Beale then leaves and is never seen again. The decades pass and eventually Morriss opens the box to find papers covered in a seemingly random series of numbers separated by commas. Beale and a small gang of associates had struck it rich in New Mexico in the late 1810s, and so Morriss suspects that these documents reveal where their treasure is hidden.

All the landlord's attempts to solve the ciphers fail, so after several more years, he takes a close friend into his confidence. The friend decodes the second cipher after discovering that each number represents the first letter of the indicated words in the Declaration of Independence. It reads:

"I have deposited in the county of Bedford, about four miles from Buford's, in an excavation or vault, six feet below the surface of the ground, the following articles, belonging jointly to the parties whose names are given in number three, herewith: The first deposit consisted of ten hundred and fourteen pounds of gold, and thirty-eight hundred and twelve pounds of silver, deposited Nov. eighteen nineteen. The second was made Dec. eighteen twenty-one, and consisted of nineteen hundred and seven pounds of gold, and twelve hundred and eighty-eight of silver; also jewels, obtained in St Louis in exchange for silver to save transportation, and valued at thirteen thousand dollars. The above is securely packed in iron pots, with iron covers. The vault is roughly lined with stone, and the vessels rest on solid stone, and are covered with others. Paper number one describes the exact locality of the vault, so that no difficulty will be had in finding it."

The friend, though, has no luck with cipher 1 (which apparently describes the exact location of the treasure) or cipher 3 (listing the various beneficiaries to whom it should go). In 1885, one J.B. Ward published the ciphers and the text above

115, 73, 24, 807, 37, 52, 49, 17, 31, 62, 647, 22, 7, 15, 140, 47, 29, 107, 79, 84, 56, 239,
10, 26, 811, 5, 196, 308, 85, 52, 160, 136, 59, 211, 36, 9, 46, 316, 554, 122, 106, 95, 53,
58, 2, 42, 7, 35, 122, 53, 31, 82, 77, 250, 196, 56, 96, 118, 71, 140, 287, 28, 353, 37,
1005, 65, 147, 807, 24, 3, 8, 12, 47, 43, 59, 807, 45, 316, 101, 41, 78, 154, 1005, 122,
138, 191, 16, 77, 49, 102, 57, 72, 34, 73, 85, 35, 371, 59, 196, 81, 92, 191, 106, 273, 60,
394, 620, 270, 220, 106, 388, 287, 63, 3, 191, 122, 43, 234, 400, 106, 290, 314, 47, 48,
81, 96, 26, 115, 92, 158, 191, 110, 77, 85, 197, 46, 10, 113, 140, 353, 48, 120, 106, 2,
607, 61, 420, 811, 29, 125, 14, 20, 37, 105, 28, 248, 16, 159, 7, 35, 19, 301, 125, 110,
486, 287, 98, 117, 511, 62, 51, 220, 37, 113, 140, 807, 138, 540, 8, 44, 287, 388, 117,
18, 79, 344, 34, 20, 59, 511, 548, 107, 603, 220, 7, 66, 154, 41, 20, 50, 6, 575, 122, 154,
248, 110, 61, 52, 33, 30, 5, 38, 8, 14, 84, 57, 540, 217, 115, 71, 29, 84, 63, 43, 131, 29,
138, 47, 73, 239, 540, 52, 53, 79, 118, 51, 44, 63, 196, 12, 239, 112, 3, 49, 79, 353, 105,
56, 371, 557, 211, 515, 125, 360, 133, 143, 101, 15, 284, 540, 252, 14, 205, 140, 344, 26,
811, 138, 115, 48, 73, 34, 205, 316, 607, 63, 220, 7, 52, 150, 44, 52, 16, 40, 37, 158, 807,
37, 121, 12, 95, 10, 15, 35, 12, 131, 62, 115, 102, 807, 49, 53, 135, 138, 30, 31, 62, 67,
41, 85, 63, 10, 106, 807, 138, 8, 113, 20, 32, 33, 37, 353, 287, 140, 47, 85, 50, 37, 49, 47,
64, 6, 7, 71, 33, 4, 43, 47, 63, 1, 27, 600, 208, 230, 15, 191, 246, 85, 94, 511, 2, 10, 38,
140, 297, 61, 603, 320, 302, 666, 287, 2, 44, 33, 32, 511, 548, 10, 6, 250, 270, 20, 39, 7,
33, 44, 22, 40, 7, 10, 3, 811, 106, 44, 486, 230, 353, 211, 200, 31, 10, 38, 140, 297, 61,
603, 320, 302, 666, 287, 2, 44, 33, 32, 511, 548, 10, 6, 250, 557, 246, 53, 37, 52, 83, 47,
320, 38, 33, 80 , 7, 44, 30, 31, 250, 10, 15, 35, 106, 160, 113, 31, 102, 406, 230, 540, 320,
29, 66, 33, 101, 807, 138, 301, 316, 353, 320, 220, 37, 52, 28, 540, 320, 33, 8, 48, 107,
50, 811, 7, 2, 113, 73, 16, 125, 11, 110, 67, 102, 807, 33, 59, 81, 158, 38, 43, 581, 138,
19, 85, 400, 38, 43, 77, 14, 27, 8, 47, 138, 63, 140, 44, 35, 22, 177, 106, 250, 314, 217,
2, 10, 7, 1005, 4, 20, 25, 44, 48, 7, 26, 46, 110, 230, 807, 191, 34, 112, 147, 44, 110, 121,
125, 96, 41, 51, 50, 140, 56, 47, 152, 540, 63, 807, 28, 42, 250, 138, 582, 98, 643, 32,
107, 140, 112, 26, 85, 138, 540, 53, 20, 125, 371, 38, 36, 10, 52, 118, 136, 102, 420, 150,
112, 71, 14, 20, 7, 24, 18, 12, 807, 37, 67, 110, 62, 33, 21, 95, 220, 511, 102, 811, 30,
83, 84, 305, 620, 15, 2, 108, 220, 106, 353, 105, 106, 60, 275, 72, 8, 50, 205, 185, 112,
125, 540, 65, 106, 807, 188, 96, 110, 16, 73, 33, 807, 150, 409, 400, 50, 154, 285, 96,
106, 316, 270, 205, 101, 811, 400, 8, 44, 37, 52, 40, 241, 34, 205, 38, 16, 46, 47, 85,
24, 44, 15, 64, 73, 138, 807, 85, 78, 110, 33, 420, 505, 53, 37, 38, 22, 31, 10, 110, 106,
101, 140, 15, 38, 3, 5, 44, 7, 98, 287, 135, 150, 96, 33, 84, 125, 807, 191, 96, 511, 118,
440, 370, 643, 466, 106, 41, 107, 603, 220, 275, 30, 150, 105, 49, 53, 287, 250, 208,
134, 7, 53, 12, 47, 85, 63, 138, 110, 21, 112, 140, 485, 486, 505, 14, 73, 84, 575, 1005,
150, 200, 16, 42, 5, 4, 25, 42, 8, 16, 811, 125, 160, 32, 205, 603, 807, 81, 96, 405,
41, 600, 136, 14, 20, 28, 26, 353, 302, 246, 8, 131, 160, 140, 84, 440, 42, 16, 811,
40, 67, 101, 102, 194, 138, 205, 51, 63, 241, 540, 122, 8, 10, 63, 140, 47, 48, 140, 288.

FIGURE IT OUT *An extract from the number series comprising the second Beale cipher. According to the story, this code was broken by identifying the first letters of the indicated words within the US Declaration of Independence, and gives teasing details of the location and nature of the treasure.*

sense—impossible to believe. Of the key characters, only Morriss can be traced with any certainty. There are queries about the ciphers, too. Why use three keys when one would do? And what about certain words including "stampede" and "improvise" that Beale supposedly wrote in his accompanying notes, but which were not in common usage in the 1820s?

Statistical analysis also suggests that the unsolved ciphers cannot be based on an English plaintext. Some linguistic experts point to similarities between the writing style of Beale and the author of the much later pamphlet, with the implication that they were one and the same person. Is it possible that the mysterious Mr Ward invented the mystery as a money-spinning publishing ruse? If that was his intention, it certainly worked—copies of the ciphers sold as quickly as they could be printed. It has even been suggested that this was a hoax designed to bring in funds for victims of a devastating fire that tore through Lynchburg in 1883.

For a while, the finger was pointed at writer Edgar Allan Poe as the controlling mind behind an elaborate practical joke. Poe used cryptographic puzzles in several of his stories. His death long before the pamphlet's publication would seem to rule him out, but a joke from beyond the grave would be just his style. Plenty of others, meanwhile, believe the ciphers are exactly what they purport to be. More often than not, there is still someone to be found searching in the vicinity of Burford's Tavern.

Just maybe the ciphers are real, and pehaps someone has *already* found the cipher keys to solve them. But if that is the case, then there may be every reason for them to continue keep the secret secret for the foreseeable future.

POE POSER *In his 40-year life, Edgar Allan Poe established himself as one of the great men of American letters. A pioneer of detective fiction, he loved a good mystery—but did he have a hand in the Beale ciphers?*

in a pamphlet entitled *The Beale Papers*. The original ciphers are then said to have perished in a fire.

The public imagination thus enflamed, throngs of treasure-hunters descended on the area around Burford's Tavern in Virginia. Some dedicated decades of their lives to pursuit of the promised riches. But no one ever managed to solve the other ciphers.

It is altogether an incredible story. For some, it is incredible in its literal

84 MV *Lyubov Orlova*

WHAT IT IS A thoroughly modern ghost ship
WHY YOU WON'T FIND IT It has been cut adrift in international waters

Built in the former Yugoslavia and launched in 1975, the *Lyubov Orlova* served out a long career as a cruise ship before being impounded in Canada in 2010 as the result of her owners' debts. Two years later, she broke free while being towed to the Caribbean and was left to drift uncrewed through international waters.

Initially registered in the USSR, the *Lyubov Orlova* was named in honor of one of the great stars of 1930s Soviet cinema. She (the ship, not the actress) cut a sizeable figure, almost 295 feet (90 m) long and weighing in at 4,183 long tons. Built to withstand icy conditions, she was a regular on the Arctic and Antarctica cruise circuits, and from 2002 was chartered by a company called Cruise North Expeditions. In September 2010, while the ship was moored at St. John's in Newfoundland, Canada, Cruise North Expeditions had reportedly made a claim for financial compensation of US$250,000 against her owners after being forced to cancel a cruise because of problems with the ship. To compound the problem, the crew of 51 Russian and Ukrainian nationals had gone unpaid for several months. So it was that the ship was seized and subsequently auctioned off.

But it was not until January 2013 that she was towed out of St. John's, destined for an ignominious end at a scrapyard in the Dominican Republic. Amid strong winds and high waves, however, *Lyubov Orlova* broke free of the ship towing her after just a day. First attempts to reattach the ships were thwarted, and it was a week before the offshore supply vessel *Atlantic Hawk* managed to secure her and draw her away from a series of offshore oil rigs. However, in early February, the Canadian transport agency announced that the ship would be cut adrift again as it no longer posed a risk to oil installations or the wider marine environment. With the ship heading for international waters, the Canadian government put responsibility for the *Lyubov Orlova* firmly back on her owners.

A month after her release, the ship was drifting several hundred miles off the Irish coast, but with her GPS navigation system no longer functioning correctly, it soon became impossible to keep track of her movements. She remains nobody's responsibility and presumably will continue to wander as a free spirit unless she poses a direct risk to shipping in someone's territorial waters—assuming she doesn't sink first.

GREENLAND

NORTH ATLANTIC
OCEAN

CUT ADRIFT *A modern ghost ship, the* Lyubov
Orlova *came to a sad end after her owners ran into
financial problems. She broke free of her shackles
off the coast of Canada and promptly began to make
her way across the Atlantic Ocean.*

SIGHTED ON
FEBRUARY 21

LABRADOR

SHIP BREAKS FREE
JANUARY 24

NEWFOUNDLAND

LAST SIGHTING,
MID-MARCH 2013

DEPARTS ST. JOHN'S
JANUARY 23

ICE QUEEN *The* Lyubov
Orlova *pictured here
in 2010 as seen from
Petermann Island in
Antarctica. All trace of
her has been lost after
she was left to her own
devices on international
waters in 2013.*

85 Harold Holt

WHO HE IS Australia's
17th prime minister
WHY YOU WON'T FIND HIM
He disappeared while
out swimming in the
mid-1960s

Harold Holt, leader of the Liberal Party, sat in the Australian parliament from 1935 and succeeded Sir Robert Menzies to become Australia's prime minister in January 1966. A career politician and enthusiastic supporter of the US war in Vietnam, he was approaching his second anniversary in office when he disappeared while swimming. The incident sparked decades of speculation.

On the weekend of December 18, 1967, Holt was spending time with friends when, on the Sunday morning, they found themselves at Cheviot Beach near Portsea on the Victoria coast. Holt was renowned as a strong swimmer so it was no surprise that he insisted on going for a dip, brushing aside concerns about dangerously strong currents. "I know this beach like the back of my hand," he contended. However, playfulness quickly turned to panic as he dived into the ocean and shortly afterward disappeared from view. The emergency services rallied all their resources but could find no sign of the prime minister.

Two days later, the government formally announced that Holt was missing, presumed dead. As Victorian state law stood at the time, no inquest could be held without a body—a situation that only encouraged speculation. Theories ranged from the credible to the absurd. A few cranks were convinced he'd been whooshed up to space by little green men. Others suggested that he faked his own death in order to elope with his mistress Marjorie Gillespie (one of the companions on that fateful weekend). A few argued that he had died by his own hand, the result of depression brought about by tensions in both his private and public lives. However, those who knew him best were adamant that this was not the case. Alien abduction aside, perhaps the most outlandish claim was made in Anthony Grey's 1983 study, *The Prime Minister Was a Spy*. Grey alleged Holt had been a Chinese double agent since the 1930s, and did not drown but was picked up by a Chinese submarine and taken away to start a new life in Asia.

The truth was almost certainly more prosaic. Holt's health had not been at its best in 1967. He had collapsed in parliament earlier in the year and suffered shoulder troubles that prompted his doctor to order a bar on swimming. When Holt ignored that advice to enter treacherous waters, he put himself in a situation beyond his control and paid the ultimate price. That, too, was the judgment of the coroner who finally ruled on the death in 2005.

86 The treasure of submarine I-52

WHAT IT IS Gold carried by a Second World War Japanese submarine
WHY YOU WON'T FIND IT It sank in the Bay of Biscay

The Imperial Japanese Navy submarine I-52 was en route to occupied France in 1944, transporting a valuable cargo to Japan's German allies when she was sunk by US forces in the Atlantic Ocean. The wreck lay undiscovered for over 40 years. Even though the vessel has now been located, the 2.2 tons of the gold she is known to have been carrying remain elusive.

I-52 set out on her fateful voyage from Kure in Japan's Hiroshima prefecture to Lorient in France in March 1944. She was carrying a varied cargo that included caffeine, molybdenum, opium, quinine, rubber, tin, tungsten—and some 146 gold bars. The plan was to deposit this haul with German forces in exchange for materials and technical knowledge to aid the Japanese war effort. Some think that her return cargo would have included large amounts of uranium

oxide, perhaps intended for use in a "dirty bomb."

But even as the I-52 made her long trip, the tide of the war was turning decisively against Germany. The planned docking in Lorient was canceled, and instead the sub was redirected to Norway. On June 22, 1944, she met, as arranged, with a German U-boat several hundred miles off Cape Verde, receiving fuel and technical equipment for the onward journey through the Bay of Biscay. But an armada of US naval ships had been tasked with tracking and destroying Japanese subs in the area, and thanks to the work of Allied codebreakers, they were able to track I-52's progress day by day. Virtually a sitting duck, she was destroyed with the loss of all hands on June 24, 1944. Despite several attempts, no one was able to locate the vessel, so she lay undisturbed at the bottom of the Bay of Biscay until the mid-1990s.

By then Paul Tidwell, a maritime researcher from Texas, had become fascinated by the story. After reviewing the available information, he and an intrepid team of deep-sea explorers tracked down the wreck in early 1995, sitting virtually upright on the seabed, 17,000 feet (5,200 m) down and 19 miles (30 kilometers) from the official estimate of her location. Tidwell and his colleagues worked closely with the Japanese authorities, who consider the sub to be a war grave. Tokyo and Tidwell agreed a long-term plan to raise the wreck and return it home in return for expenses and a share of any recovered gold. However, at the time of writing, the wreck remains in situ and while some of the crews' personal possessions have been recovered, I-52's gold remains tantalizingly out of reach.

STATE OF THE ART *The I-52 was a Type C-3 cargo submarine built by Japan's Mitsubishi Corporation and launched in 1943. She could carry a crew of just under 100, and was only struck from service on December 10 1944, almost six months after she went missing.*

87 Maxberg *Archaeopteryx*

WHAT IT IS The fossil remains of "the world's first bird"
WHY YOU WON'T FIND IT It disappeared in 1991 after the death of its owner

The Maxberg *Archaeopteryx* is a fossil of one of the earliest prehistoric birds. Discovered in Germany in the 1950s, it became the subject of a fierce bidding war, but in the end, the owner of the quarry in which it was found kept hold of the rare specimen. After he died in 1991, however, no one was able to find it, but if it should turn up again, it could command a price in excess of US$2 million.

It was in 1956 that two laborers, Ernst Fleisch and Karl Hinterholzinger, discovered a curious outline while cutting fossil-rich Solnhofen limestone in a Bavarian quarry. At first they dismissed it as unimportant, and it was stored in an onsite hut for the next two years.

In 1958, however, the quarry's owner, Eduard Opitsch, allowed geologist Klaus Fesefeldt to investigate the specimen. It was sent to Florian Heller, a paleontologist at the University of Erlangen, who realized this was only the third known fossil of *Archaeopteryx*, a creature that lived some 150 million years ago and signposted the transition from feathered dinosaurs to modern birds. Opitsch initially permitted the fossil to be put on display at the Maxberg Museum in nearby Mornsheim, but he soon came to realize there was money to be made. Berlin's Freie Universität made an opening bid of 30,000 deutchmarks for the specimen. The State Museum in Munich, keen to keep the find in Bavaria, upped the stakes by bidding 40,000, and Optisch might have accepted this offer if not for the fact that he would have had to pay 40 percent of the proceeds in tax. Instead, frustrated, he cut off negotiations in 1965. Nine years later he allowed casts of the fossil to be made, but then withdrew it from public display. Increasingly cantankerous, he turned down all requests to study the fossil, and is thought to have kept it under his bed.

Opitsch died in 1991, and his house stood empty for several weeks until his nephew (and principal heir) turned up. Alas, he found no sign of the ancient bird, although eyewitnesses claimed it had been in the building just a few weeks before. The disappearance was reported to the police but their investigations failed to find answers. Some suspected it had been stolen, or that Opitsch sold it to a private collector shortly before he died. Others suggested that perhaps the old man had hidden it as one final snub to a scientific establishment with whom he had grown weary. His gravestone bears an engraving of *Archaeopteryx*, raising the spectre that he may even have had it buried with him.

Remains of the Colossus of Rhodes

WHAT IT IS A giant statue and one of the Ancient Wonders of the World
WHY YOU WON'T FIND IT It fell during an earthquake in the third century BC

The Colossus of Rhodes was the shortest-lived of all the Seven Wonders of the Ancient World, standing for no more than 56 years. Its exact location is uncertain, and no known remains survive, though there have been various theories on that subject over the years. Today, there are plans to build a new Colossus on the island—and that may be as close to the original as we can hope to get.

Rising 100 foot (30 m) high atop a pedestal of a further 50 feet (15 m), the Colossus was sculpted by one of the great artists of the ancient world, Chares of Lindos. Crafted over 12 years from 290 BC in honor of the sun god Helios, it consisted of an iron frame weighted with large rocks, covered in a brass "skin" and finished with marble and bronze. It was built to celebrate victory in 304 BC over Demetrius, who had conquered Cyprus two years earlier. With the assistance of forces sent by Ptolemy I of Egypt, the islanders broke Demetrius's siege, then seized arms and equipment that the Cypriots left behind, plundering them for brass and iron to use in the construction of the Colossus. It was traditionally believed that the statue straddled the harbor of Rhodes but this is now thought highly doubtful. More likely, it stood on a breakwater elsewhere in the port or perhaps on a hill overlooking it.

In 226 BC, a violent earthquake shook Rhodes, and the Colossus broke apart at the joints and tumbled to the ground. No attempt was made to rebuild it, apparently because the Rhodians believed that the earthquake was a sign of the sun god's displeasure. Instead, the shattered giant lay scattered across the ground for some eight centuries. In the seventh century AD, Rhodes was conquered by Arab invaders. Writing a century later, the Byzantine chronicler Theophanes the Confessor claimed the Colossus was sold to a "Jewish merchant of Edessa" who destroyed what was left to extract the remaining bronze, using 900 camels to transport it. Some modern historians, however, suspect the statue had been broken up long before then.

In the late 1980s it was thought for a time that rock from the Colossus had been identified on the seabed close to the coast, but this idea was later discredited. More recently, German academic Dr. Ursula Vedder has suggested that foundations at a temple site on what is now Monte Smith came from the plinth on which the Colossus stood. If she is right, that may be the closest we can come to connecting with this ancient wonder.

COLOSISVS SOLIS

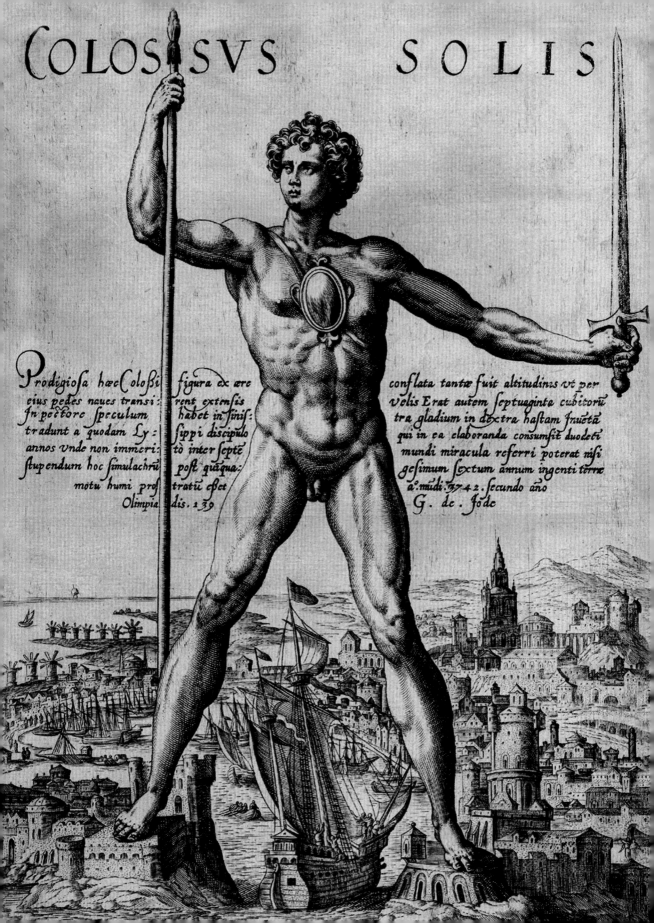

Prodigiofa hæc Coloßi figura ex ære
eius pedes naues transi: rent extensis
in pectore speculum habet in finis:
tradunt a quodam Ly: sippi discipulo
annos vnde non immeri: tò inter septe
stupendum hoc simulachrū post quaqua:
motu humi prostratū eßet
Olimpiadis. 139

conflata tantæ fuit altitudinis vt per
volis Erat autem septuaginta cubitorū
tra gladium in dextra hastam fructã
qui in ea elaboranda consumfit duodeti
mundi miracula referri poterat nisi
gesimum sextum annum ingenti terræ
aᵒ mūdi. 3742. secundo año
G. de. Jode

Lord Lucan

WHO HE IS A notorious aristocratic murderer
WHY YOU WON'T FIND HIM It is not known whether he is alive or dead, much less where he might be

An inveterate gambler, Richard John Bingham, 7th Earl of Lucan, was known to his friends and associates as "Lucky." But whether that was in any way an appropriate nickname is up for debate: in 1974, he seemingly disappeared off the face of the earth, shortly after the murder of his children's nanny and a brutal assault on their mother.

Born in 1934, Lucan was schooled at Eton, served with the Coldstream Guards in West German, and later built a career as a merchant banker. A perfectly respectable career path for a man of his station, you might think—yet Lucan had a taste for danger and glamor, too. He developed a love of gambling while still a schoolboy, adored fast cars, and raced powerboats. He was even said to have turned down the chance to audition for the role of James Bond.

In 1963, he married Veronica Duncan—the couple went onto have three children. Within a couple of months of the wedding, his father died and Lucky inherited not only the family titles, but also substantial wealth. It seemed like a perfect picture was complete, but by 1972 the marriage was crumbling and Lucan moved out of the marital home in the upmarket Belgravia area of London. There followed a bitter battle for custody of the children, with the courts eventually finding in Veronica's favor—a judgment that came as a

devastating and destabilizing blow to Lucan.

Regaining custody of his children became an obsession, and he was alleged to have started spying on his ex-wife. His mental equilibrium was almost certainly not improved when his new career as a professional gambler faltered. He was a member of the notorious Clermont gambling club in Berkeley Square, founded by his friend John Aspinall, where on a bad night, Lucan could rack up debts in five figures.

Fast forward to the early evening of November 7, 1974. Lady Lucan was at home with her children and their 29-year-old nanny, Sandra Rivett. Rivett had started working for the family a few months earlier and, on a Thursday night such as this, would normally have been out with her boyfriend. That week, though, she made the fateful decision to change her free evening to the Wednesday. After putting the children to bed, she went to the basement kitchen to make a hot drink for herself and

We know he rang his mother, asking her to pick up the children from the house. He told her that he had been driving past Veronica's house when he saw her fighting with an unknown man and then had found her alone and in a distressed state. After that call, Lucan next drove to Sussex to the home of some friends, the Maxwell-Scotts. He told Susan Maxwell-Scott a similar story, adding that Veronica had accused him of hiring a hit man. He left in the early hours of November 8 and his car was later found abandoned at nearby Newhaven. So began one of the most infamous manhunts in history. Lucan's image was plastered across newspapers and TV screens, his well-tended guardsman's mustache becoming familiar to all.

Veronica just before nine o'clock. There she was bludgeoned to death with a length of lead piping.

When Veronica descended to the top of the basement stairs to see what was keeping the nanny, she herself came under attack from a man she recognized as Lucan. As he tried to strangle her, she fought back hard and eventually he gave up his ambush. When pressed by Veronica about Rivett's fate, Lucan admitted he had killed her. Veronica insisted she could help him escape if he would cooperate with her. They went up to her room and when he went to get something from the bathroom, she saw her chance to flee. She ran to the local pub, the Plumbers Arms, and raised the alarm—but by the time the police arrived, Lucan had vanished.

An inquest named Lucan as the man responsible for Rivett's killing, rendering him the first member of the House of Lords to be identified as a murderer in over two centuries. In the weeks, months and years that followed, hundreds of sightings were reported from around the world but his fate remains a mystery. Some, including Veronica and John Aspinall, claimed that he committed suicide shortly after the attacks, while others suspect he made use of his society connections to spirit himself out of the country. One popular theory suggests he found his way to Africa and lived under an assumed identity for a further three or more decades. But whether alive or dead, it seems unlikely that we will know what happened to Lucky Lucan any time soon.

90 El Dorado

WHAT IT IS A legendary South American "City of Gold"
WHY YOU WON'T FIND IT It most likely never existed, though it has been sought since the 16th century

El Dorado, the "Lost City of Gold," was said to reside somewhere in South America, but is perhaps most valuable today as a metaphor for Man's unstinting greed for riches. The legend of El Dorado grew up among the Spanish and Portuguese Conquistadors who set out to colonize the recently discovered Americas in the 16th and 17th centuries.

"They entered a very plain house, for the door was only of silver, and the ceilings were only of gold, but wrought in so elegant a taste as to view with the richest." This understated description from Voltaire's satirical novel *Candide* captures the essence of a fantasy that dominated the European imagination during the colonization of the so-called New World.

Having had their heads turned by the phenomenal riches of, for instance, the Inca and Aztec civilizations (in modern-day Peru and Mexico, respectively), the imaginations of Conquistadors and colonists were undoubtedly receptive to the idea of an as yet undiscovered location with wealth beyond description. For more than 200 years, many great men would fall victim to their hubris, losing their power, wealth, and even lives in the pursuit of the promise that El Dorado encapsulated. Even today, some still cling to the dream of what, in reality, was never anything more than the product of rumor, exaggeration, and folklore. Indeed, the original El Dorado (which is Spanish for "the Gilded One") was not a place at all, but a person, or at least an office.

Juan Rodriguez Freyle is generally credited with providing the account that formed the basis of the legend. He reported on the rites performed by the Muisca people around Lake Guatavita (near Bogotá, the capital of modern-day Colombia). When a tribal leader was appointed, he would strip naked before being covered in powdered gold (a chronicler reporting that: "For it seemed to him that to wear any other finery ... made of gold worked by hammering, stamping, or by other means, was a vulgar and common thing"). With four other prominent dignitaries, he then sailed on a raft out into the middle of the lagoon, whereupon he cast a great hoard of treasure into the water to appease the gods. Over time, the story of this chief (known as "El Dorado") morphed into the narrative familiar to us today of a lost city of gold.

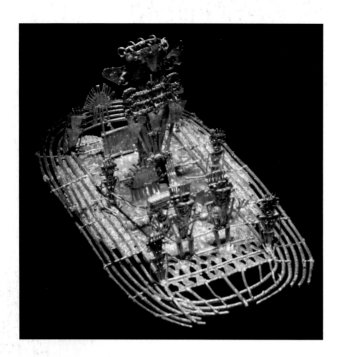

MUISCA RAFT *This stunning gold tableau, dated to between 600–1600 AD, is believed to represent the Muisca El Dorado ceremony. It was discovered in a cave near Pasca in central Colombia in 1969.*

While these later stories necessarily failed to furnish an exact location for the apocryphal metropolis, there was no shortage of volunteers willing to go in search of it. Two of the most famous were Francisco de Orellana and Gonzalo Pizarro, who set out from Quito (now the capital of Ecuador) in 1541. Despite failing to find the fabled city, De Orellana did claim to have discovered evidence of a hugely sophisticated civilization at work deep in the jungle. He was also the first European to travel to the mouth of the Amazon.

Sir Walter Raleigh, the great English explorer, was another to feel the lure of El Dorado. After an unsuccessful search in 1595, he embarked on a second mission in 1617, following the Orinoco River into Guiana. It was a disastrous trip that culminated in a lethal skirmish with Spanish forces, during which Walter's brother, Watt, was killed. When Raleigh returned to England, he felt the wrath of King James I (and VI of Scotland), who was furious that his order to avoid conflict with the Spanish had been breached. For his efforts, Raleigh was beheaded in 1618.

Others took a different approach to the quest and focused their attentions on Lake Guatavita, encountering moderate success in their search for riches. In the mid-1540s, for instance, a Conquistador scheme using local labor to drain the lake reduced the water level enough that the edges of the lake bed were exposed. Contemporary witnesses declared that a decent volume of gold was found.

Another drainage scheme in the 1580s, headed by Antonio de Sepúlveda, was even more successful, though a good many local laborers forced into participation lost their lives in a flooding accident. In the early 19th century, the revered German natural scientist, Alexander von Humboldt, calculated that Guatavita contained valuables worth some US$300 million (a figure that would run into billions in today's money). A close contemporary of von Humboldt from the Royal Institute of Paris suggested a figure of $1.8 billion as early as 1825.

Further "drain and search" operations went on well into the 20th century, though in a 30-year span from 1898 to 1929, the Company for the Exploitation of the Lagoon of Guatavita returned objects worth no more than $834. In 1965, the government of Colombia brought the lagoon under its authority as a site of nationally important heritage. As the location for the rite that birthed the El Dorado myth, Guatavita is perhaps the closest we can hope to get to the Lost City of legend. But it hardly represents the dream to which so many men sacrificed their fates and souls.

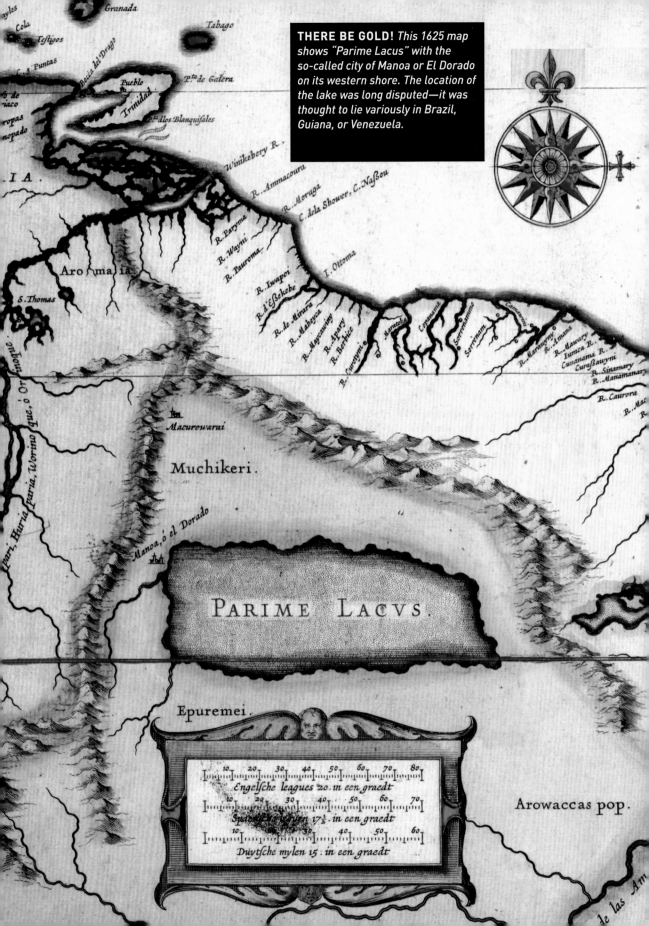

THERE BE GOLD! *This 1625 map shows "Parime Lacus" with the so-called city of Manoa or El Dorado on its western shore. The location of the lake was long disputed—it was thought to lie variously in Brazil, Guiana, or Venezuela.*

Crew of the *Mary Celeste*

WHO THEY ARE The men who sailed the most famous ghost ship of them all

WHY YOU WON'T FIND THEM Their vessel was found abandoned in 1872

It was the creator of Sherlock Holmes, Sir Arthur Conan Doyle, who did most to entrench the mystery of the *Mary Celeste* in popular folklore with a highly fictionalized short story of 1884. But what do we actually know of the famous ghost ship's last voyage? On December 5, 1872, the British-American brigantine was discovered floating near the Azores off the west coast of Portugal, with not a single person aboard.

The *Mary Celeste* had set sail from New York on November 7, captained by Benjamin Spooner Briggs. With him were seven crewmen, his wife, and their young daughter. They were headed for Genoa in Italy carrying a cargo of alcohol. The last entry in the ship's log, made in the early hours of November 25, revealed a voyage that had evidently been testing owing to bad weather but seemed hardly out of the ordinary.

Two weeks later, however, the *Mary Celeste* would be discovered by the crew of a British ship, the *Dei Gratia*, after apparently drifting unmanned for several hundred miles. Not a single person was found aboard. Instead, the crew had seemingly abandoned their possessions and hurriedly launched the ship's single lifeboat. About 40 inches (1 meter or so) of water was sloshing in the hold but the ship, its cargo, and several months' worth of provisions were all in good order. What, then, could possibly have made Captain Briggs and his entourage abandon a perfectly seaworthy ship in the middle of the ocean?

Captain Moorhouse of the *Dei Gratia* took the ship to Gibraltar, where an official inquiry was convened. Suspicion fell at first on the crew of the *Dei Gratia*, with some suspecting Moorhouse and Briggs of insurance fraud—but few today attach any blame to them. Others invoked deadly sea monsters or dastardly pirates, but if either of these was responsible, they left the ship and its valuable contents remarkably unscathed. Some have suggested that the crew might have partaken a little too enthusiastically of the alcohol on board before mutinying. But quite why they would all have abandoned ship is unclear. Was this instead a case of mass insanity brought on by alcohol fumes or even by a fungus that had infected the rye bread they ate?

Another theory is that alcohol fumes or even a minor explosion convinced Briggs that the ship was in immediate danger, and that an emergency evacuation was necessary. Once at sea, the ill-fated group would have had little chance of survival in a flimsy lifeboat with inadequate supplies.

Treasure of the Copper Scroll

WHAT IT IS A valuable hoard described on one of the Dead Sea Scrolls **WHY YOU WON'T FIND IT** Accurately deciphering the scroll has eluded generations of academics

For scholars of religion, there has been no greater find in the last 100 years than the Dead Sea Scrolls. The new light they shed on our understanding of the Bible is undoubtedly priceless, but one of them, the Copper Scroll, seemingly details a rather more material treasure—a vast hoard scattered across various locations, none of which has so far been recovered.

The Dead Sea Scrolls were discovered hidden in a series of caves in 1947. An itinerant goatherd was passing by one day in Qumram, close to the Dead Sea, when one of his animals disappeared into an opening in the rock. The herder threw a stone after the creature in a bid to encourage it out. Instead, he heard the sound of pottery smashing. When he went to investigate, he found the first of the Scrolls, stored in cylindrical jars.

Over the next few years, the area was flooded by historians, theologians, and archaeologists. In total, remnants of some 900 texts were found stored in 11 caves. The Copper Scroll was unearthed in 1952 by a French archaeologist, Henri de Contenson, and today can be seen in the Archaeological Museum at Amman in Jordan.

Discovered in two pieces and given the official designation 3Q15, it measured some 6 foot by 1 foot (2.4 m by 30 m), but crumbled when touched. At first, experts feared that any attempt to open it would destroy the contents. Then in 1955 a team from the University of Manchester delicately sawed through the first part of the scroll. The second section was opened a year later. It was already unique among the Dead Sea Scrolls for being written on copper rather than papyrus, but the text only added to the sense of something special.

Dating to somewhere between 150 BC and AD 70, it is written in a form of antiquated Hebrew unlike that seen on any of the other Dead Sea Scrolls, and probably in use some 800 years before the scroll was inscribed, and scattered with seemingly random Greek letters. And this is no religious or historical text—instead, it lists 64 locations and the treasures to be found at each, ranging from precious metals and jewelry to perfumes and clothing for use in religious rites.

Scholars found themselves at odds as to what it all meant. J.T. Milik was put in charge of translating the Copper Scroll but seemed less excited by it than his colleague John Allegro, who rushed

to his own translation first, breaking academic protocol in the process. Allegro believed the scroll's text was being supressed for fear of attracting treasure-hunters to the caves and imperiling other discoveries. In 1959 and 1960 he led two parties in search of the treasure, but on both occasions they returned empty-handed.

Each of the 64 entries follows a similar format, firstly naming a specific location, then adding some further detail and finally describing what is hidden there. Intriguingly, the last entry states: "In a dry well at Kohlit ... a copy of this document with its explanation ... and an inventory of each and every thing." Some believe that this second text must be found in order to fully comprehend the contents of the Copper Scroll.

Ancient units of measurement make it impossible to accurately estimate just

how much treasure is described, but some experts have valued the gold and silver alone in the billions of dollars. It therefore seems unlikely to have belonged to the Essenes, the ascetic Jewish sect thought to have brought the Dead Sea Scrolls together. A more credible scenario is that it came from the Second Temple in Jerusalem, hidden away in the turbulent period of the Jewish War. Indeed, some academics argue that the Romans recovered it after the sack of Jerusalem in AD 70, extracting its location through torture. A countertheory, meanwhile, links the treasure to ancient Egypt, and the reign of Pharaoh Akhenaten (see page 150).

Inevitably, there are also those ready to write the whole thing off as some kind of ancient hoax. Until someone finds at least some of the booty, or can prove just what happened to it, they will continue to make their argument.

Lord Byron's memoirs

WHAT THEY ARE The autobiography of a great Romantic poet
WHY YOU WON'T FIND THEM His circle decided to burn the manuscript after his death

Mad, bad, and dangerous to know, Lord Byron was the *enfant terrible* of the Romantic movement, with a lifestyle that would have fueled a thousand tabloid headlines. Byron died at the age of 36, with his multivolume memoirs ready for publication. Yet his friends burned them, depriving the literary world of an insight into one of its most vibrant minds.

George Gordon Byron was born in 1788, and inherited the title Baron Byron of Rochdale from his greatuncle at the age of ten. Educated at Harrow and then Trinity College, Cambridge, his first volume of poetry was published (to a critical mauling) before he was yet 20. In 1812, however, *Childe Harold's Pilgrimage*—an account in verse of his European Grand Tour—established him as a poetical superstar.

But just as greatness attached itself to Byron, so did scandal. He had a well-publicized affair with Lady Caroline Lamb, wife of the future Prime Minister Lord Melbourne. Indeed, it was Caroline who would dub him "mad, bad, and dangerous to know"). Then came allegations of an incestuous relationship with his half-sister, Augusta Leigh, possibly resulting in the birth of a daughter. In 1815, he married Anne Isabella Milbanke (known as Annabella), followed a year later by a legal separation and a new round of rumors—violence, adultery, sodomy—that did little to improve Byron's standing in polite society.

By now considered a reprehensible libertine in England, he moved to Italy and undertook some of his most important work, including what was arguably his masterpiece, *Don Juan*. In 1823, he went to fight for Greek revolutionaries against their oppressive Ottoman overlords, but he succumbed to marsh fever the following year. In Greece he was, and continues to be, considered a national hero and it is believed his heart was removed after death and buried in the country. For the British, his rehabilitation took rather longer (he was refused burial at Westminster Abbey), but few could deny him a place among the greatest poets in the English language.

Byron packed an enormous amount into his 36 years, and near the end already claimed to feel like an old man. He committed a record of his life to paper and in 1822 gave the two volumes to his close friend, Irish poet Thomas Moore, for later publication. When Moore, in the tradition of many great poets, found himself under severe financial strain, Byron agreed that he could preemptively

DEATH OF A GENIUS

In 1826, a couple of years after the event itself, Joseph-Denis Odevaere painted this vision of Byron as he lay on his deathbed. While his heart was removed for burial in Greece, Byron's embalmed body was returned to England, where it was viewed by thousands while lying in state in London. However Westminster Abbey refused him a burial on the grounds of his dubious morality.

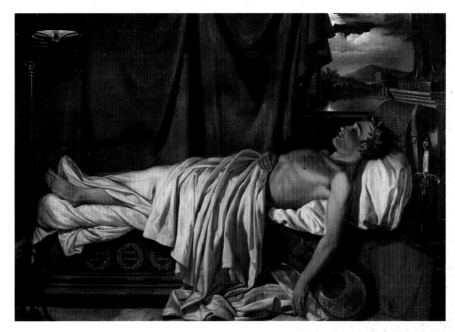

sell the memoirs to Byron's regular publisher, John Murray, for the huge sum of 2,000 guineas.

Murray, the second member of the great John Murray publishing dynasty, had not only turned Byron into a bestselling writer, but also published the likes of Jane Austen and Sir Walter Scott. Byron's memoirs would have made him a vast amount of money, yet on May 17, 1824, exactly one month after Byron's death, he hosted an extraordinary gathering in his home and offices at 50 Albemarle Street in London. For several years, this address had served as London's leading literary salon, but on that day it would bear witness to one of the greatest literary crimes.

Gathered in the building were Murray, Moore, Moore's friend Henry Luttrell, John Cam Hobhouse (an aspiring Whig politician and executor of Byron's will), plus Wilmot Horton and Colonel Doyle (the latter two representing members of Byron's family). Debate had raged between them for days about what to do

with the manuscript, with discussions coming close to blows. All but Moore wanted it destroyed, believing that publication would destroy Byron's reputation forever. Moore wanted to see through the promise he had made as Byron's literary executor but he had, of course, already sold his legal right in the work and could not now buy it back. Just what was in the manuscript nobody knows, but considering what had already been said about its author in his lifetime, the mind boggles. Murray claimed never to have read it before deciding that nobody else should either—a somewhat unusual stance for a publisher to take.

In the end, Moore was outvoted and Murray invited his teenage son to join them in witnessing the conflagration. Horton and Doyle set about tearing the memoirs apart page by page, before throwing the sheets onto the drawing-room fire. How many of England's elite breathed a sigh of relief that day will never be known, but they are surely outnumbered by bereft literary historians who have mourned the loss ever since.

94 Boudicca's grave

WHAT IT IS The last resting place of the queen of the Iceni
WHY YOU WON'T FIND IT The location of her death is disputed

Boudicca was the Briton warrior queen who fought back against Roman occupation to devastating effect. An extraordinary historical figure, the circumstances of her death are vague, but a rumor grew in the 20th century that her body lay buried beneath one of London's busiest railway stations. In truth, however, she could be almost anywhere in the country.

The Roman occupation of Britain began in earnest in AD 43, but allowed certain friendly tribal leaders to continue their rule. One of these was Prasutagus, chief of the Iceni tribe in East Anglia and Boudicca's husband. When Prasutagus died, however, the Romans decided to impose their will on the Iceni, confiscating property, and allegedly stripping and flogging Boudicca and raping her daughters. But if they thought such tactics would suppress the tribe, they had misjudged badly—in AD 60 or 61, while Britain's Roman governor Gaius Suetonius Paulinus was away in the north of Wales, Boudicca launched a massive rebellion against Roman rule.

With a force gathered from several tribes, she sacked and burned the cities of Camulodunum (modern-day Colchester, then the effective capital of Roman Britain), Londinum (London), and Verulamium (St. Albans). Tens of thousands died, raising the specter that the Romans might abandon this outer edge of their empire altogether. However, Paulinus mustered his troops

and decisively defeated Boudicca's army in the "Battle of Watling Street": Precisely where this battle took place is unknown but it was most likely on a line between London and the West Midlands. Boudicca died shortly afterward, most probably at her own hand in a bid to avoid capture.

All of which leaves us with little clue to her burial site. The curious idea that it lies under either platform 8, 9, or 10 of London's King's Cross Railway Station (not far from Platform 9¾ and the *Hogwarts Express*) seems to have emerged from a 1937 book which argued that King's Cross was on the site of a village called Battle Bridge, named in honor of an important battle between the Romans and the Iceni. In more recent years, attention has fallen on a patch of ground near a fast food restaurant in the King's Norton neighborhood of Birmingham. Roman remains have been discovered here, and this hilly, wooded area might have made a suitable location for Boudicca's final battle. However, the simple truth is that we just do not know where the final confrontation occurred.

C.H.S. del.ᵗ

Aquatinted by R. Havell

Boadicea, Queen   *of the Iceni.*

Google's search algorithm

WHAT IT IS The technology behind one of the world's biggest companies
WHY YOU WON'T FIND IT These are trade secrets worth billions of dollars

In the internet age, few things influence your online impact more than your Google Search Ranking. Whether you have goods to sell, news to spread, or opinions to share, your chances of connecting to an audience rely on how easily you can be found online. Out of all the search engines, none is bigger than Google—but their search algorithms are tightly guarded secrets.

According to Google, its search engine deals with over a billion enquiries each day in some 146 different languages. Of these, fully 15 percent of searches are unique and have not been seen before. The search ranking (where a website appears in the search results) is decided by a number of factors, processed in a series of complex calculations that Google is constantly tweaking, and is intended to rank results in order of their likely usefulness to the searcher. Teams of engineers, statisticians, and analysts have evolved increasingly refined algorithms for the purpose. The most famous is the "PageRank" algorithm, named after Google cofounder Larry Page. This works by looking at the number and quality of links pointing at a given website in order to rate its importance.

Most of the algorithms rely on automatic analysis of data, but some of them can be manually adjusted. Google argue this is essential to maintain online security, remove illegal material, make up for occasional anomalies in the automated system, and reduce spam. However, the rankings system is a highly contentious one that leaves many individuals feeling disgruntled, and some claiming to be the victims of foul play. Without solid foundation, for instance, it has been suggested that certain websites have bought their way to a high ranking.

While Google is happy to talk about its algorithms in general terms, it is much less keen to divulge the fine detail. Even though PageRank is patented (and therefore theoretically subject to full disclosure), many aspects remain vague. In fact, Google's algorithms are regarded as vital trade secrets. No one outside the company is given access to them, and employees must sign confidentiality agreements before starting work. Attempts to figure them out by rivals (along with curious geeks) have so far failed to uncover Google's secrets.

In truth, though, we can hardly expect the company to be anything less than secretive—for what is a search engine without its search technology?

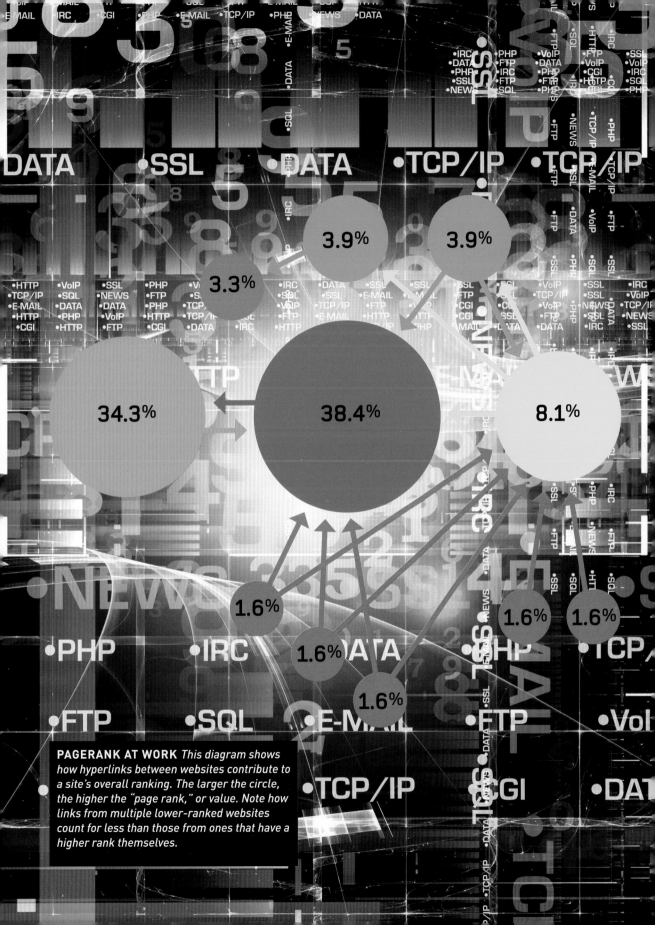

3.9%

3.9%

3.3%

34.3%

38.4%

8.1%

1.6%

1.6%

1.6%

1.6%

1.6%

1.6%

PAGERANK AT WORK *This diagram shows how hyperlinks between websites contribute to a site's overall ranking. The larger the circle, the higher the "page rank," or value. Note how links from multiple lower-ranked websites count for less than those from ones that have a higher rank themselves.*

96

Formula for Greek Fire

WHAT IT IS A deadly medieval weapon of war
WHY YOU WON'T FIND IT Knowledge of its manufacturing process died in the 12th century

For those who wish we lived in a world without weapons of mass destruction, Greek Fire is a flaming beacon of hope. This vicious chemical cocktail was used by the armies of Byzantium (the Greek-speaking descendants of the mighty Roman Empire) between the seventh and eleventh centuries. Yet the secrecy surrounding its production was so great that people eventually forgot how to make it.

Without Greek Fire, history might have been very different—the Byzantine Empire might have fallen, 800 years before its time, to the Arab fleets that besieged its capital, Constantinople, in both AD 678 and 718. The Byzantines themselves knew this fearsome weapon by names such as "artificial fire," "marine fire," or "liquid fire." One can only imagine the terror of those who

faced it: launched flamethrower-style, it rained down on the enemy, stuck to anything that got in its way, and remained alight underwater.

Incendiary weapons were by no means new, but there had never been anything as potent as this. According to the ninth-century chronicler Theophanes, it was invented by a Syrian refugee called Calinicus. However, such was the complexity not only of its basic formula but of the entire system required to use it, that modern experts suspect a network of weapons developers was involved. Special equipment was needed to heat and pressurize the core chemicals, as well as a bespoke siphon arrangement to fire it, fitted to specially decked-out ships. The secrets were restricted to a highly select group, most of whom would have known the details of only one particular aspect.

Attempts by foreigners to replicate the formula met with limited success, and while the Chinese created a similar weapon, it required the use of gunpowder (unknown to the Byzantines). Even when their enemies captured samples, they were unable to reverse engineer it. Modern chemists believe it was probably based on distilled petroleum, with resins to act as thickening agents and a further ingredient such as sulfur to create something like modern-day napalm. The mid-tenth century Emperor Constantine VII had his own take on the weapon's origins. He described how it was "shown and revealed by an angel to the great and holy first Christian emperor Constantine" and explained that the angel ordered him "not to transmit it and never to reveal it to any other nation, whatever it might be." Alas for the Byzantines, they themselves had lost track of its secrets by the 1100s.

97

Muhammad Ali's gold medal

WHAT IT IS The legendary boxer's Olympic gold medal
WHY YOU WON'T FIND IT He lost it, though exactly how remains fiercely contested

Often cited as not only the greatest boxer but also the outstanding sportsman of all time, Muhammad Ali won gold at the 1960 Olympic Games in the light heavyweight division. But his medal later went missing in circumstances that are still unclear. According to one version of events, the man himself threw it into the Ohio River in protest at racist treatment in his own country.

Born Cassius Clay in 1942, Ali became World Heavyweight Champion in 1964. He changed his name that same year, having converted to Islam. Over the course of his career, he won 56 of his 61 professional fights, was the only man to be World Heavyweight Champion three times, and took part in some of the sport's most legendary bouts. But he also transcended sport, becoming a figurehead for religious freedom and black rights as well as a high-profile critic of the Vietnam War. *Sports Illustrated* would anoint him "Sportsman of the Century," while the BBC named him "Sports Personality of the Century."

But Clay first came into the public eye with his gold medal at the 1960 Rome Olympics. According to those who saw Clay (as he then was) around the Olympic Village in the aftermath of his victory, he could not have been prouder of the medal, and kept it with him at all times. But by the time he published his autobiography in 1975, the medal was no longer in his possession. According to Ali, he threw it into the Ohio one night after being refused service at an eatery in Louisville—the very town where he grew up—and receiving abuse from a biker gang. Infuriated at this racism, he tossed away the medal that had once given him so much joy.

When the Olympics were held in Atlanta, Georgia, in 1996, Ali was given the honor of lighting the torch, and presented with a replacement for his lost medal. But now the story being put about had changed—Ali, it was claimed, had simply lost it in the chaos of a house move. Those of a revisionist bent suggested that the Ohio River tale was nothing more than the creation of Ali's ghost writer, perhaps with a political agenda of his own. Where the truth lies is anyone's guess. A full-scale dredge of the Ohio seems unlikely, but if it was mislaid on dry land, it seems extraordinary that no one has found it in the intervening years. An Olympic medal is no small thing, so it seems preposterous to think it has lain in the corner of a removal van or lodged under a chest of drawers for several decades.

GOLDEN TRIO *Ali in the days when he was still known as Cassius Clay: here he proudly wears his US Olympic kit and shows off his medal alongside fellow boxing Olympic champions, Eddie Crook and Skeeter McClure.*

PIAZZA
XVII OLIMPIADE
25 AGOSTO - 11 SETTEMBRE 1960

98

Van Gogh's *Portrait of Dr. Gachet*

WHAT IT IS One of Van Gogh's masterpieces
WHY YOU WON'T FIND IT It has not been seen in public since being auctioned in 1990

The great Dutch Postimpressionist Vincent van Gogh famously sold just one painting during his lifetime. Today he is responsible for four of the 17 artworks that have been sold for more than US$100 million (at inflation-adjusted prices). However, the most valuable of the lot, *Portrait of Dr. Gachet*, disappeared from public view in 1990, lost in a legal quagmire.

In 1890, Van Gogh painted the physician who attended him during his final illness-ravaged months. He believed the doctor's face bore "the heartbroken expression of our time." The painting challenged all the assumptions of what a portrait could be. As the artist wrote to his brother: "There are modern heads that may be looked at for a long time, and that may perhaps be looked back on with longing a hundred years later."

In fact, Van Gogh painted two versions—the second, generally considered to be inferior, was a present for the sitter, later donated by Gachet's family to the French state. The first version, meanwhile, was sold by Van Gogh's sister-in-law for a few hundred francs in 1897. By 1911 it was on display in Frankfurt, but by the 1930s the Nazis had deemed it "degenerate art" and confiscated it. That epitome of degeneracy, Hermann Goering, sold it overseas, and eventually it came into the hands of the Kramarsky family, who subsequently fled their Dutch homeland for New York to escape the Nazis and, in 1990, put Dr. Gachet up for auction.

It became the world's most expensive painting to that date, selling to Japanese industrialist Ryoei Saito, for US$82.5 million. Saito immediately put it in a climate-controlled vault, where it remained as his commercial empire came crashing down. Convicted of trying to bribe public officials and with his health deteriorating, he courted the outrage of the art world when he announced that he wanted *Dr. Gachet* cremated with him, though he would later claim this was merely a joke. Saito died in 1997, leaving the painting's future in confusion as his company, heirs, and creditors vied to claim it. The public had not seen the work since 1990 and now it was shrouded in still further secrecy. To this day, we do not know where the picture is, though there is widespread speculation that it was sold several years ago to an unknown buyer. It has been suggested that it is now in a private collection in the US, while other experts suspect France or Switzerland as its more likely home. Sadly, *Portrait of Dr. Gachet* is not the only one of van Gogh's works to have gone underground.

99

Lost works of Nikola Tesla

WHAT THEY ARE Notes, tools, and equipment belonging to one of the greatest scientific minds of all time

WHY YOU WON'T FIND THEM They went up in smoke in 1895

Nikola Tesla was one of the great scientific minds of the late 19th and early 20th centuries, standing shoulder to shoulder with the likes of Edison, Marconi, and Einstein. Yet by the time of his death in 1943, he was destitute and a figure of fun. What is worse, in 1895 a fire destroyed much of this archetypal "mad scientist's" life's work—we can only wonder at what knowledge humanity lost.

Nikola Tesla was born to Serbian parents in Smijan, a town then part of the Austrian empire and now in Croatia. In 1882, he began working in France for Thomas Edison's technological empire and two years later migrated to work at his US offices. There he tweaked and improved several of Edison's motors and generators, but relations between the two grew strained after a disagreement over pay, and by 1886 they had gone their separate ways.

Tesla carried on his work in electricity, inventing an induction motor and transformer that helped secure victory over Edison in the "War of the Currents" —a battle that raged in the 1880s between Edison's direct current and the alternating current championed by George Westinghouse. Tesla's inventions provided him with a degree of financial stability and in 1891—the year in which he became a naturalized US citizen—he set up his own laboratory on New York's South Fifth Avenue. By 1894 he was undertaking pioneering work on what we now recognize as X-rays.

However, on March 13, 1895, disaster struck. Tesla shared the building with Gillis & Geoghegan, a company manufacturing steamfitters' supplies, and just before 3 a.m. a night watchman was doing his rounds when a fire started on the ground floor. Despite his best efforts to put it out, the flames soon took hold, fed by oil kept on the premises. The first Tesla knew of the conflagration was when he turned up for work the next morning.

"It cannot be true!" he exclaimed as he strode back and forth along the street, his despair compounded by the fact that he did not have any insurance. The *New York Times* ran a story under the headline "Mr. Tesla's Great Loss" and reported the following statement from the tearful scientist:

"I am in too much grief to talk. What can I say? The work of half my lifetime, very nearly all my mechanical instruments and scientific apparatus, that it has taken years to perfect, swept away in a fire that lasted only an hour or two. How can I estimate the

loss in mere dollars and cents? Everything is gone. I must begin over again."

Aside from hardware, the fire destroyed dozens—perhaps hundreds—of detailed plans and models, copious notes, page after page of experimental results, and bundles of photographs, Even in purely financial terms, Tesla's loss was estimated to be at least $50,000, a quite staggering sum in 1895.

But while the fire may have destroyed Tesla's equipment and data, it could not consume his genius, and begin again he did. In his lifetime, he registered nearly 300 patents and there was no obvious letup in the rate immediately after the fire. Still, we may only ponder as to what other ideas and inventions he might have come up with in this richly creative phase of his life, had his momentum not been stalled by the tragedy on South Fifth Avenue. Were it not for the fire, for instance, it is possible that we would consider Tesla—and not the Italian, Guglielmo Marconi—to be the father of wireless telegraphy.

In later life, Tesla continued his work on electricity and radio waves, but continued to struggle financially thanks to his own poor business decisions and fractious relationships with potential backers. He registered his last patent in 1928 for a vertical takeoff biplane, and spent several years claiming to have developed a "death-ray"-type weapon. But by the time he died alone on January 7, 1943 in the New Yorker Hotel, his public standing had fallen as his eccentricity had grown.

To public knowledge, he never had a sexual relationship, believing that celibacy was preferential for brain development. He did, however, suspect that he had been contacted by aliens and, perhaps most strangely of all, developed a relationship with a pigeon. In his own words: "... there was one, a beautiful bird ... It was a female. I had only to wish and call her and she would come flying to me. I loved that pigeon as a man loves a woman, and she loved me. As long as I had her, there was a purpose to my life."

It is only in relatively recent years that Tesla has started to receive some of the acclaim that he is surely due. Had half his life's work not been lost, we might be more familiar with his name and accomplishments.

The missing Nixon tapes

WHAT THEY ARE Missing sections from recordings made during the Watergate scandal

WHY YOU WON'T FIND THEM All the evidence suggests they were willfully erased

Few incidents have done more to erode America's faith in its leaders than the Watergate scandal that culminated in the resignation of President Richard Nixon in 1974. His grip on power became untenable after he was caught on tape plotting to obstruct a police investigation, but another tape revealed 18½ minutes of erased recordings. What secrets might these lost conversations have held?

It is often said that politicians are not brought down by their crimes so much as the attempt to cover them up, and this was never truer than in the case of Richard Milhous Nixon. The scandal began on June 17, 1972 with the discovery of a break-in at the Democratic National Committee's headquarters in Washington's Watergate Building by five men—known as the "Plumbers"—connected to Nixon's White House administration. The motive for the crime has never been clearly established but it was not long before the FBI linked money found on the intruders to a fund for Nixon's reelection campaign.

Despite the stench of dirty tricks, Nixon easily won a new term in November 1972. However, the scandal exploded the following year when it was alleged by one of the Plumbers that the White House had influenced his criminal trial and encouraged perjury. Several of Nixon's aides fell on their swords, but at the Senate's hearings into the scandal it emerged that presidential conversations in the Oval Office were

routinely recorded. A Special Prosecutor subpoenaed the relevant tapes but Nixon at first refused to release them, citing presidential privilege. However, by April 1974 he had been persuaded to publish redacted transcripts and surrendered the tapes themselves at the end of July.

One of these became known as the "Smoking Gun" tape. In it the president is heard telling chief of staff Bob Haldeman to block FBI investigations on grounds of national security. This was, to all intents and purposes, evidence of criminal conspiracy. Within three days of the tape's public release on August 5, 1974, Nixon had stood down.

But almost as damaging was Tape 342: dating to June 20, 1972 and recording the first conversation between Nixon and Haldeman after the arrests, this is the one with the missing 18½ minutes. Nixon always claimed it was wiped as the result of an accident, but the void soon filled with suspicion. The president's personal secretary, Rose Mary Woods, took the fall, describing how she had

inadvertently recorded over a section of the tape when a phone call interrupted her in the process of transcription.

To compound the issue, however, she suggested that she had only erased about five minutes. So what of the other 13½? Later tests would show that the erasure was carried out in several instalments, seemingly negating the argument that it could have been an accident. So the inevitable question arises—what was on the tape that was so bad that it needed to be kept out of the public sphere? And why on earth leave the "Smoking Gun" tape but wipe this one? Some have sought a more innocent explanation, blaming Nixon's

famously poor grasp of technology. If he himself made the deletions, it has been argued, he might well have started with Tape 342 (chronologically the earliest of those subpoenaed), before realizing that the task was beyond him in the time he had available.

So far all attempts to recover the lost conversations have failed, though it is hoped that developments in digital technology may one day make a restoration possible. These days the tapes are kept by the National Archives at the Richard Nixon Presidential Library and Museum in Yorba Linda, California. They are kept in a temperature- and humidity-controlled vault and have only been played a handful of times in the decades since the scandal—and only then so that copies might be made.

Facing impeachment, Nixon stood down on August 9, 1974, so becoming the only US president to date to resign from office. His successor, Gerald Ford, granted him a full pardon for any crimes he had committed in the White House, but Nixon's reputation never recovered and he died in 1994 still protesting his innocence. His chances of rehabilitation remain tiny while the mystery of those missing 18½ minutes endures.

Index

Acknowledgments

Many thanks to Kerry Enzor and Richard Green at Quercus, and to my agent, James Wills. Also to Giles Sparrow and Tim Brown, who have made this book such a pleasure to look at. Finally, as ever, to Rosie.

Picture credits

Quercus

New York • London

© 2014 by Quercus Editions Ltd
First published in the United States by Quercus
in 2014

Any member of educational institutions wishing to
photocopy part or all of the work for classroom use
or anthology should send inquiries to
permissions@quercus.com.

ISBN 978-1-62365-837-3

Library of Congress Control Number: 2014931817

Manufactured in China

10 9 8 7 6 5 4 3 2 1

www.quercus.com